OUR STORIES ETCHED IN IVORY / QULIP'YUGUT IKSIAQTUUMARUAT TUUGAAMI

The Smithsonian Collections of Engraved Drill Bows with Stories from the Arctic

Tommy Soolook from Little Diomede uses his drill bow to carve ivory inside a canvas tent. A pair of completed billikens can be seen on the left. An open toolbox on the right displays sections of walrus tusk, metal files, and other carving materials. Soolook was recognized as a renowned carver. He passed away during the influenza epidemic in 1953.
Photo taken in 1946. Alaska State Library – Historical Collections, ASL-P466-02-068.

QULIP'YUGUT IKSIAQTUUMARUAT TUUGAAMI

Our Stories Etched in Ivory

The Smithsonian Collections of Engraved Drill Bows with Stories from the Arctic

AMY PHILLIPS-CHAN

editor and compiler

An ivory carver uses a drill bow on a walrus tusk engraved with scenes of whaling.
Photograph taken by J. C. Cantwell at St. Michael between 1899 and 1901.
National Anthropological Archives, Smithsonian Institution, NAA INV 01471200.

Roy Sockpick files a section of walrus bone in his carving workshop at Shishmaref. Photograph by Amy Phillips-Chan, 2012.

Published by
ARCTIC STUDIES CENTER
Department of Anthropology
National Museum of Natural History
Smithsonian Institution
www.mnh.si.edu/arctic

In cooperation with
CARRIE M. MCLAIN MEMORIAL MUSEUM
100 West 7th Avenue, P.O. Box 53
Nome, Alaska 99762
www.nomealaska.org

This volume was produced under a cooperative agreement between the Arctic Studies Center, National Museum of Natural History, Smithsonian Institution, and the Carrie M. McLain Memorial Museum.

Technical editor: Igor Chechushkov (Arius LLC)
Volume design: Igor Chechushkov and Amy Phillips-Chan
Cover design: Daria Stulova (Arius LLC)
Volume title in Ugiuvak (King Island) Inupiaq: Bernadette Y. Alvanna-Stimpfle, Yaayuk

THIS PUBLICATION IS VOLUME 10 OF THE ARCTIC STUDIES CENTER SERIES, CONTRIBUTIONS TO CIRCUMPOLAR ANTHROPOLOGY.
THE SERIES IS MADE POSSIBLE IN PART BY THE JAMES W. VANSTONE (1925-2001) ENDOWMENT.

Front cover: Drill bow, drill, and mouthpiece. Collected by the U.S. Department of the Interior, accessioned 1910. National Museum of Natural History E260132.
Back cover: (Top) An Inupiaq carver uses a drill bow to make holes for an engraved ivory cribbage board. The top features a delicate ivory rail that reads, "Nome, Alaska, 1908." Photograph by Moldt and Lomen. Carrie M. McLain Memorial Museum, 1979.1.491.
(Bottom) Carver Jerome Saclamana (Inupiaq) marks a walrus tusk before cutting it to make best use of the material during the *Material Traditions: Sculpting Ivory* artist residency at the Arctic Studies Center in Anchorage in 2015. Photograph by Ash Adams. Courtesy of the Smithsonian Arctic Studies Center.
(Right) King Island Elder Frank Ellanna uses a drill bow to carve ivory at his home in Nome, 1986. Carrie M. McLain Memorial Museum, Accession 2003.32.

Library of Congress Control Number: 2021937766

ISBN: 978-0-578-90679-9

Printed in the United States of America

contents

Volume Contributors

Whitlam Adams (*Anuġi*) was born aboard the Department of the Interior supply ship *North Star* in 1926 and grew up in Utqiaġvik, AK. He was an experienced hunter and fisherman and an active member of the local Cornerstone Church. Whitlam specialized in making jewelry and small boxes from ivory, baleen and bone. He enjoyed etching animals on his artwork and making earrings for his wife Mary.

Earl Michael Aiken lives in Utqiaġvik, AK where he was born in 1956. He is a retired whaler who has been etching baleen for almost twenty years. Earl specializes in etching rows of figures driving dog sleds, whaling, and hunting seal and caribou. He often works on artwork in the local grocery store and enjoys sharing stories about his baleen etchings.

Joseph Akaran lives in St. Michael, AK where he was born in 1976. He is an experienced small engine mechanic who enjoys hunting geese and carving with his Dremel. Joe started carving wood after high school and eventually moved on to working in ivory. He fondly recalls the time he found a walrus head with two intact tusks washed up under his house.

Bernadette Y. Alvanna-Stimpfle (*Yaayuk*) of Nome and King Island is the Kawerak Inc. Eskimo Heritage Program Director. She was an Inupiaq language and culture teacher, a classroom teacher, and English as Second Language instructor at Nome Public Schools for 25 years. She is a member of the Alaska Native Language Preservation and Advisory Council and is currently pursuing her PhD at the University of Hawaii Hilo Campus.

Francis Alvanna (*Suluk*) (1940-2018) was born on King Island and moved with his family to Nome, AK in 1952. His parents were John Alvanna and Madeline Suluk. Francis represented King Island on the Eskimo Walrus Commission and was an active member of the King Island Dance Group. He taught ivory carving to students of all ages and held traditional carving demonstrations during the Iditarod season.

Wilfred Anowlic (*Eliqutaq*) of Nome, AK is a skilled hunter and boat captain from King Island. He was born in 1948 and raised by his grandparents in a traditional subsistence lifestyle. He is a member of the King Island Dance Group and plays the acoustic guitar. Wilfred learned to carve ivory by watching his elders use drill bows and other hand tools in the King Island *qagrit*.

Sylvester Ayek of Nome, AK spent his youth exploring King Island where he was born in 1940. He is a leader of the King Island Dance Group and works with young people to make traditional drums and dance mitts. He also teaches Inupiaq hunters' language to young men in his hunting crew. Sylvester carved ivory for many years before transitioning to large-scale artwork in marble, metal, and wood.

Thomas Barr was born in Shishmaref, AK in 1971 to Delano and Minnie Barr. He spent his childhood between Nome and Kotzebue where he learned to carve alongside his father. Thomas now lives in Nome and specializes in carving ivory figures, earrings, and bracelets.

Igor Chechushkov is a book designer and an archaeologist, who collaborates with the Smithsonian Arctic Studies Center in Washington, D.C. His research interests are northern Bronze Age communities in Central Eurasia and the Quebec's Inuit communites.

Enoch Evak was born in Kotzebue, AK in 1956 and comes from a large family with nine brothers and two sisters. As a preschooler he learned to draw by copying animals made by his father. Enoch often creates art in the carving workshop of the Sulianich Art Center and specializes in detailed etchings of North Alaska animals on baleen.

Jack Frankson Jr. of Kotzebue, AK was born in 1992 and became inspired to carve through watching his father. His first project involved carving a piece of whalebone vertebrae to look like a face. Jack credits older carvers for giving him ideas on how to improve his artwork and is now teaching his brother how to carve.

John Heffle was born in 1960 in Fairbanks, AK where he learned to make traditional wood kayaks from his uncle. He learned to carve as a young boy and remembers family coming over to his house to sew and make artwork together. John spends most of his time in Utqiaġvik creating mixed-media sculptures in the Iñupiat Heritage Center.

Eben Hopson was born in Utqiaġvik, AK in 2000 and comes from a family of whalers. He started etching animals on baleen at age nine and has participated in the visiting artist program at the Iñupiat Heritage Center. Eben curently creates documentary films about the Arctic.

Glenn Ipalook (*Kachuk*) was born in 1954 and raised in Utqiaġvik, AK by his grandparents. Glenn recalls that his grandmother used to cure walrus ivory by soaking it in lake water. He enjoys visiting about Utqiaġvik's whaling history and finding glass trade beads from the old sod houses. Glenn specializes in making raven feathers and whaling ships out of baleen.

Jon Ipalook (*Natchiq*) of Kotzebue, AK was born in 1975 and has strong family ties to Point Hope and Kiana. He credits his uncles and father Allen Lane for teaching him various techniques to carve ivory and baleen. Jon enjoys making his own tools from the different materials he has collected and is skilled at using the traditional drill bow.

Henry Koonook of Point Hope, AK was born in 1955 and is an experienced hunter and whaler. He has made traditional basket sleds and small retrieving kayaks covered in sealskin. Henry enjoys using homemade tools including his drill bow and *ulimaun* to carve driftwood and whalebone masks. He also specializes in family carvings that feature figures and animals spiraling up a walrus tusk.

Joseph Kunnuk Sr. of Nome, AK was born in 1940 to parents Leo Kunnuk and Agnes Olanna. Joe grew up on King Island where he fondly recalls hunting for murre eggs among the cliffs. He is an experienced walrus hunter who emphasizes the importance of hunting and eating Native foods. Joe carves ivory animals and bracelets, repairs old carvings, and has taught ivory carving at Nome-Beltz High School.

Ken Lisbourne (1950-2017) was from Point Hope, AK where he grew up with his grandparents in a sod house and learned to carve ivory from an Iñupiaq teacher at school. Ken lived in Anchorage for a long time where he became known for his vibrant watercolor paintings that illustrate Iñupiat culture and address social issues such  as alcoholism. Ken and his wife Iva, a skilled doll maker, were married for 32 years and traveled across Alaska selling their artwork together.

Albert Matthias lives in St. Michael, AK where he was born in 1955. He is an experienced seal hunter whose wife Flora stretches spotted sealskins for making mukluks. Albert started carving beach found ivory as a teenager using only a metal file. He specializes in carving intricate ivory earrings shaped like thimbles, basket sleds, and kayaks.

Flora Matthias grew up in Kotlik where she used to snare rabbits and ptarmigans with her brothers. She learned Yup'ik from listening to Elders. In St. Michael, she taught herself how to stretch sealskins and ferment

fish eggs. She is married to Albert Matthias and enjoys wearing the ivory jewelry that he makes for her.

George Milligrock was born in 1951 in Unalakleet, AK and raised by his grandparents on Little Diomede. He grew up carving ivory alongside family members in a sod house without electricity and remembers his grandfather using a drill bow out of walrus bone. George now lives in Shishmaref with his wife Beatrice and son Elias who is also a carver.

Gilford Mongoyak Jr. of Utqiaġvik, AK was born in 1954 and enjoys sharing Native foods including *mikiaq* and his special recipe for pickled muktuk. He has assembled a small collection of local artifacts over the years and is a knowledgeable historian on past tool use and construction. Gilford etches baleen wolf scares, makes caribou jaw sleds, and participates as a resident artist at the Iñupiat Heritage Center.

Baker Ningealook of Shishmaref, AK was born at Iqpik in 1939 and recalls staying in sod houses along the coast while his father herded reindeer. Baker served in the National Guard for twenty years and participated in rifle clubs in Germany and Alaska. He is an experienced seal hunter and has made several ivory harpoon heads over the years.

James Omiak (*Sinaġuyak*) (1933-2021) of Nome, AK was born to Vincent "Bob" and Susie Omiak on Little Diomede. James shared Inupiaq culture through singing and dancing while living in Teller for almost forty years. He specialized in carving ivory bracelets and animals with his drill bow and other hand tools for over fifty  years. He also enjoyed teaching ivory carving to many students at Nome-Beltz High School.

Alzred 'Steve' Oomittuk of Point Hope, AK was born in 1962 and is an experienced whaler and member of the Tikiġaq Traditional Dance Group. He has been the mayor of Point Hope and serves as a local guide and historian to visiting researchers. Steve enjoys finding artifacts washed up from the Ipiutak site and taking students on tours of sod houses at Old Tigara.

Othniel Anaqulutuq 'Art' Oomittuk Jr. (*Anaqulutuq*) was born in 1963 and raised in Point Hope, AK. He served as the Tikiġaq Volunteer Fire Chief and is an experienced singer and drummer. Art has explored many museum collections and uses carving to tell contemporary stories. He works in wood, ivory and bronze and is well-known for his portrait-style masks.

John Penatac Sr. was born in 1940 on King Island and moved to Nome, AK at the age of eighteen. He attended the University of Alaska Fairbanks where he enjoyed working in silver, soapstone, and alabaster. John learned to carve ivory in his youth and remembers his father using an ivory drill bow along with wood drills and handmade chisels. He is an experienced drummer and singer with the King Island Dance Group.

Amy Phillips-Chan is the Director of the Carrie M. McLain Memorial Museum in Nome, AK and a research collaborator with the Smithsonian Arctic Studies Center. She works with communities in Northwest Alaska on multi-disciplinary projects that explore museum collections and their connection to traditional knowledge and oral narratives.

Vince Pikonganna (*Aŋmaluq*) (1948-2016) was born in Nome, AK and spent his childhood on King Island. His parents were Aloysius and Clara Pikonganna. Vince was a member of the King Island Dance Group and an experienced seal and walrus hunter. He participated in the Alaska Native arts program at the University of Alaska Fairbanks and worked in ivory, wood, silver and soapstone. He specialized in carving ivory cribbage boards.

John Pullock (*Ilonraaq*) of Nome, AK describes a childhood that involved walking all over King Island where he was born in 1938. John recalls his grandfather using a drill bow to carve ivory and his grandmother wielding a walrus jaw to smash seal blubber for lamp oil. Some of his first carving projects included a walrus tooth keychain and a small ivory seal he learned how to make from his cousin.

Jerome Saclamana (*Kayvanik*) was born in Nome, AK in 1963 and grew up on East End surrounded by his King Island relatives. He enjoys fishing for salmon and setting crab pots in the winter. Jerome specializes in carving whalebone shamans and ivory needle cases. He also finds inspiration from old style pictorial imagery and sometimes etches figures on his carvings.

Ross Schaeffer, Sr. (*Qualayauq*) is an experienced hunter, trapper and commercial fisherman from Kotzebue, AK. Ross was born in 1947 and has served as the Borough Mayor of Kotzebue. He carves ivory, bone and wood and actively works with Alaska Native youth to pass on traditional carving and hunting skills. He also

completed a series of wood panels illustrating seasonal activities for the Napaaqtugmiut School in Noatak.

William Simmonds was born in Anchorage, AK in 1971 and currently resides in Utqiaġvik. He started carving ivory as a teenager and eventually moved on to other art forms including walrus skull masks adorned with sealskin, and polar bear fur. William enjoys working in the Iñupiat Heritage Center and exchanging ideas with local artists.

Brian Sockpick (*Nayokpuk*) was born in Nome, AK in 1959 and spent his teenage years in Shishmaref. Brian is an experienced seal and walrus hunter who also helped his father with commercial fishing. He started etching ivory in high school after taking an art class. Brian uses his father's scribe made from a sharpened drill bit and specializes in etching ivory with dog teams and caribou herds.

Gary Sockpick was born in Nome, AK in 1967 before moving with his family to Shishmaref in 1979 where he now resides. He enjoys sharing hunting stories about walrus, ducks, and polar bears. Gary and his sons share a carving space in their home. He uses a twenty-year-old metal vise that has even survived a house fire. He specializes in etching ivory earrings and carving whalebone figures with inlaid ivory faces.

Roy Sockpick was born in Nome, AK in 1966 and moved with his older brother Gary Sockpick to Shishmaref. He worked in the National Guard for over twenty years and has also raised sled dogs. Gary and his sons share a carving space and tools including a metal file that belonged to his grandfather. Gary specializes in whalebone vertebrae masks and fishermen with inlaid ivory and baleen features.

Levi Tetpon was born and raised in Shaktoolik, AK before moving to Anchorage where he now lives. He began his career as an artist by polishing and inking his father's ivory carvings. Levi carved soapstone for many years but now works primarily with ivory he purchases from St. Lawrence Island hunters. He specializes in carving ivory hunters, drummers, and transformation pieces with inlaid baleen dots.

Kenny Tikik was born in 1953 and raised in Kotzebue, AK. Kenny credits Point Hope artists with teaching him various carving techniques such as using the structure of a whale's tail to make a face. Kenny emphasizes working in natural materials including caribou antler, sinew, and ivory. He has made traditional snow goggles, fish skin sheaths, and ivory fish hook earrings.

Edwin Weyiouanna was born in Nome in 1965 and now lives in Shishmaref, AK. He has served in the National Guard. Edwin studied art at the Institute of American Indian Arts in Santa Fe, New Mexico and developed his carving skills in the Melvin Olanna Friendship Center. He specializes in carving whalebone masks and figures with inlaid ivory and baleen designs.

Matthew Tiulana (*Kuyuruk*) of Nome, AK was born in 1952 and enjoys traveling to King Island in the summer to pick greens and salmonberries. Matthew recalls an *umiaq* with fifty walrus tusks sinking off of King Island. He prizes a carving knife passed down by his father and specializes in animal spirit ivory masks with baleen hoops and ptarmigan feathers.

 **Stanley Tocktoo** of Shishmaref, AK was born in 1970 and is a skilled hunter and fisherman. He was a former mayor and president of the Native Village of Shishmaref. He served in the National Guard and has taught bi-lingual classes for twenty years. He recalls his grandfather using a wood drill bow and drills with different sizes of bits. Stanley specializes in carving ivory bracelets with inlaid designs.

 **Damian Tom** is an experienced hunter and fisherman from St. Michael, AK. He served in the National Guard for nineteen years and currently works at the local AC store. He collects ivory and driftwood washed up on the beach to use in carving projects. Damian also weaves his own salmon and beluga nets using braided twine, a carved driftwood gauge, and a wood needle passed down from his stepfather.

1/ Strings of ivory and baleen beads surround this carver using a drill bow at Little Diomede. Hand saws, metal files, and a vise are within easy reach. c. 1930. Alaska State Library – Historical Collections, ASL-P348-212.

OUR STORIES ETCHED IN IVORY

Foreword

Quyaanavak aviqsrataaqma aglaġupluŋa ugua sanalatuatnun. Magua aŋutit ilisasaqtaqtasimaturat aŋutnanaiyaaganin. Qagzrimi naagalu iŋmini ilisasaqtazimaruat. Qiniqaaqł aŋutit sanaruat, uuktaaġatut. Tavaraŋa 'aa iŋminik sanapłutik.

Magua issanitat atuqtasimait sanak'amik; kiŋmiaq, niuqtuun, suli satkuanik. Trurauqłutik naagalu alaliuqłutik piliuqtazimaruat. Iŋiminik piliuġagait.

Ilittatutn sananamik aaŋaminin, naagalu aakaluuraaganin, aŋaminin, naagalu avaminin. Ayaqattutiraġiyait. Tavra'aa munaġiplugit naguatun ilaiyaagit.

Thank you for asking me to write the foreword for this project. I am honored to do so. As I read through the men's accounts about carving, I saw two main patterns. One is a progression for tools that were used, from handmade tools to electric ones. The other is how these artists have learned to carve ivory, bone, baleen, and wood. As it is in our Inupiaq language, it is a very observational language. These men as young people first observed their fathers, uncles, and/or grandfathers in the men's club houses or at home. Then they were given simple tools and scraps of ivory or bone to practice carving. From there, they became expert carvers.

The etchings on the bow drills are fascinating to study as they tell of a time right before Western contact. The types of tools that were used were all handmade by the artists themselves or by another family member. Inupiat had their own ingenuity in creating their own tools for artwork. Over time, some even recycled nonworking, old machinery such as a sewing machine to make beads. The bow drills allowed the carvers to make holes for making ivory bracelets, cribbage boards, salt and pepper shakers, and eyes for figurines of animals inlaid with baleen.

From father to son, uncle to nephew, grandfather to grandson, the knowledge of carving ivory, bone, antlers, and driftwood was passed on through observation and guidance. The young men practiced until their work became exquisite and elaborate carvings as the economy progressed from trade exchange to a cash economy to support their families.

Bernadette Y. Alvanna-Stimpfle, Yaayuk
Kawerak Inc. Eskimo Heritage Program

Acknowledgements

The Smithsonian Summer Institute in Museum Anthropology (SIMA) launched in 2009 and I eagerly traveled to Washington, DC in anticipation of participating in the program and spending time with collections and staff. While in D.C., I had an opportunity to examine engraved drill bows from the Bering Strait acquired by Smithsonian naturalists at the turn of the twentieth century. At the National Museum of Natural History (NMNH), SIMA Director Dr. Candace Greene encouraged me to reach out to Dr. Stephen Loring, NMNH Archaeologist, who shared a similar enthusiasm for drill bows. Those initial discussions with Dr. Loring helped to conceptualize my dissertation project that connected drill bows in Washington, D.C. with carvers, storytellers, and community members in Alaska.

After completing my dissertation in 2013, community members expressed interest in hearing extended stories from their friends and fellow carvers, as well as larger images of the engraved drill bows with written descriptions of the scenes. This book attempts to fulfill some of those requests and has been designed as a hands-on resource that makes accessible oral histories shared during the project, and museum collections of heritage items from the Arctic.

The publication could not have been completed without the generous assistance of over 40 Alaska Native community members who lent their knowledge and expertise in working with ivory and bone and shared how this vital practice connects to a subsistence lifestyle. The short biographies in the section on volume contributors only scratches the surface of their deep and historic understanding of the Arctic environment. Special appreciation goes to Henry Koonook and Jon Ipalook for demonstrating their hand-carved drills bows, Gary Sockpick and Jerome Saclamana for demonstrating how to etch on ivory, and Vince Pikonganna, James Omiak, and Matthew Tiulana for offering Bering Strait Inupiaq names of carving tools.

At the Smithsonian Arctic Studies Center (ASC), Dr. Igor Krupnik, NMNH Anthropologist, offered guidance and support to see this book through to completion. Dr. Loring generously shared his office space and unfailing enthusiasm for the project during my tenure as a Smithsonian Pre-Doctoral Fellow. Dr. Aron Crowell coordinated peer review for this publication and offered insightful comments that greatly improved the text. Dr. William Fitzhugh reviewed the manuscript and pointed me to the heated exchange over drill bows that took place in the 1890s between Smithsonian collector Edward Nelson and author Walter James Hoffman. He also contributed his considerable experience to the printing of this volume. Thank you to Nancy Shorey for helping to coordinate final printing and shipping of the books.

At the Smithsonian NMNH Museum Support Center, Felicia Pickering and David Rosenthal were instrumental in making drill bows and other carvings available for research. At the National Museum of the American Indian (NMAI), Pat Nietfeld and Tom Evans assisted with collections research and provided digital copies of engraved ivory carvings in the NMAI collection.

In Nome, Bernadette Yaayuk Alvanna-Stimpfle provided critical guidance for integration of the Inupiaq language into the text, including the translation of the volume title into Ugiuvak (King Island) Inupiaq. Her foreword offers insight into the ingenuity behind handmade tools and the importance of observational learning among carvers that continues today. Photographer Michael Burnett contributed his skills and artistic eye to creating images of objects in the Carrie M. McLain Memorial Museum. Thanks also go to Jenya Anichenko for providing a copy of N. N. Dikov's *Mysteries in the Rocks of Ancient Chukotka* (1999). Sincere appreciation goes to the two peer reviewers for suggestions that enriched this manuscript.

The creative layout of the book and its inclusion of several hundred images was accomplished under the skilled technical and design assistance of Dr. Igor Chechushkov. Thank you to the following organizations for generous permission to include photographs and object images from their collections: Alaska State Archives and Library, American Museum of Natural History, Anchorage Museum, Carrie M. McLain Memorial Museum, Field Museum, Horniman Museum and Gardens, McCord Museum, National Anthropological Archives, Smithsonian National Museum of Natural History, Smithsonian National Museum of the American Indian and the Pitt Rivers Museum. Appreciation also goes to Dr. Mikhail Bronshtein and Dr. Sergei Gusev for permission to reproduce images from their seminal publications and Dawn Biddison at the Smithsonian Arctic Studies Center for contributing photographs from *Material Traditions: Sculpting Ivory.*

The National Science Foundation provided funding for participation in SIMA that helped to launch this project; The Smithsonian National Museum of Natural History supported collections research with a Pre-Doctoral Fellowship; the ASU Graduate College and Philanthropic Educational Organization provided financial support for community discussions in Alaska. Thanks also go to the Carrie M. McLain Memorial Museum and the Smithsonian Arctic Studies Center for their support of the design, layout, and printing of this publication.

2/ Wilfred Anowlic, Sylvester Ayek, and Bernadette Yaayuk Alvanna-Stimpfle examine an engraved drill bow in the Carrie M. McLain Memorial Museum. Photograph by Amy Phillips-Chan, 2019.

Overall, some 50 people contributed their knowledge, time, and skills to the discussion of engraved drill bows and related heritage objects, and to the publication of this book. The project is the first of its kind between the Smithsonian Arctic Studies Center, the Carrie M. McLain Memorial Museum, and Bering Strait community members. We hope the publication offers new insight into the breadth of Indigenous knowledge about the Bering Strait.

Amy Phillips-Chan
Carrie M. McLain Memorial Museum

3/ Terlungna and her husband are photographed inside their tent at the Teller Reindeer Station at Port Clarence, Alaska in 1900. The drill bow being used is engraved with a row of animal skins. Photographer Edwin Tappan Adney has stepped into the frame while the image is being taken and revealed a power dynamic that non-Indigenous people often held to shape representations of Alaska Native peoples. McCord Museum, MP-1979.111.221.

Stories in Ivory
The Art and Language of Bering Strait Drill Bows

AMY PHILLIPS-CHAN

The Smithsonian National Museum of Natural History (NMNH) and National Museum of the American Indian (NMAI) care for over one hundred and thirty engraved ivory and bone drill bows (*pitiksiaq*) (Appendix 1) [1]. Among Bering Strait communities, drill bows formed part of a tool complex used with a mouthpiece (*kiŋmiaq*) and a drill (*niuun*) to create holes, start fires, and work ivory, bone, and wood (see Figs. 1, 3) [2]. Pictorial imagery on the drill bows offered visual records of life in the Arctic, and perhaps served as mnemonic aids to oral histories, within communities that relied on spoken language to pass down generational knowledge.

Engraved drill bows were eagerly acquired by Smithsonian naturalists for their animated scenes of human figures hunting, dancing, traveling, and battling mythological creatures. From field notes and museum records, we know the majority of drill bows in Smithsonian collections originated from Inupiaq communities in the Bering Strait region (Map 1, Table 1). Additional drill bows were acquired from Iñupiaq villages along the coast of North Alaska and about a dozen drill bows came from southeastern Norton Sound where the tools might have been made by Yup'ik or Inupiaq/Yup'ik carvers [3]. Although carvers on St. Lawrence Island used drill bows, the bows were not typically engraved with figural scenes (Chan 2013:246-247; Collins 1937:236-237) [4]. This is perhaps why none of the engraved drill bows in Smithsonian collections derive from the villages of Gambell or Savoonga on St. Lawrence Island.

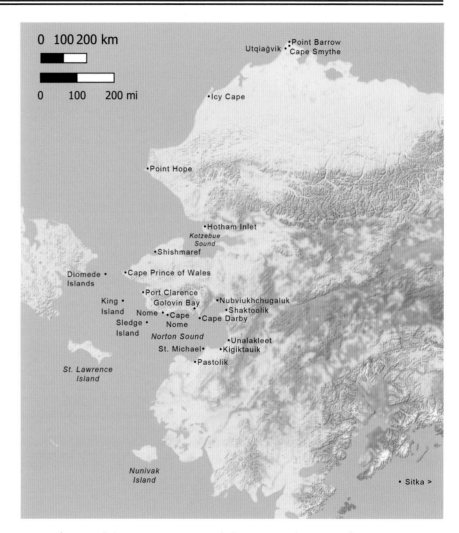

Map 1/ Map of the Bering Strait with locations where Smithsonian collectors acquired engraved drill bows.

The removal of engraved drill bows and other cultural heritage items from Alaska by explorers and ethnographers in the nineteenth century laid the foundation for a tremulous relationship between Inupiaq communities and museums [5]. As collectors procured drill bows from Alaska, the engraved tools were separated from the unique artistic and oral traditions of their home communities and often were presented as common signifiers of Arctic peoples. Over the past two hundred years, museums have displayed drill bows according to changing paradigms of representation, from curiosities and primitive tools to artistic sculptures, and, more recently, as Indigenous heritage objects (British Museum 1910:15; Chan 2013:425-453; Crowell 2020:4-8; King 1981:97; VanStone 1975:4).

The past three decades have seen significant growth in museums that commit to cross-cultural understanding through collaborative exhibitions, publications, and programs that highlight formerly repressed histories and welcome Indigenous peoples to author their own stories (i.e. Krupnik and Kaneshiro 2011; Steffian and Counceller 2020; Yohe and Greeves 2019). It is now widely recognized that active partnerships between Indigenous communities and museums can foster multi-generational dialogue, elicit oral narratives, and bring new understandings to objects in museum collections (Crowell et. al. 2010; Cruikshank 1995; Fienup-Riordan 2007). In Alaska, Inupiaq participation in collections-based projects and contemporary craft-making is fostering a revitalization of culture and language, bringing the past into the present (i.e. Phillips-Chan 2020a; Smithsonian Arctic Studies Center 2011, 2015).

Engraved drill bows with their detailed imagery of cultural activities offer a valuable knowledge bank from which to understand Indigenous worldviews and human-animal relationships in the Arctic. This catalog

Location Collected	No. Drill Bows	Location Collected	No. Drill Bows
Norton Sound (General)	22	Unalakleet / Uŋalaqłiit	3
Alaska (General)	15	Nubviukhchugaluk	2
Cape Nome / Ayasayuk	15	Pastolik	2
Kotzebue Sound (General)	10	Icy Cape / Kiyuksukuveet	1
Cape Darby / Atnuk	10	Cape Prince of Wales / Kiŋigin	2
Point Barrow / Nuvuk	9	Port Clarence	2
Sledge Island / Aziak	8	Little Diomede / Iŋaliq	1
Point Hope / Tikiġaq	7	Golovin Bay / Siŋik	1
St. Michael / Taciq	8	Nome / Sitŋasuaq	1
Diomede Islands	5	Sitka / Sheet'ká	1
Hotham Inlet	3		
Kigiktauik	3		
Shaktoolik / Saktuliq	3	TOTAL	134

Table 1/ Recorded locations of engraved drill bows in Smithsonian collections. Inupiaq and Yup'ik names for villages are *italicized*.

stems from an endeavor to reconnect Inupiaq traditional knowledge and oral histories to scenes of Bering Strait lifeways engraved on drill bows now in Smithsonian collections. The project represents a unique partnership between the Smithsonian Arctic Studies Center, the Carrie M. McLain Memorial Museum in Nome, Alaska, and Inupiaq and Yup'ik carvers in the Alaska communities of Utqiaġvik (formerly Barrow), Point Hope, Kotzebue, Shishmaref, Nome, St. Michael, and Anchorage.

In the following chapters, drill bows from the NMNH and NMAI are augmented with heritage items from the Carrie M. McLain Memorial Museum. Stories told by community members are linked to the objects and imagery, reconnecting oral knowledge to heritage items that have long resided far from their communities of origin.

Although Bering Strait carvers fashioned the drill bows more than one hundred years ago, these objects remain an integral part of Inupiaq knowledge systems and cultural identity. Many community members who contributed to this project have used drill bows or recall an older relative carving with one. During community conversations in Kotzebue, Jon Ipalook became inspired to create his own drill bow with a wood mouthpiece, drill, and bow from mineralized bone with an inlaid ivory seal and a strap of sealskin (Fig. 4). Ipalook (2012:5) shared that, "Carving is where I feel the most comfortable. Kind of brings me back to the places I've been, the people I've worked with; just being able to reconnect." For some community members, a hand-carved mouthpiece or a set of wood drills represents a cherished keepsake handed down from a respected family member. Images of drill bows elicited discussions about hand tools used to carve ivory and also fond remembrances about a time when people worked together in a shared way of life. Francis Alvanna (2012:2) recalled, "I learned to carve through my dad, in the *qagri*, men's house, community house... You used to go through the *qagri* and everybody carved in one place, like they do here in the carving shop in Nome, tell stories."

The engraved drill bows and accompanying stories also offer timely perspectives on current changes in our ecosystems and climate. The narratives shared here are rich in Indigenous observations that stem from generations of lived experience and indicate how these changes are affecting ice conditions and walrus migrations in the Arctic (Krupnik

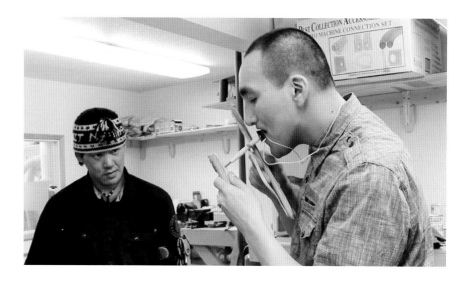

4/ Jon Ipalook demonstrates his handmade drill bow while Levi Angutiqjuaq from Igloolik, Nunavut looks on in the Sulianich Art Center. Kotzebue, AK. 2012. Photograph by Amy Phillips-Chan.

and Ray 2007). Vince Pikonganna (2012:9) remarked, "We used to watch men on King Island go down, go out to the ice, go hunting. Five, ten, fifteen miles out depending on the weather of course. Weather played a big part in everybody's life when you live in the village...But today the weather is so chaotic. You can't tell spring from summer. The winds have gotten stronger and the seasons are getting shorter. Even the ice is getting thinner... the walrus are beginning to go up earlier and earlier each year. We have to travel quite a ways out for walrus hunting, twenty, thirty miles out from Nome; maybe towards King Island or past Sledge Island and go south from there."

Ivory drill bows also speak to the continued importance of harvesting walrus for subsistence use and artwork. Wilfred Anowlic (2013:1) noted that in 2013, "We had lots of ice this year; it helped us to have a good spring season hunt. My hunting crew of three and myself went hunting and brought home a load of walrus meat, intestines, kidneys, livers, and flippers and made walrus blubber oil. We shared the meat with our Elders first. I have been having a feast, eating walrus for five days." Carvers approach a harvested walrus tusk strategically to get the most use out of the material, and even the ivory dust is carefully saved for future artwork (G. Sockpick 2012:3). Carvers who are unable to hunt their own walrus must often purchase tusks at high cost, which cuts deeply into the income they need to support their families in a cash-limited economy (Chan 2013:149-154). Decreased efforts at walrus hunting stem from multiple factors including changes in the traditional Inupiaq diet, walrus herds moving farther out from the coastline, and public perception of walrus as an endangered species.

Bering Strait communities emphasize an ongoing need to promote awareness about the legal sale of walrus ivory artwork (Baird 2016; IACB 2017). Pacific walrus are afforded protection in the United States under the Marine Mammal Protection Act (MMPA) of 1972. Under the MMPA, only Alaska Native hunters are able to harvest walrus for subsistence use. In 2016, the United States Fish and Wildlife Service (FWS) issued a near-total ban on the commercial trade in African elephant ivory. Six states (California, Hawaii, New Jersey, New York, Oregon, and Washington) followed suit and passed bans on the sale of ivory that has caused some consumers to shy away from Alaska Native artwork made from walrus ivory (Klouda 2017). FWS made an official determination in 2017 that Pacific walrus do not warrant listing as a threatened or endangered species under the Endangered Species Act (ESA). However, Alaska Native artists report that the domestic ivory ban has continued to negatively impact the art market

as it fails to acknowledge the difference between African elephant ivory and legally acquired walrus, mammoth, and mastodon ivory (Cole 2019). In 2019, a team of six delegates from the Bering Strait region traveled to Washington, DC to participate in the roundtable "Ayveq Nangaghneghput - Walrus & Our Way of Life." The presenters strove to increase public understanding on the cultural and economic significance of Pacific walrus, the importance of carving as an Indigenous way of life, and sustainable management of walrus within the changing Arctic (Kawerak, Inc. 2019).

Educational partnerships between museums and communities are bringing critical voices to the discussion of walrus and their vital role within Indigenous lifeways. In 2015, the Smithsonian Arctic Studies Center organized *Material Traditions: Sculpting Ivory*, an educational public program that documented how to process, design, and shape walrus ivory into artwork. Alaska Native carvers Jerome Saclamana (Inupiaq), Clifford Apatiki (St. Lawrence Island Yupik), and Levi Tetpon (Inupiaq) participated in a week-long residency at the Arctic Studies Center in Anchorage where they studied heritage items in collections, demonstrated carving techniques, and taught other Indigenous artists (Biddison 2016). As part of the program, Jerome Saclamana traveled to his home community of Nome where he led a two-day carving workshop at the Nome-Beltz High School (Fig. 5). This current museum-community project shares a similar approach to making space for Indigenous voices to be heard and for stories to be shared on their own terms. Discussions about drill bows and other heritage items are based on a holistic approach to knowledge that encompasses Indigenous frames of reference and multiple forms of information including oral histories, written texts, and material evidence (Griebel 2020; Kawagley 2006).

5/ Jerome Saclamana explains the different sections of a walrus tusk during a community workshop held as part of the Smithsonian Arctic Studies Center program *Material Traditions: Sculpting Ivory*. Around Jerome are left to right: Mary Jane Litchard, Moriah Sallafie, Anna Hoover, and Sierra Tucker. Nome, AK. 2015. Photograph by Amy Phillips-Chan.

Bering Strait Culture and Place

Ancient and contemporary lifeways merge in the Bering Strait, an area that broadly encompasses the northern coast of Alaska, Bering Sea islands, and the eastern Chukchi Peninsula. Along the shores, strong winds, limited rainfall, and cool temperatures restrict plant growth to dwarf shrubs and grasses. Further inland, the tundra bursts into color during long summer days with a profusion of wildflowers, edible greens, and luscious berries. The remote lands and frosty seas provide a critical habitat for hundreds of migratory birds, fish, marine mammals, and land mammals (Sutton and Steinacher 2012). Indigenous peoples have called this vast territory home for 4,000 to 6,000 years (Fitzhugh et. al. 2009; Itchoak 1978; Kaplan 1988). Finely crafted hunting equipment, tools, clothing, and artwork from the region convey a deep breadth of Indigenous knowledge that encompasses technologies for northern living, oral histories, and artistic traditions (Fienup-Riordan 2007; Fitzhugh and Crowell 1988; Fitzhugh and Kaplan 1982).

Today, the Bering Strait region of Alaska spans 23,000 square miles of coastal lands and includes 20 communities with three culturally distinct groups of people: the Inupiat, Central Yup'iit and St. Lawrence Island Yupiit. Bering Strait communities are located in rural areas primarily accessed by airplane, boat, and snow machine, and range in population from 100 to 3,600 residents. Each community has a municipal government that provides basic services to community residents and at least one Indian Reorganization Act (IRA) Council or Traditional Council that acts as the federally recognized tribal government. Communities support a mixed economy based on paid employment and subsistence practices. Challenges include inadequate housing, substance abuse, and lack of skilled job training, while community strengths include cultural and artistic activities, local schools, and close proximity to Elders [6].

Bering Strait communities are soundly connected to the outside world through smartphones, computers, social media, and other digital devices and platforms. However, like previous generations, the daily lives of many families are shaped through a close relationship with the surrounding environment (Anungazuk 2009; Zolles and Dyachkova 2009). By following a seasonal cycle of activities, communities can make efficient use of subsistence resources throughout the year (Glenn 2018). In winter (*Ugiuq*), the Bering Strait region is covered in a blanket of white with snowfall averaging around 76 inches a year. During clear weather, hunters slip on heavy parkas and warm boots to set off after

Arctic hare (*ugaliq*), wolf (*amaġuq*), red fox (*kayuqtuq*), and the elusive wolverine (*qappik*) in temperatures that can drop to well below 0°F. Polar bears (sing. *taguġaq*) are hunted for their prized fur and meat in the more northern regions. Snow machines are used to drive out on the sea ice to check pots set for king crab (*qaqquq*) while families jig for tomcod (*igałuaq*) through shore-fast ice, using netted scoops to keep the fishing holes clear and open.

Increased daylight during the spring (*Uvaġnagraq*) encourages the growth of nutritious plants including willow leaves (*sura*) and tubers from wild potato plants. Break-up of the sea ice is well under way by late April and Indigenous hunting crews follow open leads through the ice to pursue bearded seals (sing. *ugruk*), walrus (sing. *aiviq*), and bowhead whales (sing. *aġviq*) as they move north through the Bering Strait to reach summer feeding grounds in the Arctic Ocean (Fitzhugh and Crowell 2009; Koonooka 2020). Flocks of common murres (sing. *atpa*), gulls, geese, and ducks arrive soon after on warm breezes to nest among ponds, salt grass meadows, and rocky cliffs. Birds and their eggs provide a rich source of protein that can be paired with beach greens and fireweed (*pamiuqtaq*) shoots to create a spring meal bursting with nutrients and antioxidants.

During the summer (*Uvaġnaaq*), coastal waters teem with schools of salmon and herring while rivers and lakes entice anglers with freshwater and anadromous fish including grayling, pike, and whitefish. Families sweep out cabins at summer fish camps and make full use of the long daylight hours in June and July to net, cut, dry, can, or freeze hundreds of salmon in between picking and preserving berries. Autumn (*Ugiaq*) paints golden colors across the tundra and fills the skies with calls of cranes and geese as the birds embark on their southward migration. In September, the Western Arctic Caribou Herd (sing. *tuttu*) moves south through northwest Alaska and the animals are occasionally hunted among the tundra lichens and sedges of the eastern Seward Peninsula (Burch 2012). Moose (*tuttuaq*) began expanding into the Seward Peninsula from Interior Alaska during the 1930s to graze on dense clusters of willows growing on land turning over in mining during the gold rush days (Sutton and Steinacher 2012:34-35). Moose are especially prized for their large amount of lean meat that can fill up the freezer of a hunter and his family along with extended family members and friends. Expansion of the Arctic Ocean ice cap in the late fall drives marine mammals back south through the Bering Strait and offers coastal communities another opportunity to secure food and raw materials for the coming winter.

On the Hunt for Ivory

Alaska Native hunters have pursued Pacific walrus, *Odobenus rosmarus divergens*, and *aiviq* in Inupiaq, in the ice laden waters of the Bering Strait for almost two thousand years (Bruce 1895:45; Burch 2006:165-167; Curtis 1930:113). Walrus provide meat for people and sled dogs, skins for boat and kayak covers, and ivory and bone for hunting gear, tools, and artwork (Crowell 2009; Kawerak, Inc. 2019). Adult walrus average around 2,500 pounds and have two prominent ivory tusks that can grow up to 36 inches in length. A primary function of a walrus' strong, slightly curved tusks is to plough the muddy bottom of the sea for clams and other mollusks to eat. The tusks are also useful for poking breathing holes through young sea ice, anchoring onto an ice floe, fighting other walrus, and for protection from natural predators including killer whales and polar bears (Apatiki 2016). Scratches, stress lines, nicks, and even subtle shades in the coloration of a pair of ivory tusks can help us to understand the life of a walrus (Koozaata 1982; Saclamana 2016; Tetpon 2016).

Bering Strait communities hold various narratives regarding the creation of walrus. In a tale from Chukotka, Raven creates marine mammals by throwing different kinds of wood shavings into the water; pine chips turn into walrus, oak chips become seals, and black birch shavings emerge as large whales (Bogoras 1975:153). A tale told by Ticasuk from Unalakleet chronicles an exchange between walrus and ptarmigan in which ptarmigan gives his crop to walrus allowing him to float, and walrus offers up his claws that provide ptarmigan the ability to dig in the hard snow (Brown 1987:119-120). Shamans drew on the transformative power of walrus to teach lessons, assist the village, or correct improper behavior (Asatchaq 1992:118; Bogoras 1975:8). Parts of a walrus, including the bladder and skull, were considered vital to maintaining positive hunter-animal relationships and were used in special ceremonies and festivals [7]. Contemporary communities continue to enact the importance of walrus through wearing walrus gut clothing, dancing carved walrus masks, and incorporating dance movements mimicking walrus behavior (Hickman 1987; Tördal 2016).

During the winter breeding season, walrus congregate in groups of hundreds to thousands on thick ice floes from southwest of St. Lawrence Island to the Gulf of Anadyr and northern Bristol Bay. Walrus utilize sea ice for transport during the spring migration with adult females and dependent young moving into the Chukchi Sea and adult males heading to summer haul-out sites along the coasts of Alaska and Chukotka (Krupnik 2020:354-355). Subsistence hunters carry in-depth knowledge of local walrus movements with complex terminology for ice conditions and specific age-sex groupings (Koonooka 2020:152-157; Krupnik and Ray 2007). Walrus hunters must often negotiate with variable weather conditions, changing ice patterns, and large animals that can turn aggressive (Krupnik and Benter 2016). Vince Pikonganna (2012:9) recalled, "We used to watch men on King Island go down, go out to the ice, go hunting. Weather was the boss. And they have to have someone in the village that knows about the weather. A lot of people seek his advice. Of course, you learn a thing or two over the years from hunting."

Hunters pay special attention to handling and dividing the walrus meat, ivory, and skins (Burch 2006:167-169; Curtis 1930:101; Milan 1964:37) (Fig. 6). The captain often receives the flippers as well as a double portion of the meat and blubber for supplying the boat and motor (Pikonganna 2012:10). Walrus tusks might be given to the boat owner or the harpooner, or sold, and the profits divided equally among the hunting crew. The remaining walrus meat and skins are typically split between the other crewmembers. Experienced hunters continue to use the hunting process to pass on knowledge as noted by Joseph Kunnuk Sr. (2012:14) who explained, "You teach them out there, while we're hunting walrus, how to cut the heads off, cut the meat and everything." Contemporary carvers procure unworked walrus ivory through several strategies including hunting, trade, and purchase from Indigenous community members or Alaska Native organizations (Chan 2013:148-152). Active ivory carving communities include Utqiaġvik, Point Hope, Kotzebue, Shishmaref, Wales, Little Diomede, Teller, Nome, St. Michael, and Anchorage. (Chan 2013:24-59; Fair 2006:28-47). Families of skilled carvers also live in Gambell and Savoonga on St. Lawrence Island and the village of Uelen in Chukotka (Bronshtein et. al. 2002; Imperato 2017).

6/ Hunters divide walrus tusks out on the Bering Sea ice. c. 1910. Carrie M. McLain Memorial Museum, 96.1.121.

Communities of Ivory Carvers

Walrus ivory features inherent qualities of strength, endurance, and smoothness that have allowed it to be carved into multiple forms essential for daily life in the Arctic, from harpoon heads and fishing lures to needle cases and bucket handles. Ross Schaeffer Sr. (2012:2) remarked, "Dad and these guys had very little education but a lot of learning by watching. So they were real skilled at making anything. That's just natural ability from thousands of years. We made tools." Young men around the ages of nine to eleven traditionally began learning to carve through observation of relatives and gradual participation such as sanding or polishing an older carver's work (Tetpon 2012:4; Weyiouanna 2012:1; see Chapter 1, this volume). A young apprentice did not ask too many questions but paid close attention to an experienced carver and tried to follow his example. John Pullock (2012:5) affirmed that when learning to carve, "I started to copy what the older people carve. They don't show us but if we do something [wrong], they tell us, so you fix that."

Ivory carving as a male-centered activity relates to long-standing Inupiaq ideologies regarding men as the sole hunters of marine mammals (Jolles 2006:255). Ethnologist Edward Nelson (1899:197) made the general observation that in the Bering Strait, "men make very handsome ivory work [while] the women are equally skillful in beautiful ornamental needlework on articles of clothing." During this project, James Omiak (2012b:1) remarked that when growing up in Little Diomede during the 1930s, the women sewed but never carved. Likewise, Vince Pikonganna (2012:2) explained that women on King Island focused primarily on "skin sewing and stuff. They do beautiful work. They have very delicate hands."

In other communities, increased tourism and an expanded art market encouraged women to carve. Levi Tetpon (2012:13) recalled that his mother and father both carved and sewed as a source of employment while he was growing up in Shaktoolik. Today, an increasing number of Indigenous women are interested in ivory carving as seen at the carving workshop in Nome in 2015 (see Fig. 5). In Little Diomede, Vera Ozenna specializes in carving ivory bracelets with engraved animals. Artist Susie Silook from Gambell has been carving sinuous ivory sculptures for over thirty years and is leading recent discussions on the legal use of walrus ivory by Alaska Native artists (Hovey 2017).

Rather than a solitary pursuit, carving in the past traditionally occurred within a larger realm of physical activity related to construction and repair of implements inside the *qagri* or men's house. A *qagri* (pl. *qagrit*) often served as the physical, social, and spiritual center of a community where men worked together and the entire community gathered for drum dancing, feasts, and celebrations (Anderson 2005:34; Burch 2006:220-222; Jensen 2012:147). Edward Nelson (1899:286) observed that during the 1880s, "men are nearly always to be found in the kashim [*qagri*] when in the village, this being their general gathering place, where they work on tools or implements of the chase, or in preparing skins." Sitting with legs outstretched in the *qagri*, men could chat and relay stories while carving and undertaking the painstakingly slow task of engraving miniature scenes across narrow ivory surfaces. Carvers-in-training would have had an opportunity to observe tools and techniques being used and to listen to stories of ancient creatures and hunting exploits. King Island elder Sylvester Ayek (2012:4) noted, "As boys we were always in the clubhouse. Where all the carving, and tool-making and implement construction, *qayaq* construction, took place."

Traditional *qagrit* began to disappear during the late nineteenth century under the influence of traders and missionaries, with attendant

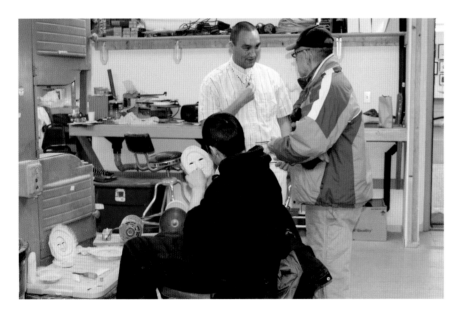

7/ Jon Ipalook discusses his ivory and baleen necklace with Kenny Tikik while Emmanuel Hawley carves a whalebone mask inside the community carving workshop at the Sulianich Art Center. Kotzebue, AK. 2012. Photograph by Amy Phillips-Chan.

transformation of internal power relations and religious beliefs (Cassell 2000:122; Phillips-Chan 2020b:176-178). However, many carvers continued to work side-by-side under skin boats at summer camps or in repurposed spaces such as metal Quonset huts in Nome and Utqiaġvik (Chan 2013:173-175; Mongoyak 2012:3; Omiak 2012a:7) (see Fig. 119). Forms of contemporary *qagrit* with areas for carvers to work together can be seen today at the King Island Native Community carving shop in Nome, Iñupiat Heritage Center Traditional Room in Utqiaġvik, and the Sulianich Art Center in Kotzebue (Chan 2013:180-185). Bone and ivory carvers in Kotzebue enjoy access to a ventilated workshop with drawers to store their supplies, use of large power tools, and free bones to carve that are brought in by local hunters (Fig. 7). The Center also serves as a teaching space where experienced carvers Ross Schaeffer and Jon Ipalook have demonstrated carving techniques to younger artists, including working with whalebone and how to use a drill bow (see Fig. 4).

Drill Bow Technology

The transformation of unprocessed walrus tusks into finely-crafted implements and artwork requires a toolkit of specialized items that are needed to split, shape, polish, and engrave the ivory (see Appendix 2). Contemporary carvers utilize a variety of hand tools such as chisels and files as well as power tools including electric drills with interchangeable bits (Fig. 8). However, carvers from the Old Bering Sea and Ipiutak cultures had to draw from surrounding natural resources to assemble toolkits, which included stone-bladed adzes, side-hafted knives, scrapers, and burins. Engraving appears to have been done with ivory styluses fitted with bits of animal teeth or non-meteoric iron obtained in trade from Siberia (Chan 2013:219-221; Larsen and Rainey 1948:83).

8/ Joseph Kunnuk Sr. holds up an ivory bracelet link inside his carving workshop. Nome, AK. 2012. Photograph by Amy Phillips-Chan.

Vince Pikonganna (2012:8) commented, "I don't know how they carved in those days, with the tools they had, very limited tools. But they were making some of the most beautiful items I've ever seen in my life."

Drill bows of ivory and antler became part of carving toolkits by around 1200 A.D. and appear to have been introduced into the Bering Strait with the rise of the Western Thule culture (Chan 2013:188-190; Collins 1937:180, 236-237). The incorporation of drill bows into toolkits of the overlapping Birnirk-Thule and Punuk-Thule cultures can be related to the integration of metal tools and a change to a bolder engraving style accompanied by the emergence of pictorial imagery (see pp. 30-34, this volume). In addition to drill bows, toolkits from this historic period (approx. 1200-1890 A.D.), typically included an adze, carving knife, chisel, scraper, whetstone, and red ocher. These tools were often carefully stored in a bentwood toolbox or hide satchel (Gordon 1917:222; Murdoch 1892:189; Nelson 1899:93-94) (see Figs. 27, 156).

Oral narratives from Inupiaq and Yup'ik communities describe the introduction of drill bow technology through lessons of trial and error and from supernatural creatures. Inupiaq Elder William Oquilluk (1973:267) explained that the people of Qawiaraq learned to use drill bows to ignite fires following a great disaster that decimated the area. In a legend from the Yukon-Kuskokwim Delta, Raven teaches men how to make fire with a drill bow:

> Here the R. [Raven] stopped and spent considerable time teaching the men various things, among others how to make a fire with a drill and a piece of wood, with a cord to make drill revolve... They were now taught to make a fire with drill and to place the burning spark or timber in a bunch of dry grass and wave it back and fro to make a blaze and to put upon this dry wood [8].

Creation of an ivory drill bow begins with removal of the paper-like outer cementum of a walrus tusk, often with the use of an adze (*qayuun*) (Hoffman 1897:774-775; Koonook 2010:2) (see Fig. 50). Next, an adze, hacksaw, or coping saw is used to cut the tusk vertically into four or more sections, forming the general outline of the drill bow (Saclamana 2012a:15) (Fig. 9). Metal files, gravers, burins, chisels or small knives serve to refine the shape (see Figs. 42, 46, 59). A carver can then use a drill or knife to hollow out lashing holes on the ends of the bow. The time-consuming task of polishing comes next with ivory, stone, or sandpaper used to smooth the surface until it gleams (Alvanna 2012:8). Engraved imagery is added with fine-tipped metal tools including knives, engravers, drills, and dentistry tools (B. Sockpick

2012:6). Dark soot, India ink, or red ocher can then be rubbed into the engravings with the extra coloring buffed off (G. Sockpick 2012:16) (Fig. 10). Finally, a strap of animal skin, typically from bearded sealskin or young walrus, is strung through the end holes and knotted on one end.

Drill bows are used in conjunction with a mouthpiece (*kiŋmiaq*) and a drill (*niuun*), which allows the carver to have one hand free to hold the object on which he is working (see Fig. 1). Contemporary carvers speak of the skill required to make and use a drill bow. Ross Schaeffer Sr. (2012:4) stated, "It took a lot of work to make a drill bow real flat, especially with the kinds of tools they had." Vince Pikonganna (2012:13) shared, "Using a drill bow is how my father got such a strong neck. I used my father's drill bow before…It wore out my neck and jaw gripping the mouthpiece."

Drill bows were taken care of as prized tools and passed down through the generations (Gordon 1917:233; Hoffman 1897:774). Contemporary carvers speak with respect about drill bows that belonged to family members and whose parts they have inherited. Sylvester Ayek (2012:4) mentioned the only belonging of his father's he has left is his wood mouthpiece. John Penatac Sr. (2012:1) remembered his father using an ivory drill bow and has carefully saved his father's set of wood drills. James Omiak used his own drill bow for many years to carve ivory bracelets while Francis Alvanna used his drill bow to demonstrate traditional ivory carving to tourists in Nome (Alvanna 2012:1-2; Omiak 2012a:1-2). In Point Hope, Henry Koonook often relies on his handmade drill bow when he is creating holes for ivory bracelets or cribbage boards (Fig. 11). Henry Koonook (2010:12) emphasized that, "it's important to have people like myself and others that use these tools. It's important to pass all this on to the next generation because they may have to use these tools someday. Who knows…

9/ Gary Sockpick uses a vise and hacksaw to cut through a section of walrus tusk in his outdoor carving space. Shishmaref, AK. 2012. Photograph by Amy Phillips-Chan.

10/ Gary Sockpick rubs off a layer of black ink to reveal a pair of walrus he engraved onto the ivory. Shishmaref, AK. 2012. Photograph by Amy Phillips-Chan.

11/ Henry Koonook demonstrates a handmade drill bow inside his home. A vise, hacksaw, and *ulimaun* (adze) are within easy reach on the table. Point Hope, AK. 2010. Photograph by Amy Phillips-Chan.

we might have to go back and live the old way." As can be seen, drill bow technology remains a form of Indigenous science, valued within traditional Inupiaq knowledge systems. However, engraved drill bows in Smithsonian collections were crafted over a hundred years ago and knowledge of their makers has been lost to time (Pullock 2012:1). To help us understand the pictorial imagery, we need to turn to some of the earliest known cultures in the Bering Strait.

Tracing the Origins of Pictorial Engraving

Artistic origins of the pictorial system of figures and animals engraved on drill bows remains a point of debate between archaeologists and art historians (i.e. Bronshtein 2006; Fitzhugh and Crowell 2009; Fitzhugh and Kaplan 1982:242-243; Mason and Alix 2019). Beginning around 100 A.D., communities on both sides of the Bering Strait utilized walrus ivory for creating the majority of their hunting implements, tools, and household articles (Fitzhugh et. al. 2009). Waves of cultural settlement by Okvik, Old Bering Sea, Ipiutak, Birnik, and Punuk peoples resulted in design systems of interconnected lines that wrapped around the contours of ivory carvings in elaborate patterns that indicate organized methods of learning and production (Bronshtein 2006; Bronshtein and Dneprovsky 2009:108; Chan 2013:218-221). Archaeologist Henry Collins made one of the earliest attempts to retrace the source of pictorial imagery and argued it derived from Old Bering Sea linear designs in Eastern Siberia (Collins 1939).

The Old Bering Sea (100-800 A.D.) artistic tradition consists of curvilinear designs, nucleated circles with multiple rings, and straight, dashed, and barbed lines that are delicately engraved onto the ivory surface. Around 800 A.D., the Old Bering Sea design system shifted into a simplified method of linear motifs related to the Punuk culture (800-1200 A.D.). Punuk design elements include straight lines with pairs of barbs, barbed bands, ladder or checkered lines, bevel lines, nucleated circles, and zigzag like motifs (Bronshtein 2006:166) (Table 2).

The Birnirk culture (800-1200 A.D.) overlapped with the Punuk culture but with their sparse ornamentation, Birnirk engravings appear to have been a derivative rather than a successor in the Old Bering Sea artistic continuum (Carter 1966; Collins 1939:1). Birnirk design motifs include spurred lines, curved double lines, rows of dots or broken lines, straight lines with widely spaced barbs, prongs or double-prongs, and a horizontal line with vertical bars (Bronshtein 2006:165; Collins 1973:10) (Table 3).

Both the Birnirk and Punuk cultures contributed to the rise of the Thule culture (1000-1500 A.D.) and its artistic traditions (Dumond 2009:75; Fitzhugh 2009:88). This confluence appears to have resulted in two styles of early pictorial imagery on bone and ivory that combined linear elements and figural motifs, a Birnirk-Thule style and a Punuk-Thule style. Birnirk-Thule figural motifs tend to have irregular outlines with a sketch-like appearance while Punuk-Thule figures tend to be larger with straight outlines and darkened centers that result in a bold appearance. These two early pictorial styles can be seen at several village sites along the coast of the Bering and Chukchi seas (Chan 2013:218-249).

One of the most vivid examples of the Birnirk-Thule style of engraving was uncovered during the summer of 2007 by a team of Russian-American researchers led by Sergei Gusev and Daniel Odess at the Un'en'en site near the modern whaling village of Nunligran on the southern coast of the Chukotka Peninsula (Fisher 2008; Gusev 2014; Luukkanen and Fitzhugh 2020:169; Powell 2009). The ivory carving from Un'en'en is of a slightly curved form with a lashing hole on one end and a vertical groove on the other end indicative of use as a drill bow or bag handle (Fig. 12). The carver has engraved barbed lines around the lashing hole and a row of figures on each broad side that depict hunting whales with the aid of harpoons and sealskin floats, harpooning walrus on the ice, hunting polar bears with spears, hunting in a kayak, dancing, dogs, birds, and conical tents. The carver pressed hard to engrave the lines and dug out the centers or used dense cross hatching to darken the figures. Distinctive Birnik-Thule pictorial elements seen on the carving include figures with rectangular bodies and heads and extended or droopy arms; polar bears with elongated necks and distended stomachs; barbs or lines to indicate figures in a skin boat (often with a transparent side); and a kayak with a rectangular figure in the center (Chan 2013:221-249).

12/ Walrus ivory tool engraved with scenes of whaling and hunting from the Un'en'en site on the southern coast of the Chukotka Peninsula (from Gusev 2014:209).

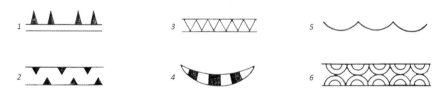

Table 2/ Basic motifs of Punuk graphic design (from Bronshtein 2006:166).

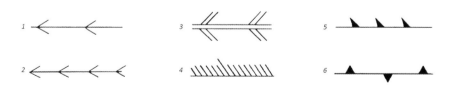

Table 3/ Basic motifs of Birnirk graphic design (from Bronshtein 2006:165).

13/ Tayaġnailitaq WRIST GUARD
Cape Smythe (Utqiaġvik)
Collected by Vilhjalmur Stefansson, accessioned 1912
American Museum of Natural History 60/9732
Bone; Length 10.4 cm (4 in)

14/ Pitiksiaq DRILL BOW
Point Hope
Collected by John Borden, accessioned 1927
Field Museum 177754
Walrus ivory, sealskin; Length 38 cm (15 in)

Birnirk-Thule elements on the Un'en'en carving, including rectangular figures in skin boats and the depiction of bowhead whales in full profile, are stylistically similar to petroglyphs found along the Pegtymel River in north Chukotka that date back to the Old Bering Sea period (Dikov 1999:57-58, 143, 154, 156). Likewise, pictorial motifs on the Un'en'en carving including skin boats, whales, and tall figures with staffs appear to have been carried forward into the nineteenth century as seen on

a painted sealskin with hunting and village scenes collected by William Hulme Hooper at Indian Point (Ungaziq) in southern Chukotka in 1849 (Chan 2013:249-250; Hooper 1853:106). These examples suggest that elements of a rich pictorial tradition were transmitted and expressed through over a thousand years of successive cultures along the coast of Chukotka.

A fluid exchange of culture and artistic traditions seems to have also existed between the Birnirk peoples of Chukotka and North Alaska. Some of the earliest known carvings from Alaska to combine Birnirk linear elements with pictorial motifs derive from collections made by Vilhjálmur Stefansson in the area of Cape Smythe (Utqiaġvik) in 1912 (Chan 2013:231-234) [9]. One of these pieces is a bone wrist guard that features a roughly engraved bow hunter with a rectangular torso shooting a single caribou on top of a pronged line (Fig. 13). Down the coast, the Birnirk culture appears to have existed close to Ipiutak settlements near the modern village of Point Hope but with limited control of the area (Mason 1998). In 1927, John Borden collected a drill bow at Point Hope with sketch-like motifs related to early Birnirk-Thule artistry including tall rectangular figures and figures standing in an umiaq with a transparent side (Borden 1928) (Fig. 14).

A Punuk-Thule engraving style appears to have found expression in North Alaska as well as in Chukotka and St. Lawrence Island (Chan 2013:227-228). Punuk-Thule engraving often features barbed bands and nucleated circles paired with large simple motifs such as a standing figure or a row of animals. An engraved ivory plate acquired by Stefansson at Utqiaġvik in 1912 offers a good example of Punuk-Thule artistry. The plate features a V-shaped notch at the top, wide lashing holes on the sides, and two large figures with rectangular torsos and raised arms engraved on the front (Fig. 15). A drill bow from Point Hope also relates to Punuk-

15/ IVORY PLATE
Cape Smythe (Utqiaġvik)
Collected by Vilhjalmur Stefansson, accessioned 1912
American Museum of Natural History 60.1/1015
Walrus ivory; Length 6.9 cm (2.7 in)

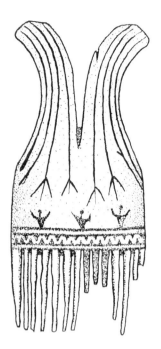

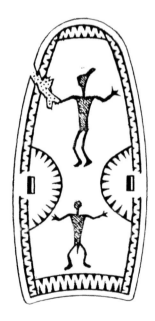

17/ Illaiyutit COMB
Kurigitavik site at Wales
Collected by Henry Collins, accessioned 1936
National Museum of Natural History A395118
Walrus ivory; Length 7.5 cm (3 in)

16/ Tayaġnailitaq WRIST GUARD
Kurigitavik site at Wales
Collected by Henry Collins, accessioned 1936
National Museum of Natural History A392832
Bone; Length 5.8 cm (2.3 in)

18/ BOAT HOOK
Bering Strait
Collected by Caroline Coons, accessioned 1985
Carrie M. McLain Memorial Museum 1985.3.140
Walrus ivory; Length 21 cm (8.3 in)

Thule engraving with its combination of barbed lines and nucleated circles and its row of large caribou, wolves, whale flukes, and figures (Fig. 36). Excavations in the Kurigitavik mound at Cape Prince of Wales in 1936 by Henry Collins uncovered several carvings with Punuk-Thule imagery including a bone wrist guard with a barbed band around the edge, two arched lines with barbs, and two standing figures in the center (Fig. 16).

Bering Strait coastal communities such as those at Cape Prince of Wales served as a crossroads of cultures, languages, and artistic traditions. For example, stratigraphic layers at Kurigitavik reveal a Birnirk settlement followed by Punuk-Thule houses (Jenness 1928; Mason 1998). Artistic elements from these overlapping cultures can be seen on an ivory comb from Kurigitavik engraved with three figures and spurred lines (Birnirk) and a barbed band (Punuk) (Fig. 17). A portion of an engraved ivory boat hook from North Alaska also combines Birnirk and Punuk elements including a row of dashed lines and barbs to indicate figures in a skin boat (Birnirk) along with barbed ladder lines and a large standing figure and polar bear (Punuk) (Fig. 18). This combination or borrowing of Birnirk-Punuk-Thule design elements persisted into the nineteenth century and can be seen on several drill bows including one acquired by Lucien Turner in Norton Sound that is engraved with spurred lines (Birnirk), barbed bands (Punuk), and a row of caribou figures (Thule) (Fig. 108). It was out of the pervasive Thule culture that pictorial engraving on ivory and bone reached new heights of complexity and flourished for almost a hundred years from the late 1700s to the late 1800s.

The Art of Engraving Drill Bows

The Bering Strait experienced a vibrant artistic movement during the nineteenth century with a proliferation of pictorial imagery on material culture items made from ivory, bone and wood (see Appendix 3). The imagery speaks to the region's rich artistic traditions as well as a wealth of traditional ecological knowledge that has sustained Indigenous communities for generations (Chan 2013:604-639; Ray 1977:22-28). Communities carried unique histories and practices that influenced the content, or characters, on engraved drill bows including different techniques for hunting animals, construction of houses and kayaks, kinds of celebrations, and forms of mythological creatures (see Appendix 4). Artistic traditions within a community influenced the shape of a drill bow along with the techniques used to compose the figural scenes and to engrave and darken the imagery. These distinct cultural and artistic traits, along with associated written documentation, help us to identify some of the home communities for Bering Strait drill bows.

Museums records and field notes offer a starting point toward understanding the origins of engraved drill bows. Smithsonian naturalist Edward Nelson paid attention to the proveniences of drill bows and recorded the names of sixteen locations and villages (see Appendix 1). Other collectors noted more general areas, such as Lucien Turner who attributed almost all the drill bows he secured to "Norton Sound." Complicating the record is that community members traveled from distant villages to trade with collectors but their home villages were not always recorded. For instance, we know Edward Nelson purchased engraved drill bows from King Islanders who were visiting St. Michael, but Nelson did not label any drill bows as "King Island" [10]. Likewise, Nelson labeled ten drill bows as "Kotzebue Sound" but they most certainly represent the artistry of several village groups who had traveled to the region for summer fishing and perhaps the international trading fair at Hotham Inlet (Ray 1982:258) (see Figs. 61, 133).

Content within engraved scenes, including sleds, kayaks, and dwellings, feature design traits that offer further insight into where drill bows originated (Chan 2013:157-161, 269-271) (see also Appendix 4). Various forms of kayaks depicted on drill bows is a good example of this diversity (Table 4). Indigenous kayaks in Alaska were strongly built with light wood frames typically covered with sealskin that were

NMNH E48524	NMNH E360422	NMNH E44209	NMNH E24556
North Alaska	Bering Strait	Norton Sound	Aleutians

Table 4/ Kayaks engraved on ivory drill bows with construction traits that relate to four areas of Alaska including: North Alaska (left), Bering Strait (center left), Norton Sound (center right) and the Aleutians (right).

uniquely designed for rough water and weather conditions outside coastal communities (Zimmerly 2000). Kayaks from North Alaska feature a sharp rise to the deck in front of the cockpit while those from the Bering Strait are characterized by an upturned bow and sloped stern. Norton Sound kayaks are typically longer than their northern counterparts and feature a straight line along the deck ridge and handgrips on the ends. Kayaks from the Aleutian Islands often include two or three hatches and a prominent bifurcated bow (Fitzhugh and Crowell 1988:159).

Besides design differences in kayaks and other household items, a particular engraving style could have communicated the owner's social identity, similar to clothing, dance masks, and other forms of artistic expression (Driscoll Engelstad 2020; Phillips-Chan 2020b:168-174). Museum anthropologist George Byron Gordon traveled to northwest Alaska in 1905 and remarked, "All of the western Eskimo are adept in the art [of carving ivory] but some individuals excel to such a degree that their work is known throughout their respective tribes" (Gordon 1906:80). During a visit to the Anchorage Museum in 2012, Levi Tetpon (2012:8) readily identified stylistic traits of ancestral carvings from his home community of Shaktoolik as well as artistic elements related to King Island and St. Lawrence Island. Likewise, although field collectors did not record the names of drill bow owners, the work of particular artists would have doubtless been known to others in their home communities. Vince Pikongganna (2012:1) explained, "Over the years, you learn whose carving it is, by watching. Today, you can recognize people's carvings, who they are."

Through close examination of how drill bows are carved and engraved we can begin to see stylistic distinctions. Bering Strait carvers principally utilized walrus ivory to craft their drill bows, but members of the Pastolik community appear to have preferred bone or antler from more readily accessible caribou (Chan 2013:335-343) (see Figs. 54, 99). The technique used for splitting a walrus tusk resulted in a variety of drill bow forms including rectangular, flat, square, triangular, or cylindrical bows with either squared or rounded edges. Jerome Saclamana (2012a:15) of King Island said, "My father Mike Saclamana Sr. used to split a walrus tusk into four for making drill bows. He used the female tusks with a natural curve for the drill bow and did the old style of etching." In Little Diomede, carvers often fashioned shorter drill bows of rectangular form with squared edges (see Figs. 39, 44, 101, 144). In contrast, carvers from Sledge Island preferred longer bows with two sloped sides divided by a ridge in the center (see Figs. 84, 131, 148). Carvers from Point Hope often added a carved caribou head or whale's fluke to the end of their bows (Chan 2013:553-554) (see Figs. 36, 63).

A new drill bow presented a blank surface on which to engrave figures and scenes. Organization of the engraved scenes varied between villages but most drill bows feature lower and/or upper baselines to orient the figures, similar to a sheet of lined paper (see Figs. 72-75). Upside-down figures on a drill bow sometimes illustrate the continuation of a scene and a carver reading or narrating the story could have rotated the drill bow to continue the tale, similar to turning the pages of a book (see Figs. 81, 84, 86). Artists arranged other scenes by season or location, such as a drill bow acquired at Cape Darby, which has separate sides illustrating a winter celebration, spring whaling, and autumn caribou hunting (Fig. 127).

Drill bow artists engraved characters in a representational style that often communicated a lot of action in a few lines. To make symmetrical circles for heads on figures, carvers could rotate a wooden drill shaft with a metal bit. One could also hold a wooden drill like a pencil and use the metal bit to draw outlines of characters. Carving knives, gravers, and three-cornered files were used in the same manner by pressing their pointed ends into the ivory (Hoffman 1897:785). The centers of drill bow characters were hollowed out and filled in with vertical lines, hatching, and scribbles (Chan 2013:268-269). Ivory carvers in a community often worked together and followed local artistic traditions, which resulted in village styles of pictorial engraving. For instance, drill bows acquired at Hotham Inlet were probably made by carvers from the Kigiktauik settlement in Kotzebue Sound or Sheshalik on the north side of Hotham Inlet (Jackson 1893:1277). These drill bows regularly feature deeply etched scenes with irregular outlines and scraped out centers (see Figs. 98, 105). Drill bows collected at Cape Nome appear to have originated from the local village of Ayasayuk or were made by visitors from Ugiuvak on King Island (Chan 2013:321-326; Jackson 1893:1273; Ray 1992:104-106). Cape Nome drill bows feature complex scenes with delicate figures and straight lines (see Figs. 77, 122, 124). Drill bows labeled Diomede Islands derive from the village of Iŋaliq on Little Diomede, and possibly the settlement of Imaqłiq on Big Diomede (see Curtis 1930:111-117; Hughes 1985:248). Diomede drill bows are recognizable by their block-like characters with broad square hatching and white bands (Figs. 44, 101, 144).

After characters had been engraved, carvers rubbed a dark fill across the drill bow to make the images stand out against the creamy white background. Lucien Turner observed Bering Strait carvers using a mixture of powdered charcoal from burnt grass mixed with oil (Hoffman 1897:790). Edward Nelson (1899:196) recorded that carvers used a mixture of gunpowder and blood and John Murdoch (1892:390) explained that the dark red color on Point Barrow imagery came from red ocher. Jerome Saclamana (2012b:2) commented that seal oil lamps in the past would have generated a residue that carvers could apply to their etchings. Saclamana (2012b:1) also remembered older relatives from King Island who rubbed cigarette or tobacco ash from their ashtrays over the engraved imagery.

Several drill bows in the Smithsonian collection feature two or more engraving styles (see Figs. 41, 45, 55, 80, 143). The presence of multiple art styles indicates that drill bows might have been passed down to younger carvers, circulated among different villages, or traded to other carvers who added their own imagery for personal enjoyment or to make them more appealing to collectors. An ivory drill bow collected by Edward Nelson at Cape Darby seems to have been passed between three different artists (Table 5, Fig. 55). The drill bow appears to have originated at Wales where Artist 1 engraved small motifs with gouged out centers including a row of caribou swimming in the water. The drill

Artist 1 (Wales)	Artist 2 (Little Diomede)	Artist 3 (St. Michael)

Table 5/ Caribou engraved on ivory drill bow NMNH E44209 relate to three villages including: Wales (left), Little Diomede (center), and St. Michael (right). Collected by Edward Nelson at Cape Darby between 1877 and 1881. Length 34 cm.

bow then seems to have traveled to Little Diomede where Artist 2 added a row of caribou etched with square hatching. Artist 3 squeezed six small and delicate caribou onto the end in an artistic style predominant at St. Michael. This third carver was probably the last to add imagery to the drill bow before selling it to Nelson between 1877 and 1880. The circulation of drill bows such as this one encourage us to not simply label them with one origin but to consider the complex social lives of the carvings as they moved around the Bering Strait region.

The emergence of tourist markets at Port Clarence and St. Michael in the late 1800s and at Nome in the early 1900s fostered the use of new engraving techniques and materials including pencils for sketching outlines, metal dentistry tools for etching fine lines, and black ink to quickly darken characters (Gordon 1906:80-81; Ray 1977:43-44) (Figs. 19, 157). Many ivory artists transferred their engraving skills to profitable curios such as pipes, whole tusks, and cribbage boards (Figs. 2, 66, 70, 141, 190, 191). However, a handful of carvers continued to fashion drill bows and engrave them for the curio trade (see Figs. 67-68). Drill bows made for sale during the early 1900s often feature a modified style of pictorial engraving with larger or formulaic characters

darkened with a zigzag technique created by rocking a metal etcher back and forth (Chan 2013:343-350) (see Figs. 39, 201). Carvers may have also made drill bows at the request of collectors such as Superintendent of Education Walter C. Shields who received a drill bow engraved by an artist from Wales in 1915 (Fig. 20).

The curio market in Nome also nurtured the rise of a new style of pictorial engraving characterized by traditional Inupiaq subject matter, i.e. northern animals and activities, etched according to Western artistic principles including realism and perspective (Phillips-Chan 2019:43-48). While most drill bow artists of this era remained anonymous to

19/ Three young carvers from St. Lawrence Island are engraving walrus tusks outside a tent on the beach. c. 1905. Carrie M. McLain Memorial Museum, 96.12.4.

20/ Pitiksiaq DRILL BOW
Wales
Collected by Walter C. Shields, dated April 14, 1915, accessioned 2015
Carrie M. McLain Memorial Museum 2015.2.2
Walrus ivory, sealskin; Length 53 cm (21 in)

outsiders, a few of their twentieth-century successors became well-known including Angokwazhuk "Happy Jack," Guy Kakarook, and Joe Kakarook (Ray 1996:105-109; Ray 2003). Pictorial engraving at this time shifted in purpose and took on a new social and economic value outside the traditional use as illustrations of personal records or oral narratives [11].

Stories in Ivory

Ivory carvers drew from a rich catalog of images or characters to illustrate scenes on drill bows including marine and land mammals, birds and fish, plants, human figures, mythical creatures, and objects related to living in the Arctic (see Appendix 3). Engraved stories featuring subsistence activities communicate a deep understanding about the seasonal cycle that structures community life (Pikonganna 1988). One characteristic sequence of events can be seen on a drill bow that shows hunters harpooning a bowhead whale, cutting the whale up on the beach, and villagers celebrating the successful hunt (Fig. 127). Sylvester Ayek (2012:4) observed, "Because our culture is oral culture

too, this is how they told their views about village life. And what it takes to be a hunter and gatherer. And they did very well." Today, the engraved imagery offers us a detailed record of Bering Strait lifeways in the 1800s. Edwin Weyiouanna (2012:3) of Shishmaref commented, "On some of these carvings, they tell their story on how they lived. That's why they have these etchings. They didn't have any paper or books a long time ago. They didn't know how to read. But they knew how to do artwork."

Oral stories are essential to passing on family records, cultural values, and traditional ecological knowledge (Oquilluk 1973:xviii). In North Alaska, a respected storyteller is known as a *unipkaaqti*, a historian, who safeguards the community's collective knowledge of the past. Herbert Anungazuk (2003:77-78) of Wales emphasized that, "Oral history is a time-honored way to teach, and it is based on the learning and experiences of the ancestors." Contemporary ivory carvers draw on oral narratives for visual inspiration as noted by Henry Koonook (2010:2), "As an artist and carver, all my carvings come from hunting experiences, whaling experiences, stories told by my relatives and sometimes from dreams." However, identities of the carvers who created the Smithsonian pieces lie outside of current memory, so how are we to understand the stories they communicated through drill bow imagery?

To start, we can turn to the field notes or publications of collectors who acquired these objects. Edward Nelson (1899:84) considered the engraved imagery on drill bows to represent personal stories or hunting tallies of the owner, although he did not record any associated narratives. Lucien Turner told John Murdoch that engraved drill bows from Norton Sound included accurate records of hunting and other events "that no one ever ventures to falsify" (Murdoch 1892:177). Although Murdoch acquired two drill bows engraved with figures and animals, he was unable to determine if the imagery related to real events (Chan 2013:591; Murdoch 1892:177). This may be due to the very old age of the drill bows, as the engraving appears related to the Birnirk-Thule culture. On the other hand, Murdoch acquired a bag handle engraved with a row of whales, along with a similarly engraved drill bow (Fig. 91), that the owner said corresponded with the number of whales his crew had landed (Murdoch 1892:177). In 1881, the same year that Murdoch arrived at Point Barrow, Captain Hooper of the U.S. Revenue Steamer *Corwin* stopped at Cape Blossom and traded for two ivory drill bows that he described as being covered with images that give "reference to events covering a series of years, perhaps a life-time" as well as more recent images including the ships and buildings that were connected with the Western Union Telegraph Service (Hooper 1884:111).

George Byron Gordon, ethnographer and collector for the University of Pennsylvania Museum, recorded some of the most detailed interpretations of drill bow imagery while he was in Alaska. In 1905, Gordon collected four engraved drill bows from Wales including one covered with mythical creatures. Gordon attempted a detailed reinterpretation of the creatures, identifying four by name including "Amakum" a "huge monster that formerly lived on the tundra and frequented pools" (Gordon 1917:246-247) [12]. Two years later Gordon acquired another engraved drill bow at the mouth of the Yukon River from a carver who said that it had been in his family for eleven generations. Gordon (1917:233) states, "On it [the drill bow] are engraved pictures that he [the carver] identified as those of Aglu, Keelugbuk, Tunook and a big deer not extinct. There are also pictures of men and walrus and whales and deer and trees and villages on this old relic" [13]. Gordon's accounts reveal a distinct fascination with Indigenous mythology, and he contextualizes the drill bows with attempts to translate the stories that he was told. However, Gordon would have looked at drill bows as a non-Indigenous ethnographer who did not speak the Inupiaq language.

Of more benefit perhaps are Gordon's observations of story-telling in the early 1900s: "The men are the storytellers and the custodians of legends...The stories are learned by the young men from their Elders, carefully memorized and practiced with much industry and attention to detail. The same story is always told in the same words, with the same innotations [sic] and the same gestures. If a story teller makes a mistake someone among his hearers is sure to correct him. Some of the stories are very long and occupy hours in the telling. Many of them refer to the doings of mythical beings, animals, and men." (Gordon 1917:233). This account encourages us to remember that ivory carvers often worked together in the *qagri*, which also functioned as a gathering space animated by stories, dances, and celebrations. Sylvester Ayek (2012:6) said that on King Island, "There were a lot of things that we passed time with. One good one is listening to myths and legends inside the clubhouses." As carvers shared stories of legendary exploits or travel along the coast, the associated imagery may have been engraved onto a drill bow or other ivory object. The images could have then been used as visual aids to retell or pass down the story with less apprehension about missing a significant part or being publicly corrected.

Drill bow engravings also correspond with traditional genres of Inupiaq narratives. These narratives include legends, myths, family histories, and personal accounts (Kaplan 1988; Kaplan and Kingston 2007:127-132). A courageous hero who overcomes obstacles and assists others often appears in a *unipkaaq*, or legend from the distant past, of people and events not remembered today (Anderson 2005:42; Killigivuk 2007:151-168; Norton 2005b). A drill bow acquired at Cape Darby offers one example of larger-than-life heroes or giants assisting to land and cut up a bowhead whale (Fig. 127). Another *unipkaaq* depicted on a drill bow from Cape Darby illustrates a row of spear-wielding figures marching across a rope to confront a fierce mythological creature (Fig. 134).

Over twenty drill bows in the Smithsonian collections feature imagery that relate to stories of supernatural creatures, giants, and transformational human-animal figures (see Brower 1994:167-168; Brown 2005:115-116; Chan 2013:294-295, 401-405; Cleveland 2005:250; Nelson 1899:441-450). A drill bow collected in Kotzebue Sound reveals several fantastic creatures including a skin boat with the head of a *tirisiq* (a mythical creature with an elongated head and two antenna-like horns), followed by tall creatures with bent necks and outstretched arms, and anthropomorphic wolves and caribou (Fig. 52). A drill bow acquired at St. Michael features an astounding diversity of mythological characters including ferocious creatures, transformational

seal and walrus figures, and giants prowling outside a row of *qagrit* (Fig. 140). This drill bow may have belonged to a shaman and is similar to one acquired by Daniel Neuman at Wales, which he described as "Shaman's drill bow covered with engravings of mythical creatures" (Chan 2013:105-108) [14]. Likewise, Vince Pikonganna considered that a shaman must have owned the drill bow that illustrates a shaman taking flight from a *qagri* (Fig. 133). Pikonganna (2012:4) remarked, "There were good and bad shamans in those days. The good shamans were to help the village of course, hunting, weather, foreseeing the future. A bad shaman would be only to himself, help himself gain wealth, get another wife, or use his power in a not so good way."

Some *unipkaaq* narratives are about ancient wars or battles between Arctic communities (Auliye 1977; Norton 2005a). Sylvester Ayek (2012:5) remarked, "Villagers come into another village and kill as many men as possible. King Island was one of the very difficult places to invade. There's a war song, warrior's song that we know today. There are no dance motions to it, they just sang it. Telling the other villagers, that there's no place to hide on our island, because it's so small." Scenes of warfare with invaders carrying spears, attacking people, entering houses, and engaging in sexual activity appear on several drill bows in museum collections including two (Figs. 75, 124) acquired by Edward Nelson at Sledge Island and Cape Nome (Chan 2013:403-405).

In contrast to legends or stories about a time long ago, a *quliaqtuaq* or *uqaluktuaq* narrative generally recounts a known historical event, personal encounter, or family experience (Anderson 2005:19-20; Kaplan and Kingston 2007:130-131). Inupiaq oral tradition holds many stories about celebrations and gift-giving festivals including the Wolf Dance (*nigla*) and Kivgiq (the Messenger Feast) (Ellanna 1988a; Kingston et. al. 2001; Lockwood 1978:2-4). The arrival of guests from other communities for Kivgiq may have prompted carvers to memorialize this significant event on drill bows (Fig. 127). Another drill bow (Fig. 133) appears to feature a close-up scene from Kivgiq with drummers, dancers, perhaps wearing loon headdresses, and a competitor doing the two-foot high kick. Jerome Saclamana (2012b:1) described the imagery, "The dancers may be from the Inviting in Dance during the Messenger Feast in Barrow. The right drummer with his head lifted up is singing."

Inupiaq historical narratives also recount particular incidents such as encounters with non-Indigenous people (Irrigoo 1977:7-9; Oquilluk 1973:216-218). One example is an engraved drill bow that illustrates figures working at a forge. This bow may represent the crew of the HMS *Rattlesnake* that was sent north in 1853 to serve as a depot ship at Port Clarence where crewmen built a driftwood house, set up a blacksmith shop, and assembled carpenters' sheds (Maguire 1988:44; Ray 1977:220) [15]. A drill bow collected by Edward Nelson illustrates the crew of another ship, the *W. F. March*, who delivered a group of miners to Golovin Bay in the summer of 1881 (Bair and Pratt 2009:322; Chan 2013:356-362) (Fig. 40).

Some drill bow scenes seem to illustrate a particular chapter of history such as the presence of the whaling fleet in the Bering Strait from the 1850s to the early 1910s (Bockstoce et. al. 2005; Phillips-Chan 2020b:174-176) (see Figs. 147-150). Commercial whaling ships and stations became embedded in Inupiaq oral traditions and remained long after the collapse of the baleen industry in 1914 (Green 1959:6-7; Oquilluk 1973:221-223). John Pullock (2012:6) remembers hearing stories from his grandfather about the U.S. Revenue Cutter *Bear* that used to patrol the whaling fleet and carry supplies to King Island and other northern communities. In Shishmaref, Baker Ningealook (2012:1)

recalled a story of some of the first whalers giving community members gold coins that they considered non-functional buttons and promptly tossed overboard.

Oral tradition is comprised of stories held collectively by a culture or a community as well as individual narratives within that tradition. In Inupiaq oral tradition, many personal stories shared and passed down by men focus on hunting and whaling activities (Anungazuk 2007; Ellanna 1988b; Saclamana 1979). During the course of this project, engraved scenes of hunting marine mammals elicited stories about the importance of learning how to hunt from experienced family members, being prepared with the right clothing and tools, and the appropriate manner to harvest and share the animals (see Chapter 2, this volume). Francis Alvanna shared (2012:9), "My brother-in-law, my oldest sister's husband taught me how to hunt in the moving ice; I was sixteen, seventeen years old. They made me sealskin pants, mukluks, everything the hunters use…We use the harpoon for *ugruk* (bearded seals) and the gun for both *aiviq* (walrus) and *ugruk*" (see scenes of seal hunting on Figs. 40, 80, 98). Engraved scenes may have also been related to memorable hunting encounters. Gary Sockpick (2012:15) recounted an unusual time when he and his crew were out walrus hunting and came across walrus that "were on ice like a martini glass, way up there. The ice lifted up somehow. They jumped off, there was a bunch of them, and we shot the three biggest ones. Those other ones had to jump down a long ways. First time I ever saw that." Another singular experience may have prompted the scene of hunters protecting their skin boats from a herd of enraged walrus on a drill bow collected at Wales (Fig. 71).

Perhaps the most straightforward images are engraved rows of whales and animal skins that might have represented a hunting tally kept by the carver (Murdoch 1892:177; Nelson 1899:84) (Figs. 91-92, 105-106). For instance, the ten bowhead whales engraved on a drill bow from Point Barrow might represent the skill and prestige of a respected *umialik* (whaling captain) (Fig. 91). The continued significance of visually communicating the number of whales one has caught is expressed by Henry Koonook (2010:5) who asserted, "When I get the fifth whale for my father, I'm going to put in *tuutaq*, labrets."

Drill bow engravings illustrate the different genres of Inupiaq narratives described above, and often incorporate both legends and lived histories on the same piece (Figs. 51, 84, 122). Attempts at literal interpretation of these narratives can prove difficult due to their age as well as practices of adding imagery over time and of secondary carvers engraving their own scenes (see Figs. 45, 80, 143). Othniel Oomittuk Jr. (2010:8) remarked, "Each carver has his own story to tell. It might take a week looking at a piece to figure out part of the story. Somebody else might know another part of the story." A young person listening to these stories might have learned to follow the related imagery, which would have seemed to come to life when the drill bow moved from side to side while being used (see Fig. 26). As a drill bow was passed down, the new owner might recall stories from his childhood and engrave imagery that continued the existing narrative (see Fig. 41). Of primary importance today is not that we know the specific stories but that the vivid imagery can be used to reawaken traditional knowledge and revitalize oral historical practices.

The Smithsonian Collections of Bering Strait Drill Bows

Details of time and place found in printed records help us to follow the histories of Bering Strait drill bows after they left the hands of carvers and circulated among collectors and museums. Perhaps the most circuitous journey belongs to the first drill bow known to have been collected by a Westerner, Captain James Cook aboard the HMS *Resolution* in 1778 (Chan 2013:64-67; Cook 1999:1333; Pennant 1784:144). The ivory bow appears to have been acquired by Cook at a Chukchi or Siberian Yupik village in Chukotka (Beaglehole 1967:1333; King 1981:20). It features a carved caribou head on one end and four sides engraved with human figures hunting whales, caribou, and ducks; mythological creatures swimming in the water; and three people wearing suits of Siberian slat armor (Fig. 21). The British Museum accessioned the drill bow in 1780 along with other ethnographic items from Cook's third voyage (King 1981:23). While it was at the British Museum, Thomas Pennant (1784:Pl. VI) created an illustration of the drill bow next to a wooden club from a Nuu-chah-nulth community (Vancouver Island, British Columbia) for his three-volume series *Arctic Zoology*, a publication that decontextualized Indigenous materials and treated them as specimens from Western exploration of distant lands (Thomas 1994:118). In 1803, the British Museum seems to have sold the drill bow along with other Arctic items through Sotheby's auction house where the drill bow was purchased by the Royal Canterbury Museum in Kent (King 1981:39). Sometime later, the Royal Canterbury Museum sold or exchanged the drill bow with the Horniman Museum in south London where it now resides [16].

Subsequent explorers to the Bering Strait in the early 1800s may have been familiar with *Arctic Zoology* and its illustration of this intriguing drill bow. During the summer of 1816, Otto von Kotzebue sailed the *Rurik* around the northern coast of Seward Peninsula and stopped at Cape Espenberg, where he traded tobacco, small beads, knives, and mirrors for two engraved drill bows and a handful of carved ivory animals and figures (Chamisso 1986:87; Choris 1822:10; Kotzebue

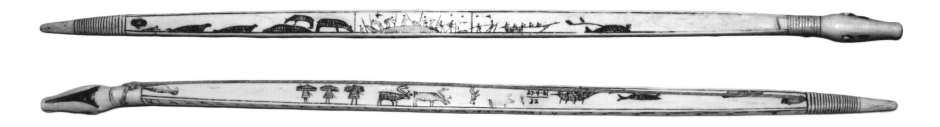

21/ Pitiksiaq DRILL BOW
Bering Strait
Collected by Captain James Cook, 1778
Horniman Museum and Gardens 27.4.61/32
Walrus ivory, sinew, bead; Length 48 cm (19 in)

22/ Pitiksiaq DRILL BOW
Kotzebue Sound
Collected by Frederick W. Beechey, accessioned 1886
Pitt Rivers Museum 1886.1.693
Walrus ivory; Length 35.2 cm (14 in)

1967:209-210). Ten years later in the summer of 1826, Frederick W. Beechey guided the HMS *Blossom* into the same area and set anchor in Hotham Inlet. The annual Siberian-Alaskan trading fair appears to have been in full-swing and Beechey, along with crewmembers Edward Belcher and George Shuldham Peard, traded Western goods for at

least fifteen engraved drill bows, now in museums in England (Beechey 1831:340-408; Bockstoce 1977; Chan 2013:526-527; Pearce 1976; Peard 1973) (Fig. 22). Beechey observed that the images appeared to relate to an established artistic tradition. He remarked, "On the outside of this and other instruments there were etched a variety of figures of men, beasts, and birds, &c., with a truth and character which showed the art to be common among them" (Beechey 1831:344).

During the early to mid-nineteenth century, European explorers made dozens of expeditions to the Bering Strait but collected fewer than 40 engraved drill bows in all (Bockstoce 1977; Chan 2013:64-75; 526-530). However, Smithsonian naturalists Lucien Turner, Edward Nelson, and John Murdoch, managed to acquire over 100 pictorial drill bows from the Bering Strait region. What could have prompted Inupiaq carvers to trade with Smithsonian collectors and part with such a great number of drill bows in the late nineteenth century?

First, creation of an ivory drill bow required access to walrus tusks through hunting or trade as well as specialized knowledge and tools to carve a bow and the accompanying wood mouthpiece and drills (Chan 2013:196-217; Hoffman 1897:774-775; Koonook 2010:14; Saclamana 2012a:15). Even the finest carved drill bows work by means of intermittent rotations that can cause the drill bit to get stuck. The last quarter of the nineteenth century saw mass production and distribution of metal hand braces and geared drills that provided continuous drilling motion and interchangeable parts (De Decker 2010). Ready-made metal drills would have offered a technological advancement and a time-saving alternative to procuring and fashioning raw materials into a handmade drill bow.

The role of pictorial engraving as a visual device for oral histories and cultural knowledge was also undergoing a transition in the late 1800s due to the burgeoning curio market and proliferation of non-Native speakers (Krauss 1980). Increased trade with outsiders and demand for ivory souvenirs encouraged carvers to create a style of engraving with formulaic motifs that could be quickly etched and replicated on items such as ivory pipes and cribbage boards (Chan 2013:353-379;

Ray 1977:22-28). Engraved imagery began to take on representational and economic value outside of its original social and cultural contexts.

Finally, the internal dynamics of many Inupiaq communities were changing. Outside influences from missionaries, school teachers, and traders were altering the political and religious structure of communities, particularly the *qagri* that served as a center for tool-making, ivory carving, and community gatherings (Burch 2013; Cassell 2000:122; Lowenstein 2008:321-325; Phillips-Chan 2020b:176-178). Decline of the *qagrit* would have reduced time spent as a group engraving imagery and recounting stories. During this period of increased access to manufactured tools and growth of a commodity-driven market, the first of the Smithsonian collectors arrived in the Bering Strait region.

William H. Dall (1865-1868)

The Western Union Telegraph Expedition from 1865 to 1868 brought naturalist William Healey Dall (1845-1927) to Alaska where he joined the expedition as a scientist in charge of invertebrates and fish (Bartsch et. al. 1946). Dall collected several thousand natural and cultural history items for the Smithsonian Institution including four drill bows from Port Clarence (Chan 2013:75-77). Only one of these features a significant amount of pictorial engraving, showing mythical creatures and dancers in motion (Fig. 23). Dall observed that carvers still used engraved drill bows, which may have contributed to his difficulty in purchasing more examples. He remarked, "I have seen an ivory bow, used in conjunction with a drill, and made of an entire walrus tusk, which had depicted on each of the four sides every pursuit followed by the Innuit from birth to internment" (Dall 1870:237). Dall made subsequent trips to Alaska from 1871 to 1880 and acquired additional cultural material that he sold to

23/ Pitiksiaq DRILL BOW
Port Clarence
Collected by William H. Dall, accessioned 1880
National Museum of Natural History E46054
Walrus ivory, sealskin; Length 36.2 cm (14.3 in)

individuals and museums (Bartsch et. al. 1946:7; Chan 2013:76-77). Dall retained some pieces for his private collection, including an engraved drill bow that was donated by Dall's grandchildren to the Alaska State Museum in 2003 (Chan 2013:76, 302, 528).

Lucien M. Turner (1874-1877)

Lucien McShan Turner (1848-1909) traveled to Alaska in 1874 to assume duties with the U.S. Army Signal Corps. For the next three years, Turner used the Alaska Commercial Company trading post at St. Michael as home base to record meteorological, atmospheric, and tidal data for the Corps and assemble ethnological material for the Smithsonian Institution (Loring 2001). Turner accepted a second term of employment with the Corps and from 1878 to 1881 strove to establish meteorological stations primarily in the Aleutians (Loring 2001:xiii). Turner's research in Alaska resulted in a collection of over 1,500 ethnological objects including twenty-five pictorial drill bows (Chan 2013:77-79). Turner labeled the majority of them with the general provenience of "Norton Sound." However, the variety of engraved imagery relates to several coastal communities. For example, the collection includes a unique group of nine engraved drill bows with broad outlines and diagonal hatch marks in a style characteristic of Pastolik, a Central Yup'ik community, once located near the western mouth of the Yukon River (see Figs. 32-34).

During the 1890s, Turner struck up a correspondence with Walter James Hoffman, a medical doctor, who was at that time working on an extensive report about imagery on Arctic objects in the Smithsonian Institution [17]. Turner found an enthusiastic audience in Hoffman who was eager to hear firsthand accounts from field collectors and printed large sections of Turner's letters in his completed report *Graphic Art of the Eskimos* (1897:774-814). Turner's letters include some of the most detailed information we have on nineteenth century construction and use of drill bows and their cultural value to Bering Strait communities [18]. Turner writes:

> The drill bow or other implement or utensil was not produced in a day or even in a month, as these articles were usually created for personal use. I have known of such articles being taken along while on a protracted hunting expedition and there worked upon to while away the oftentimes tedious hours of watching game. Again I have known when a native had requested a friend to etch some design, and in their festivals, commemorating their dead, these articles were often presented and highly cherished as gifts. Other articles of ivory often passed as a legacy from a relative to another, and highly valued by the owner (Hoffman 1897:774).

Edward W. Nelson (1877-1881)

The completion of Lucien Turner's service with the U.S. Army Signal Corps at St. Michael in 1877 overlapped with the arrival of his replacement and fellow naturalist Edward William Nelson (1855-

1934). Nelson and Turner shared a similar passion for collecting ethnographic material. Soon after Nelson's arrival at St. Michael, the two colleagues visited the nearby village of Taciq where Nelson remarked, "In the evening, Mr. Turner and I went to the Indian village and traded for some ivory dolls and small parkies" [19]. Over the next four years, Nelson traveled across Alaska by kayak, dog sled, and the U.S. Revenue Cutter *Corwin*, amassing over 10,000 objects of material culture from both sides of the Bering Strait, the Yukon-Kuskokwim Delta, and Lower Yukon (Fitzhugh and Kaplan 1982; Nelson 1899) [20].

Native community members quickly realized that Nelson purchased almost any cultural item offered for sale. When the *Corwin* stopped at King Island in the summer of 1881, Captain Calvin Hooper and Nelson discovered that community members had already left carrying a large number of ivory carvings in hopes of meeting and trading with Nelson. Hooper (1884:37) remarked that Nelson's "custom of buying these carvings, and many other things which were of no value except as specimens for a museum, pleased the natives very much, and to many to whom his name was not known, he was described as 'the man who buys good-for-nothing things.'" To make sure he didn't miss out on any collecting opportunities, Nelson hired Native traders to visit additional villages and exchange manufactured goods for artifacts that they then delivered to him in St. Michael [21]. An ivory carving with engraved imagery epitomized Nelson's idea of a good museum specimen. On a return journey to St. Michael in the winter of 1880, Nelson stopped in the village of Kvikh in northern Norton Sound (Nelson 1899:99). He visited the home of Isaac, an Iñupiat from Kotzebue Sound, who was employed as a trader for the Western Fur and Trading Company. Nelson remarked, "In the evening I bought some articles among which

a drill bow and an ivory-handled skin scraper are the two finest I have seen of the kind" [22].

Nelson went on acquire a total of 81 pictorial engraved drill bows as well as a substantial number of engraved bag handles, pipes, household articles, and hunting equipment. The drill bows feature some of the most intricate scenes of engraved imagery, showing figures hunting animals, battling mythological creatures, and trading with whalers (see Figs. 92, 140, 148). Nelson labeled the drill bows as coming from the general regions of Norton Sound and Kotzebue Sound, and from fourteen specific places including Point Hope, Hotham Inlet, Diomede Islands, Cape Prince of Wales, Sledge Island, Cape Nome, Cape Darby, Golovin, Nubviukhchugaluk, Shaktoolik, Unalakleet, Kigitauik, St. Michael, and Pastolik. Although we know Nelson acquired drill bows from Kvikh as well as from villagers of King Island, these place names do not appear in the museum records. This reminds us that although recorded place names may indicate where Nelson obtained items, some had probably passed through many hands and circulated between villages, making their place of origin difficult to ascertain or remember.

Nelson's service with the U. S. Army Signal Corps ended in 1881 and he concluded his fieldwork with a final prodigious collecting trip aboard the *Corwin*, making stops along the coasts of North Alaska and Chukotka. Back in the Lower 48, Nelson spent almost twenty years organizing his extensive ethnographic notes, photographs, and object descriptions into what would become the seminal nineteenth century report on Bering Strait lifeways titled *The Eskimo about Bering Strait* (1899). In the report's section on drill bows, Nelson (1899:84) remarks that the engravings represent, "various incidents in the life of the owner, such as a record of the animals killed by him on various hunts, the number of skins he has possessed, or other personal data." These observations on the personal nature of pictorial imagery may have originated with Nelson or could have been borrowed from earlier reports by his colleagues Lucien Turner and John Murdoch (Hoffman 1897:774; Murdoch 1892:177-178).

Patrick H. Ray and John Murdoch (1881-1883)

Lt. Patrick Henry Ray (1842-1911) established a meteorological and magnetic observation station at Point Barrow in 1881 where he carried out diverse scientific and cultural field research in partnership with John Murdoch (1852-1925) and other members of the International Polar Year Expedition (IPY). Edward Nelson encountered the IPY schooner *Golden Fleece* at Plover Bay during the summer of 1881 and received assurance from Ray that although Murdoch was primarily employed as an ornithologist, he also intended to give "due attention to the native customs and beliefs" [23]. Over the next two years, Murdoch and Ray assembled one of the largest collections of cultural, ornithological, and geological material from North Alaska (Krupnik et. al. 2009; Murdoch 1892; Ray 1885). The majority of cultural objects originated from the Iñupiaq communities of Nuvuk at Point Barrow and Utqiaġvik at Cape Smythe but several items were also purchased from visiting community members of Icy Cape and Point Hope.

Murdoch (1892:175) remarked that, "The use of the drill bow appears to be universal among the Eskimo. Those at present employed at Point Barrow do not differ from the large series collected at the Mackenzie and Anderson rivers by [Roderick] MacFarlane." However Ray (1885:46) held the opinion that drill bows were being swiftly set aside in favor of modern steel tools and that the scientists only "found the ancient fire drill still in use among some of the old, conservative

men." Murdoch and Ray managed to acquire sixteen ivory drill bows described as "Flat bows of ivory of bone, often carved, or engraved, with a string of rawhide" (Ray 1885:69). Murdoch (1892:176) observed that "These bows are often highly ornamented both by carving and with incised patterns colored with red ocher or soot." The majority of drill bows from their collection are engraved with geometric designs and only four drill bows include a significant amount of pictorial imagery (Murdoch 1892:178) (see Fig. 91). A handful of items including an ivory harpoon rest, bone box, and sections of ivory have rows of animals or "hunting records" engraved upon their surface but the lack of complex scenes suggest that pictorial engraving had not been as widely practiced in North Alaska and had almost disappeared by the late-nineteenth century (Murdoch 1892:323,342, 361-363).

George G. Heye (1897-1957)

George Gustav Heye (1874-1957) grew up in New York among comfortable surroundings made possible by the fortune his father Carl Heye had made in the petroleum industry (McMullen 2009:70-71). After receiving a degree in electrical engineering, George Gustav Heye was sent by his employer to Arizona in 1897, where he became intrigued by Native American culture and purchased a Diné (Navajo) man's shirt. Heye worked in investment banking from 1901 to 1909 but must have found the hours tedious as he left to focus on expanding his collection of Native American art and artifacts. Heye traveled across the country to acquire objects in person, purchased large collections from traders, and sponsored field expeditions. In 1916, after Heye's collection had grown to include some 58,000 objects, he partnered with some of his affluent friends to build the Museum of the American Indian (MAI) in New York. The museum opened to the public in 1922 with a professional staff who printed guidebooks and organized exhibits. Heye kept collecting over the next three decades, carrying on through the Depression and two world wars, to leave an astonishing collection of almost 700,000 items upon his passing in 1957.

Heye collected Native American art and artifacts from more than 1,200 Indigenous cultures across the Americas. The Arctic portion of the collection includes approximately fifty ivory carvings with older pictorial-style imagery on fifteen drill bows in addition to bag handles, pipes, net gauges, and harpoon rests. Heye purchased the first of these drill bows in 1905 (Fig. 36) from John Hackman, who had established a shore-based whaling station with his cousin Heinrich Koenig at Point Hope in 1889 (Bockstoce 1986:240; Lowenstein 2008:69-78). Hackman married an Iñupiaq woman while in Point Hope and acquired several thousand ethnographic items that he later sold to collectors such as Heye and to curio dealers including Joseph E. Standley (Duncan 2000:46-47). Heye in turn looked to Standley to fill the exhibit halls of the new MAI in New York, and in 1916 spent five thousand dollars to purchase Alaska Native items that Standley had exhibited at the Alaska-Yukon-Pacific Exposition in Seattle in 1909 (Chan 2013:429-431) [24]. Among the cribbage boards, masks, and baskets purchased in 1916 were three engraved drill bows, including one (Fig. 62) that Standley described as "Ancient record drill bow covered all over with records. It is 16 inches long carved out of ivory tusk. Wonderful" [25].

As an avid collector, Heye must have looked longingly at the immense field collections acquired by Lucien Turner and Edward Nelson in Alaska during the 1870s-1880s. In 1908, Heye brokered an exchange with the U.S. National Museum (now the Smithsonian National Museum of Natural History) for a number of Arctic items including an engraved drill bow (Fig. 128) originally acquired by Edward

Nelson at Cape Darby. In his acquisition of the drill bow and other items from the U.S. National Museum, Heye may have also been attempting to align himself intellectually with the esteemed nineteenth century ethnologists. In 1989, Heye's entire collection was transferred to the Smithsonian Institution to form the core collections of the National Museum of the American Indian.

Collectors and Communities

For George Heye, the impetus to collect was closely tied to the goal of acquiring large quantities of material to fill exhibit halls in his new museum (McMullen 2009:75-77), while Smithsonian collecting strategies aligned with the late nineteenth century paradigm of "salvage ethnography." This meant assembling encyclopedic representations of cultures before they became relics of the past or disappeared entirely (Macdonald 2006; Pearce 1992). Captain Hooper observed Edward Nelson's all-inclusive collecting approach at Point Hope during the summer of 1881 [26]:

> We went on shore to examine their houses and learn something of their mode of living. Mr. Nelson, who was ever on the alert for anything of etymological [sic] interest, took his camera and a small package of trade goods. Upon reaching the settlement Nelson established himself under the lee of a turned-up oomiac near the shore, and signified through the interpreter his desire to buy any old worthless things they might possess. A general raid was made on the old collections or rather accumulations of the settlement. Carved images, drill bows (for making fires), and implements of various kinds, made of ivory and stone, were brought out and offered for sale by the natives, each trying to be the first to trade, as if afraid

OUR STORIES ETCHED IN IVORY

the supply of beads, calico, tobacco, &c., would not hold out, or that the market for articles of native manufacture might be overstocked. Each article offered was taken by Nelson and examined, and if of any value as a specimen the interpreter was told to ask what was wanted in return, and upon being told what the native most wanted a fair quantity was given (Hooper 1884:107).

Despite the rapidity at which collections were assembled, Smithsonian collectors did recognize and value finely made drill bows. During the summer of 1877, a group of travelers from King Island arrived by skin boat at St. Michael and spent the night in the Alaska Commercial Company bathhouse. The Inupiaq visitors met with Nelson the next morning and offered dried fish and seal oil for trade, which did not interest Nelson. A long day of bargaining ensued that caused Nelson to remark, "The cause of the difficulty in trading with these northern natives is that a great many whalers do more or less trading with them and pay almost anything they charge for their goods and thus give them an exaggerated idea of their value." The King Island party eventually brought out drill bows and other ivory carvings to exchange. Nelson praised the craftsmanship of the carvings stating, "During the day a number of drill bows (ivory) and various ivory carvings were brought me by the natives to trade, some of which were very good" [27].

Smithsonian naturalists paid primary attention to where they acquired drill bows as well as the basics of construction and use. Field notes reveal few details on individual carvers or narratives connected to the engraved scenes. A lack of recorded information on drill bow engravings can be partly attributed to the swiftness with which objects

were acquired, leaving little time to transcribe oral stories. Likewise, language barriers between collectors and Inupiaq communities posed a challenge to understanding local histories. Finally, without long-term relationships built on trust and reciprocity, community members were perhaps hesitant to share personal histories and cultural knowledge with outsiders. A photograph from around 1910 reveals the uncomfortable dynamic that often existed between artists and collectors. In this image, three men in hats lean in to scrutinize the engraved scene on a walrus tusk, while the carver attempts to finish his work under their close gaze (Fig. 24). This catalog attempts to subvert the power relations inherent in this photograph and prioritize community members' perspectives and voices.

24/ Three non-Indigenous men gather around a Bering Strait carver as he works on an engraved walrus tusk. c. 1910. Carrie M. McLain Memorial Museum, 2002.18.1.

Creating the Catalog

Production of this catalog went through several phases over a ten-year journey. The first phase involved hands-on research with Arctic collections in the Smithsonian's NMNH and NMAI in 2009 and from 2011 to 2013. Over 150 engraved drill bows and 100 engraved bag handles, pipes, hunting implements, and household items were examined to record their construction, use wear, engraving styles, and pictorial scenes. Contextual information about the drill bows was sought in field diaries, catalog records, and photographs at the Smithsonian Institution Archives, NMNH Museum Support Center, and National Anthropological Archives. Additional collections research at fifteen North American and European museums from 2011 to 2013 advanced understanding of the history and stylistic diversity of engraved drill bows from the Bering Strait region. Object records from the Smithsonian and other museums were correlated with collectors' accounts and ethno-historical sources to create a dataset of almost 300 engraved drill bows. While this catalog focuses on the Smithsonian collections, additional discussions of drill bows in other museums, collector biographies, contexts of creation and use, oral narratives, and regional styles of engravings can be found in my dissertation (Chan 2013).

With photographs and information about engraved drill bows in hand, I made several trips to Alaska between 2010 to 2012 to seek community input on traditional ecological knowledge and oral stories connected to the engraved imagery on drill bows. Community-based research was approached from a perspective of radical empiricism that replaces the quest for authoritative facts with an attempt to explore micro-histories and local ideologies (Jackson 1989).

Forty-seven cultural knowledge bearers in Utqiaġvik, Point Hope, Kotzebue, Shishmaref, Nome, St. Michael and Anchorage shared their thoughts on drill bow construction and use, activities portrayed in engraved scenes, and how carving connects to a wider realm of physical activity and oral knowledge. Photographs of drill bows served as a form of visual repatriation that prompted stories about hunting and carving in addition to reanimating the objects by conferring contemporary meaning to the historic imagery (e.g. Fienup-Riordan 1996). Stories were recorded during informal interviews at contributor's homes or carving workshops and shared through emails and personal conversations (Fig. 25). Twenty-one project participants in Alaska demonstrated the use of hand tools including drill bows, adzes, and files, and explained how to engrave on ivory, etch on baleen, and carve ivory and whalebone. Demonstrations were video recorded and offer insight into the social aspects of carving, including the use of materials and stylistic choices. Project contributors also expressed ideas behind their own work,

25/ Henry Koonook reviews photographs of engraved drill bows in museum collections with Amy Phillips-Chan. Point Hope, AK. 2010.

concerns about passing on cultural traditions, and suggestions for future collaborations.

During the spring of 2012, community presentations featuring photographs of the engraved drill bows were held at the Iñupiat Heritage Center (Utqiaġvik), the Northwest Arctic Heritage Center (Kotzebue), and the Carrie M. McLain Memorial Museum (Nome). Following a community presentation in Nome, Jerome Saclamana became inspired to dust off his engraving tools and replicate imagery from a drill bow depicting figures drumming and dancing during Kivgiq, which he transferred to an ivory letter opener. This particular drill bow (Fig. 133) was collected by Edward Nelson in Kotzebue Sound between 1877 and 1881 and features the engraving styles of two separate carvers. It has appeared in publications and exhibitions, while the imagery has been copied by Indigenous and non-Indigenous artists (Chan 2013:16-21). The active social life of the drill bow speaks to the agency that these heritage items continue to hold for Bering Strait communities.

Following community conversations in Alaska, photographs of engraved drill bows from museum collections, as well as transcribed interviews and photos taken during community visits, were sent to all of the project participants. During my trips to Alaska, it became clear that engraved drill bows continue to carry cultural value and artistic inspiration within Bering Strait communities. Contributors expressed particular interest in the content of the figural scenes and what other community members had shared about the engraved imagery. In 2014, Dr. Igor Krupnik in the Smithsonian Arctic Studies Center and I discussed the potential for a catalog that would feature photographs of drill bows from the Smithsonian collection with an emphasis on the description of imagery and their relation to community stories. A similar pairing of historical photographs with oral histories had proved successful in the Smithsonian Contributions to Circumpolar Anthropology volume, *Faces We Remember / Neqamikegkaput: Leuman M. Waugh's Photography from St. Lawrence Island, Alaska, 1929-1930* (Krupnik and Kaneshiro 2011).

Carrying several drafts of the catalog, I returned to Nome and Kotzebue in 2014 to revisit community members and seek their input on the proposed content and design of the publication. Soon after this last visit to Alaska, I accepted the position of Director at the Carrie M. McLain Memorial Museum in Nome, and the drill bow project was paused while building a new museum from 2015 to 2017. The project received a reboot in 2018 following a reimagining of the volume as a collaboration between the Smithsonian Arctic Studies Center, Carrie M. McLain Memorial Museum, and Bering Strait communities.

The catalog pairs drill bows and stories in a manner similar to how tales would be shared in a *qagri*, as people worked together and enjoyed one another's company. Full-page images of 87 drill bows are presented alongside oral histories in three chapters organized by what contributors considered important to share: lessons in carving, records of hunts, and stories of community. Community stories have been illustrated with almost 40 heritage objects from the Carrie M. McLain Memorial Museum. The collector and location of acquisition appears under each drill bow next to a brief description of the engraved imagery. Additional discussion of collectors, Inupiaq terms for carving tools and materials, examples of material culture objects with pictorial imagery, and a detailed look at drill bow characters appear in the appendices.

The final publication in your hands has been shaped by many voices over the years. First and foremost, stories shared by community contributors provided the structure and content for the catalog. Without their participation, the drill bows in this book would have remained silent within museum cabinets. The foreword by Bernadette Yaayuk Alvanna-Stimpfle skillfully situates the drill bows within the social context of Inupiaq communities. At the Arctic Studies Center, Dr. Igor Krupnik championed the project from the start, Dr. Aron Crowell carefully reviewed the text, and Dr. William Fitzhugh shepherded the book through publication. The clean look and engaging layout are the work of designer Dr. Igor Chechushkov whose organizational skills are to be commended.

Cultural knowledge is not lost and can be reawakened through community-directed storytelling and interaction with heritage items. It is hoped that this publication will foster community empowerment by increasing access to knowledge of the past and by holding space for Indigenous knowledge and perspectives to be heard.

Notes

1. Inupiaq terms in this essay follow the dialect and spelling of King Island Inupiaq (Kaplan 1994). Regional dialects and spelling have been retained in community member stories.

2. The drill bow tool complex, consisting of a bow, drill, and mouthpiece, is also known as a bow drill. The term drill bow is used throughout this publication to refer both to the bow and tool complex for uniformity of text.

3. Use of a tilde, Inupiaq or Iñupiaq, is often dependent upon the location of the community and dialect(s) of Inupiaq spoken. In general, community members in the Bering Strait region speak Inupiaq while those in North Alaska speak Iñupiaq. One can also use Inupiaqtun to refer to the language being spoken, lit. "speaking like an Inupiaq."

4. The Smithsonian NMNH cares for a traditional drill bow from St. Lawrence Island that consists of a walrus rib bone bow, wooden drill, ivory mouthpiece, and a wood hearth on which to start a fire. The drill bow (E280465) is stored in a sealskin pouch with tinder and was made by a St. Lawrence Island Yupik carver with the family name of Wongittilin. It was collected by anthropologist Riley D. Moore before 1913.

5. Collectors acquired over 300 drill bows engraved with pictorial imagery from the Bering Strait between 1778 and 1920. The majority of these drill bows are now in museums in the United States and the United Kingdom with significant collections also in Germany and Russia (Chan 2013:515-536).

6. Bering Strait Comprehensive Economic Development Strategy 2019-2024, Kawerak, Inc. Available: https://kawerak.org/bering-strait-comprehensive-economic-development-strategy-published/; 2019 Community Needs Assessment: Bering Strait Region, Kawerak, Inc. Available: https://www.mcdowellgroup.net/wp-content/uploads/2020/02/community-needs-assessment-key-findings.pdf

7. Smithsonian Institution Archives. "Record Unit 7364: Edward William Nelson and Edward Alphonso Goldman Collection, circa 1873-1946 and undated. Box 11, "Field Journals," December 15, 1878. Hereafter referenced as SIA, *Nelson Field Journals*.

8. SIA, *Nelson Field Journals*, December 26, 1880.

9. See American Museum of Natural History, Anthropology Archives, 1912-168, V. Stefansson Museum Expedition.

10. SIA, *Nelson Field Journals*, August 19, 1877.

11. The 1918 Influenza took the lives of many Inupiaq artists on the Seward Peninsula and advanced the decline of pictorial engraving. Only a few Inupiaq carvers continue to practice pictorial engraving, among them, Gary Sockpick in Shishmaref and Brian Sockpick in Nome. Engraving is more

commonly practiced in Gambell and Savoonga where St. Lawrence Island Yupik artists, including Miller Kingeekuk and Fred Kingeekuk, incorporate engraved scenes into their imaginative ivory sculptures.

12. Gordon made two trips to Alaska in 1905 and 1907 and collected over 3,000 cultural objects including seven pictorial engraved drill bows that he deposited with the Penn Museum (Chan 2013:89-91). The drill bow (NA461) described here was loaned out with drill bow NA1517 over thirty years ago and never returned to the Penn Museum (Personal communication with Bill Wierzbowski, University of Pennsylvania Museum Keeper of Collections). Photos of the two missing drill bows appear alongside three other bows collected by Gordon in the article by J. Alden Mason, 1927, "Eskimo Pictorial Art," *The Museum Journal*, University of Pennsylvania 18: 248-83.

13. This description refers to drill bow NA1517 no longer in the Penn Museum (see above).

14. Dr. Daniel S. Neuman lived in Nome from 1910 to 1920 and acquired several thousand objects from both sides of the Bering Strait through trade, purchase, and as payment for his medical services (Chan 2013:105-108). Neuman created an illustrated catalogue of many objects in his collection including the "Shaman's drill bow" described here, now in the Alaska State Museum (ASM II-A-9). Alaska State Museum Accession Files, Neuman Collection, *Catalogue*.

15. This drill bow was collected by Mr. Spark, a crewmember of the *Rattlesnake*, and is now in the British Museum (Am1855.1126.227) (Chan 2013:545).

16. Horniman Museum Records.

17. Edward W. Nelson was carrying out fieldwork in Mexico during the 1890s while Hoffman was in Washington, DC going through the Smithsonian's Arctic collection. Nelson wrote to his colleagues in DC and implored them to keep Hoffman from gaining access to the bows as he wanted to feature them in his forthcoming publication *Eskimo about the Bering Strait* (1899). Nevertheless, Hoffman procured access to the bows and wrote up interpretations of the engraved imagery for his book *Graphic Art of the Eskimos* (1897). Nelson's bitterness at this infringement upon his collection resulted in only a cursory nod to drill bows in *Eskimo about the Bering Strait* (Nelson 1899:84-85, Pl. XXXVI). Personal communication with William W. Fitzhugh, November 4, 2020.

18. Turner's letters to Hoffman span a two-year period from the winter of 1894 to the spring of 1896 (Hoffman 1897:774-775, 768, 798).

19. SIA, *Nelson Field Journals*, June 21, 1877.

20. A number of educational materials were produced during the 1980s to accompany the exhibition *Inua: Spirit World of the Bering Sea Eskimo*, which featured the expansive collection of objects, photographs, and stories assembled by Edward. W. Nelson (Fitzhugh and Kaplan 1982). The Smithsonian Institution Office of Elementary and Secondary Education (1981) created a lesson plan around the exhibit that encouraged students to imagine themselves living in the Arctic and the relevant objects and skills they would need to survive. The Smithsonian Institution developed the lesson plan into a curriculum packet that featured slides, booklets, and worksheets structured to develop students' research and writing skills in subjects that included anthropology, geography, and art history (Bay and Selig 1983). Copies of the curriculum unit traveled with 120 objects from the *Inua* exhibition (including drill bow NMNH E38521) to Alaska and the United States and were offered to schools and organizations, including the Carrie M. McLain Memorial Museum in Nome. Indigenous voices are largely absent in these early educational resources but in 1983 the Alaska

State Museum organized a training program that brought a group of 20 Elders, students, and museum staff to Juneau to examine objects in the *Inua* exhibition. Indigenous knowledge shared by Elders during the program equipped students to act as guides when the traveling exhibition came to their communities. The program also resulted in a rich body of information published in Inupiaq and Central Yup'ik as *Inua: Return of the Spirit through the Eyes of the Elders* (Alaska State Museum 1989).

21. Nelson remarked that less than a year after arriving at St. Michal, he had acquired over 1,200 artifacts, "besides the considerable amount that is yet to come in from traders to whom I have given goods." SIA, *Nelson Field Journals*, March 22, 1878.

22. SIA, *Nelson Field Journals*, March 29, 1880.

23. SIA, *Nelson Field Journals*, August 24, 1881.

24. National Museum of the American Indian Archives, Box 142, Folder 25, J. E. Standley Alaska Purchase Lists, 1916.

25. Ibid.

26. Nelson recorded a provenience of Point Hope for four engraved drill bows: E63802, E63803, E63804 and E63805. The drill bows were accessioned as part of 82A00003, a later accession date that indicates the drill bows were probably acquired during the 1881 exchange described by Hooper.

27. Nelson and Rudolph Neumann, manager of the Alaska Commercial Company post at St. Michael, made a brief visit to the village of Taciq where they came across a group from King Island who had apparently just arrived in their *umiaq*. Shortly thereafter, the King Islanders paddled across to the ACC post to request shelter for the evening. SIA, *Nelson Field Journals*, August 19, 1877.

References

Alaska State Museum. 1989. *Inua: Return of the Spirit through the Eyes of the Elders.* Juneau: Alaska State Museum.

Alvanna, Francis. 2012. Interview with Amy Phillips-Chan, 21 April. Nome, Alaska.

Anderson, Wanni. 2005. *The Dall Sheep Dinner Guest: Iñupiaq Narratives of Northwest Alaska.* Fairbanks, AK: University of Alaska Press.

Anowlic, Wilfred. 2013. Personal communication with Amy Phillips-Chan. Nome, Alaska.

Anungazuk, Herbert. 2003 "Ootenna." In *Eskimo Drawings,* ed. Suzi Jones, pp. 76-83. Anchorage: Anchorage Museum of History and Art.

_____ 2007. "An Unwritten Law of the Sea." In *Words of the Real People: Alaska Native Literature in Translation,* ed. Ann Fienup-Riordan and Lawrence D. Kaplan, pp. 189-199. Fairbanks, AK: University of Alaska Press.

_____ 2009. "The Sea is our Garden: A Hunter's View." In *Gifts from the Ancestors: Ancient Ivories of Bering Strait,* ed. William W. Fitzhugh, Julie Hollowell, and Aron L. Crowell, pp. 42-45. Princeton, NJ: Princeton University Art Museum.

Apatiki, Clifford. 2016. "Sculpting Ivory (7 of 17): Materials – Walrus Tusk (Ivory)." *Material Traditions: Sculpting Ivory,* ed. Dawn Biddison. Smithsonian Arctic Studies Center. Available: https://www.youtube.com/playlist?list=PL3wBN-dh9DMRrXiXA10N3mOsiKzvN2Hiy

Asatchaq. 1992. *The Things That Were Said of Them: Shaman Stories and Oral Histories of the Tikigaq People as Told by Asatchaq.* Translated by Tom Lowenstein and Tukummiq. Berkeley: University of California Press.

Auliye, Fritz. 1977. "The Angatuk Anguyaktuk (The Medicine Man Fights)." In *"I remember . . .",* ed. Bill Karp, pp. 71-75. Village Library Project, ESAA Title VII. Nome, AK: Kegoayah Kozga Library Association.

Ayek, Sylvester. 2012. Interview with Amy Phillips-Chan, 16 April. Nome, Alaska.

Bair, Gerald A. and Kenneth L. Pratt. 2009. "History and Native Art." In *Chasing the Dark: Perspectives on Place, History and Alaska Native Land Claims,* ed. Kenneth L. Pratt, pp. 322-328. Anchorage, AK: United States Department of the Interior Bureau of Indian Affairs, Alaska Region.

Baird, Kevin. 2016. "Ivory Ban Affects Native Arts." 21 October. *Daily News-Miner.*

Bartsch, Paul, Harald Alfred Rehder and Beulah E. Shields. 1946. *A Bibliography and Short Biographical Sketch of William Healey Dall.* Washington, DC: Smithsonian Institution.

Bay, Ann and Ruth Osterweis Selig. 1983. *Of Kayaks and Ulus: The Bering Sea Eskimo Collection of Edward W. Nelson "The Man Who Collected Good-For-Nothing Things."* Washington, DC: Smithsonian Institution Press.

Beaglehole, J. C., ed. 1967. *The Journals of Captain James Cook on His voyages of Discovery, vol. 3: The Voyage of the Resolution and the Discovery,* 1776-1789. Cambridge: Cambridge University Press for the Hakluyt Society.

Beechey, Frederick. 1831. *Narrative of a Voyage to the Pacific and Beering's Strait to Co-operate with the Polar Expeditions.* London: Colburn & Bentley.

Biddison, Dawn. 2016. *Material Traditions: Sculpting Ivory.* Available https://www.youtube.com/playlist?list=PL3wBN-dh9DMRrXiXA10N3mOsiKzvN2Hiy

Bockstoce, John R., Daniel B. Botkin, Alex Philip, Brian W. Collins, and John C. George. 2005. "The Geographic Distribution of Bowhead Whales, *Balaena mysticetus,* in the Bering, Chukchi, and Beaufort Seas: Evidence from Whaleship Records, 1849-1914." *Marine Fisheries Review,* 67:1-43.

Bockstoce, John R. 1977. *Eskimos of Northwest Alaska in the Early Nineteenth Century based on the Beechey and Belcher Collections and Records Compiled during the Voyage of the H.M.S. Blossom to Northwest Alaska in 1826 and 1827.* Oxford: Pitt Rivers Museum, University of Oxford.

_____. 1986. *Whales, Ice, and Men: The History of Whaling in the Western Arctic.* Seattle: University of Washington Press.

Bogoras, Waldemar. 1975. *Chukchee Mythology.* New York: AMS Press.

Borden, Mrs John. 1928. *The Cruise of the Northern Light.* New York: The Macmillan Company.

British Museum. 1910. *Handbook to the Ethnological Collection.* London: British Museum Press.

Bronshtein, Mikhail, Irina Karakhan, and Jury Shirokov. 2002. *Bone Carving in Uelen: The Folk Art of Chukchi Peninsula.* Moscow: State Museum of Oriental Art.

Bronshtein, Mikhail M. and Kirill A. Dneprovsky. 2009. "Archaeology at Ekven Chukotka." Translated by Anna Samarova. In *Gifts from the Ancestors: Ancient Ivories of Bering Strait,* ed. William W. Fitzhugh, Julie Hollowell, and Aron L. Crowell, pp. 94-109. Princeton: Princeton University Art Museum.

Bronshtein, Mikhail. 2006. "Variability in Ancient Eskimo Graphic Designs: On the Problem of the Ethnic and Cultural History of the Bering Sea from the 1st millennium B.C. to the 1st millennium A.D." Translated by M. Slobodina. *Alaska Journal of Anthropology,* 4(1-2):162-171.

Brower, Charles D. 1994. *Fifty Years Below Zero: A Lifetime of Adventure in the Far North.* Fairbanks, AK: University of Alaska Press.

Brown, Emily Ivanoff "Ticasuk." 1987. *Tales of Ticasuk: Eskimo Legends and Stories.* Fairbanks, AK: University of Alaska Press.

Brown, John Patkuraq. 2005. "Half Squirrel and Half Beaver." In *The Dall Sheep Dinner Guest: Iñupiaq Narratives of Northwest Alaska,* ed. Wanni Anderson, pp. 115-116. Fairbanks, AK: University of Alaska Press.

Bruce, Miner. 1895. *Alaska: Its History and Resources, Gold Fields, Routes and Scenery.* Seattle: Lowman & Hanford Stationery and Printing Company.

Burch, Ernest S. Jr. 2006. *Social Life in Northwest Alaska: The Structure of Iñupiaq Eskimo Nations.* Fairbanks, AK: University of Alaska Press.

_____. 2012. *Caribou Herds of Northwest Alaska, 1850-2000,* ed. Igor Krupnik and Jim Dau. Fairbanks, AK: University of Alaska Press.

_____. 2013. "The Iñupiat and the Christianization of Arctic Alaska." In *Iñupiaq Ethnohistory: Selected Essays by Ernest S. Burch, Jr.,* ed. Erica Hill, pp. 59-83. Fairbanks, AK: University of Alaska Press.

Carter, Wilbert. 1966. "Archaeological Survey of Eskimo, or Earlier, Material in the Vicinity of Point Barrow, Alaska." Final Report, 31 January. Report to Office of Naval Research and Arctic Institute of North America.

Cassell, Mark S. 2000. "Iñupiat Labor and Commercial Shore Whaling in Northern Alaska." *Pacific Northwest Quarterly,* 91(3):115-123

Chamisso, Adelbert von. 1986. *A Voyage Around the World with the Romanzov Exploring Expedition in the Years 1815-1818 in the Brig Rurik, Captain Otto von Kotzebue.* Translated and edited by Henry Kratz. Honolulu: University of Hawaii Press.

Chan, Amy. 2013. *Quliaqtuavut Tuugaatigun (Our Stories in Ivory): Reconnecting Arctic Narratives with Engraved Drill Bows.* PhD Dissertation. Arizona State University.

Choris, Louis. 1822. *Voyage Pittoresque Autour Du Monde, avec Des Portraits de Sauvages d'Amérique, d'Asie, d'Afrique, et des Îles du Grand Océan: Des Paysages, des Vues Maritimes, et Plusieurs Objets d'Histoire Naturelle.* Paris: F. Didot.

Cleveland, Flora Kuugaaq. 2005. "The Goose Feather People." In *The Dall Sheep Dinner Guest: Iñupiaq Narratives of Northwest Alaska,* ed. Wanni Anderson, p. 250. Fairbanks, AK: University of Alaska Press

Cole, Dermot. 2019. "How State-Level Ivory Bans are Hurting Alaska Native Hunters and their Communities." 1 July. *Arctic Today.*

Collins, Henry B. 1937. *Archaeology of St. Lawrence Island.* Washington, DC: Smithsonian Institution.

_____. 1939. "On the Origin and Relationships of the Old Bering Sea Culture." National Anthropological Archives, Smithsonian Institution, Henry B. Collins Papers, Box 45.

_____. 1973. "Eskimo Art." In *The Far North: 2000 Years of American Eskimo and Indian Art,* ed. Henry B. Collins, Frederica de Laguna, Edmund Carpenter, and Peter Stone, pp. 1-131. Bloomington: Indiana University Press.

Cook, James. 1999. *The Voyage of the Resolution and the Discovery, 1776-1780.* Vol. 3, ed. J. C. Beaglehole. Rochester, NY: Boydell Press.

Crowell, Aron L., Rosita Worl, Paul C. Ongtooguk and Dawn Biddison, eds. 2010. *Living Our Cultures, Sharing Our Heritage: The First Peoples of Alaska.* Washington, DC: Smithsonian Institution Press.

Crowell, Aron L. 2009. "Sea Mammals in Art, Ceremony, and Belief: Knowledge Shared by Yupik and Iñupiaq Elders. In *Gifts from the Ancestors: Ancient Ivories of Bering Strait,* ed. William W. Fitzhugh, Julie Hollowell, and Aron L. Crowell, pp. 206-225. New Haven: Princeton University Art Museum and Yale University Press.

_____. 2020. *Living Our Cultures, Sharing Our Heritage:* "An Alaska Native Exhibition as Indigenous Knowledge Nexus." *Alaska Journal of Anthropology,* 18(1):4-22.

Cruikshank, Julie. 1995. "Imperfect Translations: Rethinking Objects of Ethnographic Collection." *Museum Anthropology,* 19(1):25-38.

Curtis, Edward. 1930. *The North American Indian, being a Series of Volumes Picturing and Describing the Indians of the United States, the Dominion of Canada, and Alaska.* Vol. 20. Norwood, MA: The Plimpton Press.

Dall, William H. 1870. *Alaska and its Resources.* Boston: Lee and Shepard.

De Decker, Kris. 2010. "Hand Powered Drilling Tools and Machines." *Low-tech Magazine.* Available: https://www.lowtechmagazine.com/2010/12/hand-powered-drilling-tools-and-machines.html

Dikov, N. N. 1999. *Mysteries in the Rocks of Ancient Chukotka (Petroglyphs of Pegtymel).* Translated by Richard L. Bland. Anchorage, AK: U. S. Department of the Interior, National Park Service, Shared Beringian Heritage Program.

Driscoll Engelstad, Bernadette. 2020. "Averting Animal Crashes: Function and Symbolism in Arctic Clothing Design." In *Arctic Crashes: People and Animals in the Changing North,* ed. Igor Krupnik, Aron L. Crowell, pp. 235-253. Washington, DC: Smithsonian Scholarly Press.

Dumond, Don E. 2009. "Chronology of Bering Strait Cultures." In *Gifts from the Ancestors: Ancient Ivories of Bering Strait,* ed. William W. Fitzhugh, Julie Hollowell, and Aron L. Crowell, pp. 70-77. Princeton, NJ: Princeton University Art Museum.

Duncan, Kate. 2000. *1001 Curious Things: Ye Olde Curiosity Shop and Native American Art.* Seattle: University of Washington Press.

Ellanna, Frank. 1988a. "How the Wolf Dance First Came to King Island." In *Ugiuvangmiut Quliapyuit King Island Tales: Eskimo History and Legends from Bering Strait,* ed. Kaplan, Lawrence D., pp. 106-115. Fairbanks, AK: Alaska Native Language Center and University of Alaska Press.

_____. 1988b. "The Boys' Share of the Hunt." In *Ugiuvangmiut Quliapyuit King Island Tales: Eskimo History and Legends from Bering Strait,* ed. Kaplan, Lawrence D., pp. 136-143. Fairbanks, AK: Alaska Native Language Center and University of Alaska Press.

Fair, Susan W. 2006. *Alaska Native Art: Tradition, Innovation, Continuity.* Fairbanks, AK: University of Alaska Press.

Fienup-Riordan, Ann. 1996. *The Living Tradition of Yup'ik Masks: Agayuliyarrput (Our Way of Making Prayer).* Seattle: University of Washington Press.

_____. 2007. *Yuungnaqpiallerput. The Way We Genuinely Live. Masterworks of Yup'ik Science and Survival.* Seattle: University of Washington Press.

Fisher, Kerynn. 2008. "Russian-American Research Team Examines Origins of Whaling Culture." *UAF News and Events,* 2 April. Available: http://www.uaf.edu/files/news/a_news/20080402153648.html.

Fitzhugh, William W. and Aron Crowell, eds. 1988. *Crossroads of Continents: Cultures of Siberia and Alaska.* Washington, DC: Smithsonian Institution.

Fitzhugh, William W. and Aron L. Crowell. 2009. "Ancestors and Ivories: Ancient Art of Bering Strait." In *Gifts from the Ancestors: Ancient Ivories of Bering Strait,* ed. William W. Fitzhugh, Julie Hollowell, and Aron L. Crowell, pp. 18-27. Princeton, NJ: Princeton University Art Museum.

Fitzhugh, William W. and Susan A. Kaplan, eds. 1982. *Inua: Spirit World of the Bering Sea Eskimo.* Washington, DC: Smithsonian Institution Press.

Fitzhugh, William W. Julie Hollowell, and Aron L. Crowell, eds. 2009. *Gifts from the Ancestors: Ancient Ivories of Bering Strait.* Princeton, NJ: Princeton University Art Museum.

Fitzhugh, William W. 2009. "Notes on Art Styles, Cultures, and Chronology." In *Gifts from the Ancestors: Ancient Ivories of Bering Strait,* ed. William W. Fitzhugh, Julie Hollowell, and Aron L. Crowell, pp. 88-93. Princeton, NJ: Princeton University Art Museum.

Glenn, Alice Qannik. 2018. "Episode 2: All About Native Foods (Part 1)." *Coffee and Quaq. Podcast.* Available: https://www.coffeeandquaq.com/post/allaboutnativefoodspart1

Gordon, George Byron. 1906. "Notes on the Western Eskimo." University of Pennsylvania *Transactions of the Free Museum of Science and Art* 2:69-101

_____. 1917. *In the Alaskan Wilderness.* Philadelphia: The John C. Winston Company.

Green, Paul. 1959. *I am Eskimo – Aknik my Name.* Bothell, WA: Alaska Northwest Books.

Griebel, Brendan. 2020. "Oral History, Oral Present, Oral Future: The Language of Inuinnait Heritage Research." 2020 Annual Ernest S. Burch Lecture. Washington, DC: Smithsonian National Museum of Natural History and Arctic Studies Center.

Gusev, Sergei V. 2014. "Excavations of the Unenen Settlement (The Ancient Whaling Culture) in Eastern Chukotka in 2007-2014." *Journal of Cultural Research* 3(17):205-212.

Hickman, Pat. 1987. *Innerskins / Outerskins: Gut and Fishskin.* San Francisco: San Francisco Craft and Folk Art Museum.

Hoffman, Walter James. 1897. *The Graphic Art of the Eskimos.* Washington, DC: Government Printing Office.

Hooper, Calvin L. 1884. *Report of the Cruise of the U.S. Revenue Steamer Thomas Corwin, in the Arctic Ocean, 1881.* Washington, DC: Government Printing Office.

Hooper, William Hulme. 1853. *Ten Months among the Tents of the Tuski, with Incidents of an Arctic Boat Expedition in Search of Sir John Franklin, as far as the Mackenzie River, and Cape Bathurst.* London: J. Murray.

Hovey, Davis. 2017. "Confusion over Legalities is Hurting Alaskan Ivory Market, Locals Say." *KNOM-Nome,* 17 June.

Hughes, Charles S. 1985. "Siberian Eskimo." In *Handbook of North American Indians, Volume 5, Arctic*, ed. David Damas, pp. 247-261. Washington, DC: Smithsonian Institution.

Imperato, Eleanor M. 2017. *Carving Life: Walrus Ivory Carvings from the Bering Sea.* New York: QCC Art Gallery Press.

Indian Arts and Crafts Board (IACB). 2017. "Alaska Native Ivory." Washington, DC: U.S. Department of the Interior. Available: https://www.doi.gov/sites/doi.gov/files/uploads/iacb_alaska_ivory_brochure_2017_web.pdf

Ipalook, Jon. 2012. Interview with Amy Phillips-Chan, 2 April. Kotzebue, Alaska.

Irrigoo, Samuel. 1977. "Story of Old Gambell House." In *"I remember…",* ed. Bill Karp, pp. 6-11. Village Library Project, ESAA Title VII. Nome, AK: Kegoayah Kozga Library Association.

Itchoak, Noralee, ed. 1978. *"I remember II…"* Village Library Project, ESAA Title VII. Nome, AK: Kegoayah Kozga Public Library.

Jackson, Sheldon. 1893. *Education in Alaska, 1889-90.* Washington, DC: Government Printing Office.

Jackson, Michael. 1989. *Paths toward a Clearing: Radical Empiricism and Ethnographic Inquiry.* Bloomington: Indiana University Press.

Jenness, Diamond. 1928. "Archaeological Investigations in Bering Strait." Annual Report for 1926. *Bulletin 50.* Ottawa: National Museum of Canada.

Jensen, Anne. 2012. "The Material Culture of Iñupiat Whaling: An Ethnographic and Ethnohistorical Perspective." *Arctic Anthropology,* 49(2):143-161.

Jolles, Carol Zane. 2006. "Iñupiaq Society and Gender Relations." In *Circumpolar Lives and Livelihood:A Comparative Ethnoarchaeology of Gender and Subsistence*, ed. Robert Jarvenpa and Hetty Jo Brumbach, pp. 238-262. Lincoln: University of Nebraska Press.

Kaplan, Lawrence D. with Deanna Paniataaq Kingston. 2007. "Introduction to Iñupiaq Narratives." In *Words of the Real People: Alaska Native Literature in Translation,* ed. Ann Fienup-Riordan and Lawrence D. Kaplan, pp. 127-132. Fairbanks, AK: University of Alaska Press.

Kaplan, Lawrence D., ed. 1988. *Ugiuvangmiut Quliapyuit King Island Tales: Eskimo History and Legends from Bering Strait.* Fairbanks, AK: Alaska Native Language Center and University of Alaska Press.

_____. 1994. *Dictionary of King Island Inupiaq (Preliminary Draft).* Fairbanks, AK: Alaska Native Language Center, University of Alaska Fairbanks.

Kawagley, A. Oscar. 2006. *A Yupiaq Worldview: A Pathway to Ecology and Spirit.* Longrove, IL: Waveland Press.

Kawerak, Inc. 2019. *Ayveq Nangaghneghput – Walrus & Our Way of Life.* Available: https://www.youtube.com/watch?v=eOPSXTAtahU

Killigivuk, Jimmie. 2007. "A Long Unipkaaq." In *Words of the Real People: Alaska Native Literature in Translation*, ed. Ann Fienup-Riordan and Lawrence D. Kaplan, pp. 151-168. Fairbanks, AK: University of Alaska Press.

King, Jonathan C. H. 1981. *Artificial Curiosities from the Northwest Coast of America: Native American Artefacts in the British Museum Collected on the Third Voyage of Captain James Cook and Acquired through Sir Joseph Banks.* London: British Museum.

Kingston, Deanna M., Lucy Tanaqiq Koyuk and Earl Aisana Mayac. 2001. "The Story of the King Island Wolf Dance, Then and Now." *Western Folklore,* 60(4):263-278.

Klouda, Naomi. 2017. "Campaigns Continue to Remind Alaskan Ivory Products are Legal." *Alaska Journal of Commerce.* Available: https://www.alaskajournal.com/2017-10-25/campaigns-continue-remind-alaskan-ivory-products-are-legal

Koonook, Henry. 2010. Interview with Amy Phillips-Chan, 8 August. Point Hope, Alaska.

Koonooka, Merlin (Paapi). 2020. "Observing Marine Mammals in Gambell, Alaska, at a Time of Change." In *Arctic Crashes: People and Animals in the Changing North,* ed. Igor Krupnik, Aron L. Crowell, pp. 152-163. Washington, DC: Smithsonian Scholarly Press.

Koozaata, Harry. 1982. "Interview: Harry Koozaata." *Journal of Alaska Native Arts,* (July/August).

Kotzebue, Otto von. 1967. A *Voyage of Discovery into the South Sea and Beering's Straits.* Amsterdam: N. Israel; New York: Da Capo.

Kunnuk, Joseph Sr. 2012. Interview with Amy Phillips-Chan, 19 April. Nome, Alaska.

Krauss, Michael E. 1980. *Alaska Native Languages: Past, Present, and Future.* Alaska Native Center Research Paper No. 4. Fairbanks, AK: Alaska Native Language Center.

Krupnik, Igor and Vera Oovi Kaneshiro, eds. 2011. "Neqamikegkaput / Faces We Remember: Leuman M. Waugh's Photography from St. Lawrence Island, Alaska, 1929-1930." *Contributions to Circumpolar Anthropology* 9. Washington, DC: Smithsonian Arctic Studies Center.

Krupnik, Igor and Brad Benter. 2016 "A Disaster of Local Proportion: Walrus Catch Falls for Three Straight Years in the Bering Strait Region." *Arctic Studies Center Newsletter,* 23:34-36.

Krupnik, Igor and G. Carleton Ray. 2007. "Pacific Walruses, Indigenous Hunters, and Climate Change: Bridging Scientific and Indigenous Knowledge." *Deep-Sea Research II*, 54:2946-2957.

Krupnik, Igor, Michael A. Lang, and Scott E. Miller, eds. 2009. *Smithsonian at the Poles: Contributions to International Polar Year Science.* Washington, DC: Smithsonian Institution Scholarly Press.

Krupnik, Igor. 2020. "Pacific Walrus, People, and Sea Ice: Relations at Subpopulation Scale, 1825-2015." In *Arctic Crashes: People and Animals in the Changing North,* ed. Igor Krupnik, Aron L. Crowell, pp. 351-374. Washington, DC: Smithsonian Scholarly Press.

Larsen, Helge and Froelich Rainey. 1948. *Ipiutak and the Arctic Whale Hunting Culture.* New York: American Museum of Natural History.

Lockwood, Michael. 1978. "Boyhood Days." In *"I remember II...",* ed. Noralee Itchoak, pp. 2-8. Village Library Project, ESAA Title VII. Nome, AK: Kegoayah Kozga Public Library.

Loring, Stephen. 2001. "Introduction to Lucien M. Turner and the Beginnings of Smithsonian Anthropology in the North." In *Ethnology of the Ungava District, Hudson Bay Territory,* by Lucien M. Turner, vii-xxxii. Washington, DC: Smithsonian Institution.

Lowenstein, Tom. 2008. *Ultimate Americans: Point Hope Alaska: 1826-1909.* Fairbanks, AK: University of Alaska Press.

Luukkanen, Harri and William W. Fitzhugh. 2020. *The Bark Canoes and Skin Boats of Northern Eurasia.* Washington, DC: Smithsonian Books.

Macdonald, Sharon. 2006. "Collecting Practices." In *A Companion to Museum Studies,* ed. Sharon Macdonald, pp. 81-97. Oxford: Blackwell.

MacLean, Edna Ahgeak. 2012. *Iñupiatun Uqaluit Taniktun Sivunniuġutiŋit: North Slope Iñupiaq to English Dictionary.* Fairbanks, AK: University of Alaska Fairbanks.

Maguire, Rochfort. 1988. *The Journal of Rochfort Maguire, 1852-1854: Two Years at Point Barrow, Alaska, Aboard HMS Plover in the Search for Sir John Franklin,* ed. John Bockstoce. London: Hakluyt Society.

Mason, Owen K. and Claire M. Alix. 2019. "Birnirk in its Element: Ferment, Experimentation and Migration in the 11th – 12th centuries AD." Paper presentation. 46th Annual Meeting of the Alaska Anthropological Association, Nome, AK.

Mason, Owen K. 1998. "The Contest between the Ipiutak, Old Bering Sea, and Birnirk Polities and the Origin of Whaling during the First Millennium A.D. along the Bering Strait." *Journal of Anthropological Archaeology,* 17:240-325.

McMullen, Ann. 2009. "Reinventing George Heye: Nationalizing the Museum of the American Indian and its Collections." In *Contesting Knowledge: Museums and Indigenous Perspectives,* ed. Susan Sleeper-Smith, pp. 65-105. Lincoln: University of Nebraska Press.

Milan, Frederick. 1964. "The Acculturation of the Contemporary Eskimo of Wainwright, Alaska." *Anthropological Papers of the University of Alaska,* 11(2):1-95.

Mongoyak, Gilford Jr. 2012. Interview with Amy Phillips-Chan, 22 May. Barrow, Alaska.

Murdoch, John. 1892. *Ethnological Results of the Point Barrow Expedition.* Washington, DC: Government Printing Office.

Nelson, Edward W. 1899. *The Eskimo about Bering Strait.* Washington, DC: Government Printing Office.

Ningealook, Baker. 2012. Interview with Amy Phillips-Chan, 9 June. Shishmaref, Alaska.

Norton, Nora Paniikaaluk. 2005a. "The Kobuk River Massacre." In *The Dall Sheep Dinner Guest: Iñupiaq Narratives of Northwest Alaska,* ed. Wanni Anderson, pp. 132-134. Fairbanks, AK: University of Alaska Press.

_____. 2005b. "One Who Walked Against the Wind." In *The Dall Sheep Dinner Guest: Iñupiaq Narratives of Northwest Alaska,* ed. Wanni Anderson, pp. 153-157. Fairbanks, AK: University of Alaska Press.

Omiak, James. 2012a. Interview with Amy Phillips-Chan, 20 April. Nome, Alaska.

_____. 2012b. Interview with Amy Phillips-Chan, 21 April. Nome, Alaska.

Oomittuk, Othniel Anaqulutuq "Art" Jr. 2010. Interview with Amy Phillips-Chan, 9 April. Point Hope, Alaska.

Oquilluk, William A. 1973. *People of Kauwerak: Legends of the Northern Eskimo.* Anchorage: Alaska Pacific University Press.

Pearce, Susan M. 1976. *Towards the Pole: A Catalogue of the Eskimo Collections.* Exeter: Royal Albert Memorial Museum.

_____. 1992. *Museums, Objects, and Collections: A Cultural Study.* Washington, DC: Smithsonian Institution Press.

Peard, George. 1973. T*o the Pacific and Arctic with Beechey: The Journal of Lieutenant George Peard of H.M.S. Blossom, 1825-1828,* ed. Barry M. Gough. Cambridge: Published for the Hakluyt Society at the University Press.

Penatac, John Sr. 2012. Interview with Amy Phillips-Chan, 28 September. Nome, Alaska.

Pennant, Thomas. 1784. *Arctic Zoology. Vol. I. Introduction. Class I. Quadrupeds.* London: Henry Hughes.

Phillips-Chan, Amy. 2019. *Nome. Images of America.* Charleston: Arcadia Publishing.

_____. 2020a. "Bering Strait Narratives and Collaborative Processes of Exhibit Development in Nome, Alaska." *Alaska Journal of Anthropology,* 18(1):23-50.

_____. 2020b. "The Impact of Bowhead Whale Fluctuations on Iñupiat-Whale Relations and Masked Dances in North Alaska." In *Arctic Crashes: People and Animals in the Changing North,* ed. Igor Krupnik, Aron L. Crowell, pp. 164-182. Washington, DC: Smithsonian Scholarly Press.

Pikonganna, Aloysius. 1988. "The Ways of the King Islanders." In *Ugiuvangmiut Quliapyuit King Island Tales: Eskimo History and Legends from Bering Strait,* ed. Kaplan, Lawrence D., pp. 40-49. Fairbanks, AK: Alaska Native Language Center and University of Alaska Press.

Pikonganna, Vince. 2012. Interview with Amy Phillips-Chan, 15 April. Nome, Alaska.

Powell, Eric A. 2009. "Origins of Whaling." *Archaeology* 62(1). Available: archive.archaeology.org/0901/topten/origins_of_whaling.html

Pullock, John. 2012. Interview with Amy Phillips-Chan, 26 April. Nome, Alaska.

Ray, Dorothy Jean. 1977. *Eskimo Art: Tradition and Innovation in North Alaska.* Seattle: University of Washington Press.

_____. 1982. "Reflections in Ivory." In *Inua: Spirit World of the Bering Sea Eskimo,* ed. William W. Fitzhugh and Susan A. Kaplan, pp. 254-267. Washington, DC: Smithsonian Institution Press.

_____. 1996. *A Legacy of Arctic Art.* Seattle: University of Washington Press.

_____ 2003. "Happy Jack and Guy Kakarook: Their Art and Heritage." In *Eskimo Drawings,* ed. Suzi Jones, pp. 18-33. Anchorage, AK: Anchorage Museum of History and Art.

Ray, Patrick H. 1885. *Report of the International Polar Expedition to Point Barrow, Alaska, in Response to the Resolution of the [U.S.] House of Representatives of December, 11, 1884.* Washington, DC: Government Printing Office.

Saclamana, Jerome. 2012a. Interview with Amy Phillips-Chan, 11 April. Nome, Alaska.

_____. 2012b. Interview with Amy Phillips-Chan, 13 April. Nome, Alaska.

_____. 2016. "Sculpting Ivory (10 of 17): Cutting Ivory." *Material Traditions: Sculpting Ivory,* ed. Dawn Biddison. Smithsonian Arctic Studies Center. Available: https://www.youtube.com/playlist?list=PL3wBN-dh9DMRrXiXA10N3mOsiKzvN2Hiy

Saclamana, Mike. 1979. "Nick Wongittilon Recalls Hunting Whales on St. Lawrence Island." In *Surah,* pp. 26-29. Nome, AK: Nome-Beltz High School.

Schaeffer, Ross Sr. 2012. Interview with Amy Phillips-Chan, 2 April. Kotzebue, Alaska.

Smithsonian Arctic Studies Center in Alaska. 2011. Smithsonian Learning Lab Collection: "Iñupiaq Lessons: Language and Culture." *Smithsonian Learning Lab.* December 10, 2019. Accessed October 19, 2020.

_____. 2015. Smithsonian Learning Lab Collection: "Sculpting Walrus Ivory Videos." *Smithsonian Learning Lab.* December 13, 2019. Accessed October 19, 2020.

Smithsonian Institution Office of Elementary and Secondary Education. 1981. "Of Kayaks and Ulus: The Bering Sea Eskimo Collection of Edward W. Nelson 'The Man Who Collected Good-For-Nothing Things.'" *Art to Zoo* (Spring/Summer). Available: http://www.smithsonianeducation.org/educators/lesson_plans/eskimo_collection/ATZ_CollectionofEdwardWNelson_SprSum1981.pdf

Sockpick, Brian. 2012. Interview with Amy Phillips-Chan, 26 April. Nome, AK.

Sockpick, Gary. 2012. Interview with Amy Phillips-Chan, 4 June. Shishmaref, AK.

Steffian, Amy and April Counceller. 2020. "Exploring Alutiiq Heritage One Word at a Time." *Alaska Journal of Anthropology,* 18(1):57-70

Sutton, Anne and Sue Steinacher. 2012. *Alaska's Nome Area Wildlife Viewing Guide: Exploring the Nome Roadways.* Juneau: Alaska Department of Fish and Game.

Tetpon, Levi. 2012. Interview with Amy Phillips-Chan, 18 June. Anchorage, Alaska.

_____. 2016. "Sculpting Ivory (7 of 17): Materials – Walrus Tusk (Ivory)." *Material Traditions: Sculpting Ivory,* ed. Dawn Biddison.

Smithsonian Arctic Studies Center. Available: https://www.youtube.com/playlist?list=PL3wBN-dh9DMRrXiXA10N3mOsiKzvN2Hiy

Thomas, Nicholas. 1994. "Licensed Curiosity: Cook's Pacific Voyages." In *The Cultures of Collecting,* ed. John Elsner and Roger Cardinal eds., pp. 117-136, 281-282. London: Reaktion Books.

Tiulana, Matthew. 2012. Interview with Amy Phillips-Chan, 12 April. Nome, AK.

Tördal, Amanda. 2016. "Wales Celebrates 17th Annual Kingikmiut Dance Festival." 8 September. *The Nome Nugget.*

VanStone, James W. 1975. "Nineteenth Century Alaskan Eskimo Art: A New Exhibit Opens December 11." *Field Museum of Natural History Bulletin,* 46(11):3-7.

Weyiouanna, Edwin. 2012. Interview with Amy Phillips-Chan, 8 June. Shishmaref, Alaska.

Yohe, Jill Ahlberg and Teri Greeves, eds. 2019. *Hearts of Our People: Native Women Artists.* Minneapolis: Minneapolis Institute of Art in association with University of Washington Press.

Zimmerly, David W. 2000. *Qayaq: Kayaks of Alaska and Siberia.* Fairbanks, AK: University of Alaska Press.

Zolles, Carol Jane and Galina Dyachkova. 2009. "Artists and Contemporary Life." In *Gifts from the Ancestors: Ancient Ivories of Bering Strait,* ed. William W. Fitzhugh, Julie Hollowell, and Aron L. Crowell, pp. 240-247. Princeton, NJ: Princeton University Art Museum.

Engraved Drill Bows
from the Smithsonian Collections

26/ William Kiminock from Little Diomede uses a drill bow under the close observation of his grandson. c. 1970. Carrie M. McLain Memorial Museum.

1

Lessons in Carving

Eliqutaq *Wilfred Anowlic, 2013:*

When I was growing up at King Island, I used to watch my grandfather and other young men use the Eskimo drill. The men carved cribbage boards and drilled holes to make eyes on polar bears and seal figurines. Drill bows and engravings on drill bows were done before I was born. I use a Dremel tool to drill. I did see plain drill bows that were used by my grandfather, father, and uncle. Beautiful etchings were done on their carvings. I do etching on my cribbage boards, ivory cups, and walrus tooth key holders [see Figs. 47, 66, and 112 for holes created with a drill bow on a cribbage board and eyes on a seal and polar bear].

Sylvester Ayek, 2012:

For people my age, this is how we learned to drill holes on ivory a long time ago, using our father's drill bow. The only thing I have left of my father is a mouthpiece. It wasn't all that hard as long as your drill bit was sharp; it goes through ivory pretty fast. When I was growing up, they had those drills that you crank to make big, big holes for pipes. Some of the good ones,

when they make a pipe or cigarette holder, they drill from both ends. That's hard to do, for a very small hole like that, to hit the other side [see the ivory pipe shown in Fig. 141].

Ilonraaq *John Pullock, 2012:*

These are drill bows; they had fancy ones. I saw those used, but not ivory ones. You don't see these kinds of drill bows in King Island, they are plain. I used these drill bows when I was a young, young man, my grandfather's. Sometimes they use wood and bone, and sometimes ivory like this, curved, they bend it. Some of these are way before me [see a carver from King Island using a drill bow in Fig. 154].

Kuyuruk *Matthew Tiulana, 2012:*

My dad Paul Tiulana used a drill bow to carve ivory. My grandfather had one of those old wooden toolboxes, *ayupqat;* he gave it to my cousin as a namesake but now everyone uses plastic. My cousin gives me ivory to carve or sometimes I find ivory on the beach; that saves money [see bentwood toolboxes shown in Figs. 27 and 119].

27/ Ayupqat BENTWOOD TOOLBOX (Bering Strait Inupiaq)
Bering Strait
Collected by Robert Renshaw, accessioned 1977
Carrie M. McLain Memorial Museum 1977.1.2
Wood with ivory plates, sealskin hinges, and a repaired ivory handle; Length 61 cm (24 in)

28/ Pitiksiaq DRILL BOW
Cape Darby
Collected by Edward W. Nelson, accessioned 1880
National Museum of Natural History E44210
Walrus ivory; Length 31.3 cm (12.3 in)

TOP: Caribou graze on the tundra. A figure with a spear and hunting bag stands in the center.

BOTTOM: A herd of caribou graze and rest on the tundra. Three seals appear on the right end.

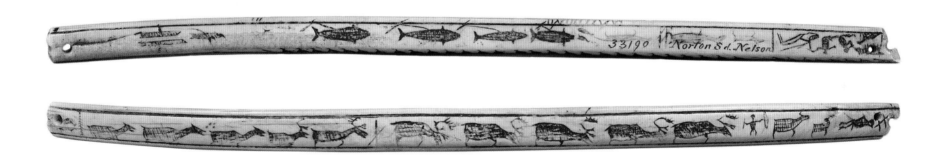

29/ Pitiksiaq DRILL BOW
St. Michael
Collected by Edward W. Nelson, accessioned 1878
National Museum of Natural History E33190
Walrus ivory; Length 38 cm (15 in)

TOP: A pair of hunters in kayaks harpoon a walrus. Four harpooned whales float across the top, a wolf chases a caribou and calf, and two figures smoke pipes.

BOTTOM: A long row of caribou face a bow hunter on the right end. The crossed post in the center may represent a snare made from willows.

Nayokpuk *Brian Sockpick, 2012:*

They used to always use those drills a long time ago. Most of them are ivory but some are from bone, depends on what they catch or what time of the year. These engraved drill bows are pretty old since they're yellow; really been used [see Figs. 32-34 for drill bows made from caribou bone].

George Milligrock, 2012:

My grandfather had a drill bow out of walrus rib bone, not etched. I used to have the whole thing including the mouthpiece. They used to carve in a sod house in Little Diomede, with no electricity. Everyone in my family carved, my father, grandfather, even my mother. It was the only way we had to make money back then [see Fig. 1 of a carver using a drill bow at home in Little Diomede].

Qualayauq *Ross Schaeffer Sr., 2012:*

It took a lot of work to make a drill bow real flat, especially with the kinds of tools they had. They didn't have any grinders at all. I haven't tried the drill bow much. I made one a couple of years ago, just for show [see carving tools shown in Figs. 46, 50, 59, and 60].

Aŋmaluq *Vince Pikonganna, 2012:*

I used to watch my father use his drill bow to make over 120 holes in his cribbage boards. Using a drill bow is how my father got such a strong neck. I used my father's drill bow before. I tried drilling holes out of curiosity before I had my own drills and Foredom. It wore out my neck and jaw gripping the mouthpiece [see the many holes required for a cribbage board in Fig. 66, wood mouthpieces shown in Figs. 30, 37, and 39, and an ivory carver gripping a mouthpiece shown in Fig. 1].

30/ Kiŋmiaq MOUTHPIECE (Bering Strait Inupiaq)
Little Diomede
Donated by Sylvia Milligrock Eningowuk, accessioned 2011
Carrie M. McLain Memorial Museum 2011.16.1
Wood with a stone socket, used by carver Lincoln Milligrock;
Length 61 cm (24 in)

31/ Niuutit DRILLS (Bering Strait Inupiaq)
Seward Peninsula
Collected by Wilfred A. McDaniel, accessioned 2001
Carrie M. McLain Memorial Museum 2001.5.12 (left), 2001.5.11 (right)
Wood with metal bits lashed on with copper wire (left) and sealskin (right);
Length 19.5 cm (7.7 in) (left), Length 13.5 cm (5.3 in) (right)

OUR STORIES ETCHED IN IVORY

32/ Pitiksiaq DRILL BOW
Norton Sound
Collected by Lucien M. Turner, accessioned 1876
National Museum of Natural History E24551
Caribou bone; Length 33.4 cm (13.1 in)

Crossed lines appear on the ends. The center features a herd of caribou and a figure standing between wolves.

33/ Pitiksiaq DRILL BOW
Norton Sound
Collected by Lucien M. Turner, accessioned 1876
National Museum of Natural History E24552
Caribou bone; Length 34.5 cm (13.6 in)

A kayak on the left is followed by a bow hunter who takes aim at a wolf chasing a herd of caribou. A porcupine and pair of beavers appear on the right end.

34/ Pitiksiaq DRILL BOW
Norton Sound
Collected by Lucien M. Turner, accessioned 1876
National Museum of Natural History E24550
Caribou bone; Length 30.6 cm (12 in)

A nucleated circle appears on the left end followed by various species of fish.

Stanley Tocktoo, 2012:

I was raised by my grandparents. My grandfather had a drill bow made of wood, not fancy like these. His drill bow was strung with rawhide and the drills had different sizes of bits. I mostly use power tools to carve in the school shop. Not much time to carve with the kids around at home. Some kids stop by to watch when I am carving. I've done etching before but hardly anyone does those story carvings anymore; they must have passed away. The circle-dot motifs and line etchings appear on some of the artifacts we have found [see circle-dot engravings, also known as nucleated circles, shown in Figs. 35-36].

John Penatac Sr., 2012:

My father had an ivory drill bow that he used. I can't remember if it was etched. I still have my father's wooden drills. Carvers used to use only hand tools like chisels in the old days [see the wood drills shown in Fig. 31 and the chisel in Fig. 46].

Levi Tetpon, 2012:

Some of these carvings are really, really old. They don't do this type of thing anymore. These guys really took their time because time had a different meaning. There also aren't very many people who do this sort of thing because it takes so much material.

Baker Ningealook, 2012:

My father used a drill bow, *niuqtuun,* made from ivory, but it wasn't etched. He used it with a hardwood mouthpiece and a stone socket. Some of the old mouthpieces are ivory [see Fig. 30 for a wood mouthpiece with a stone socket].

Kenny Tikik, 2012:

I never used a drill bow but I hear they're real fast. They drill real accurate. If you want to drill something like a bracelet, they drill real straight. The tip was three sides, made out of a nail. I sure wouldn't mind making one of those [see the bracelet made from ivory and baleen in Fig. 42].

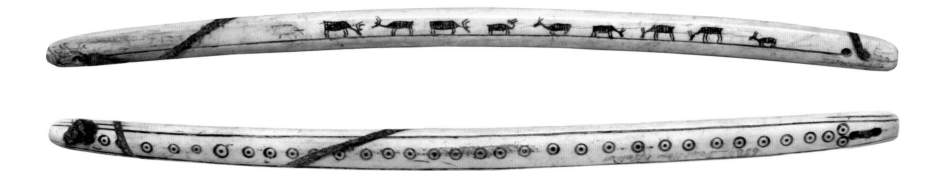

35/ Pitiksiaq DRILL BOW
Point Hope
Collected by Edward W. Nelson, accessioned 1882
National Museum of Natural History E63803
Walrus ivory, sealskin; Length 37.9 cm (15 in)

TOP: A herd of caribou graze on the tundra.

BOTTOM. A row of nucleated circles extends across the side.

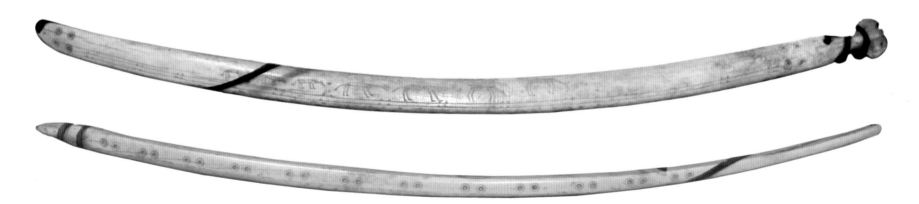

36/ Pitiksiaq DRILL BOW
Point Hope
Purchased by George Heye from John Hackman in 1905
National Museum of the American Indian 4488
Walrus ivory, sealskin; Length 44.5 cm (17.5 in)

TOP: A row of five wolves pursue two caribou. Four nucleated circles appear on each end. The right end has been carved into a whale fluke.

BOTTOM: Pairs of nucleated circles extend across the side.

Sinaġuyak *James Omiak, 2012:*

My drill bow is really curved; this is an almost straight one. In Little Diomede, we call it *kiŋmiaq* (mouthpiece), *niuqtuun* (drill), *satquaq* (drill bow). This is a sealskin strap; sometimes they use *ugruk* when they have no sealskin. We use bleached sealskin now for the drill bow; it gets real soft when you use it. They used a tool of some kind, like a homemade drill, for engraving. I had a drill that I used for carving. I made it from a three-corner file; that's what we had, homemade. An old man down in Diomede, 1943 or 1944, he made a mouthpiece and put a rock in it for my brother; that rock's still there. When the mouthpiece is worn out you put in another piece to replace it. My brother used the mouthpiece before he quit carving and I used it to make lots of bracelets [see the drill bow set from Little Diomede shown in Fig. 39].

Edwin Weyiouanna, 2012:

This was their Eskimo bow drill; they used that a long time ago. They always had their own mouthpiece and own design.

They used to use bow drills to drill holes for bracelets a long time ago. My dad used to use those a long time ago when I was growing up. They were made out of wood but these are good carvers, they make them out of ivory [see the mouthpiece with a unique seal design shown in Fig. 37].

Suluk *Francis Alvanna, 2012:*

I know my dad had an ivory drill bow but I don't remember if it was etched. I used to borrow my brother-in-law's drill bow. A bow drill set is called *niuutiq*: *kiŋmiaq* (mouthpiece), *pitiksiaq* (drill bow), *niuun* (drill). I made a *pitiksiaq* out of *tuttu* (caribou) antler. I made a mouthpiece out

of an old hickory pick handle. I have a *qayuun* (adze), made from a twelve-inch flat file but I have a drugstore scraper. I cut a knife and shaped it for etching. I try to etch but I'm not very good at it. Do you know why a whole bunch of the drill bows are engraved? They had nothing to do, no television, no radio [see the mouthpiece and drill bow shown in Figs. 37-38 and the adze in Fig. 50].

37/ Kiŋmiaq MOUTHPIECE (Bering Strait Inupiaq)
Alaska
Collected by Victor J. Evans, accessioned 1931
National Museum of Natural History E360422
Wood with a stone socket and carved seal heads on the ends;
Length 14 cm (5.5 in)

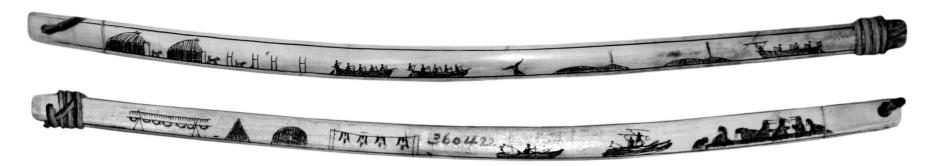

38/ Pitiksiaq DRILL BOW
Alaska
Collected by Victor J. Evans, accessioned 1931
National Museum of Natural History E360422
Walrus ivory, sealskin; Length 46.6 cm (18.3 in)

TOP: Hunters in skin boats pursue bowhead whales outside a village with rounded reindeer hide tents in the style of Chukchi or Siberian Yupik houses.

BOTTOM: A summer camp on the left features tents and racks holding fish and reindeer skins. On the right, hunters in kayaks aim their harpoons at walrus resting on a cake of ice.

39/ Pitiksiaq DRILL BOW   Kiŋmiaq MOUTHPIECE   Niuun DRILL
Little Diomede
Purchased by MAI from an unknown source in 1919
National Museum of the American Indian 9/4635
Walrus ivory, sealskin (drill bow), wood, stone, sealskin (mouthpiece), wood, metal (drill);
Length 48 cm (18.9 in) (drill bow), 15 cm (5.9 in) (mouthpiece), 25.3 cm (10 in) (drill)

A group of dancers and drummers perform between a village with sod houses and storage caches and a summer camp with a fish rack, tent, and a skin boat on its side. A hunter spears a polar bear on the right end.

Sylvester Ayek, 2012:

Because our culture is oral culture too, this is how they told their views about village life. What it takes to be a hunter and gatherer. They did very well. I really enjoy something like this because sometimes they have some really good ideas, how they see village life to be [see Fig. 40 for scenes of spring hunting, summer fish camp, and winter village life].

Anaqulutuq *Othniel Anaqulutuq "Art" Oomittuk Jr., 2010:*

These stories on the drill bows kind of tell the same thing that I'm telling when I create something. Each carver has his own story to tell. It might take a week looking at a piece to figure out part of the story. Somebody else might know another part of the story. You don't see these images in contemporary times. It started to change and change, that's what is happening in this culture. It could be that now we create a lot for tourism, people don't make this type of engraving. So the mindset changed. We transitioned from creating these marks. We started to get sloppy and forgot. Then it was just the ivory shapes, animals that are still carved [see carved ivory animals shown in Figs. 47 and 112 and animal carvings for sale on top of a toolbox in Fig. 119].

Edwin Weyiouanna, 2012:

On some of these carvings they tell their story on how they lived. That's how come they have these etchings. That's how come they recorded, put them on ivory. They didn't have any paper or books a long time ago. They didn't know how to read. But they knew how to do artwork.

Henry Koonook, 2010:

When boys come and watch me carve they're real quiet. I will say, "You guys want to ask questions, you are more than welcome to ask questions," and then they start talking. They forget about the questions so they just start talking. I tell them stories. I tell them how I got started with my artwork. I tell them it's a big part of my life in Point Hope. It shows who I am as an Iñupiaq. I am Kamaktoaq. I come from that clan over there [see Figs. 35, 36, and 63 for an etching style from Point Hope that features nucleated circles and a row of animals].

40/ Pitiksiaq DRILL BOW
Golovin Bay
Collected by Edward W. Nelson, accessioned 1897
National Museum of Natural History E176172
Walrus ivory; Length 34.6 cm (13.6 in)

TOP: This scene appears to depict the wreck of the schooner *W. F. March* that was blown ashore without loss of life at Golovin Bay on August 15, 1881. The ship carried a crew of seven along with ten miners, provisions, ore, and mining tools. Members of the ship are shown wearing broad-brimmed hats, disembarking in small skiffs, and setting up four-paneled tents on the beach. A summer fish camp and boulder are illustrated on the left.

MIDDLE: A person pushes a basket sled to a group of hunters cutting up a walrus. Figures run across the ice and a hunter prepares to throw his harpoon at a seal coming up to breathe. On the right, hunting crews in skin boats are pursuing a bowhead whale and walrus.

BOTTOM: This side features a village with a figure practicing the two-foot high kick, a giant standing outside a tent with people inside smoking pipes, wrestling, dancing and drumming inside a *qagri*, and a row of thirteen whale flukes.

Kayvanik *Jerome Saclamana, 2012:*

My father Mike Saclamana Sr. used to split a walrus tusk into four for making drill bows. He used the female tusks with a natural curve for the drill bow and did the old style of etching. He used to have a copper socket in his mouthpiece. Seeing these old ivory engravings makes me want to engrave. I'm amazed that they know how to make motion with the least amount of detail. Some of these engravings were maybe just to fill the space. I had an old mammoth tusk and engraved all around it and had a large empty space when I was done. So I etched a dancer in it just to fill the void [see Fig. 50 for an adze used to carefully split a walrus tusk into a drill bow].

Henry Koonook, 2010:

Some of this knowledge I learned from my grandparents, my aunts and uncles, my father, and mom. This is something that a lot of the younger generation don't know about or care about. I think that's why it's important to have people like myself and others that use these tools. It's important to pass all this on to the next generation because they may have to use these tools someday. Who knows, we might not have any of this stuff a hundred years from now. We might have to go back and live the old way. They will at least have a piece of information that can be used, which was used, five hundred years ago [see examples of multi-generational learning in Figs. 7 and 26].

Joseph Kunnuk Sr., 2012:

They did amazing work in those days. My dad used to etch. He tried to teach me how to etch. He taught me how to do things, how to correct me, and where my mistakes are. My dad used to tell me not to touch his tools. He just gave me a file and whatever I wanted, whatever I have to use, when I carve. I used to help him, making bracelets, sand them up, sand them down. Most of the time, we learned how to do things by watching. We listened to our people and what we were supposed to be doing [see Fig. 8 of carver Joseph Kunnuk Sr. working on an ivory bracelet and Fig. 41 for a scene repeated in different etching styles that may have been used as a teaching tool].

Aŋmaluq *Vince Pikonganna, 2012:*

Before I do any carving, I like to take my time and think about what I'm going to be doing for two or three days. I like to have a little plan. I get into my own world when I'm carving ivory. Maybe I'm looking for some kind of answer.

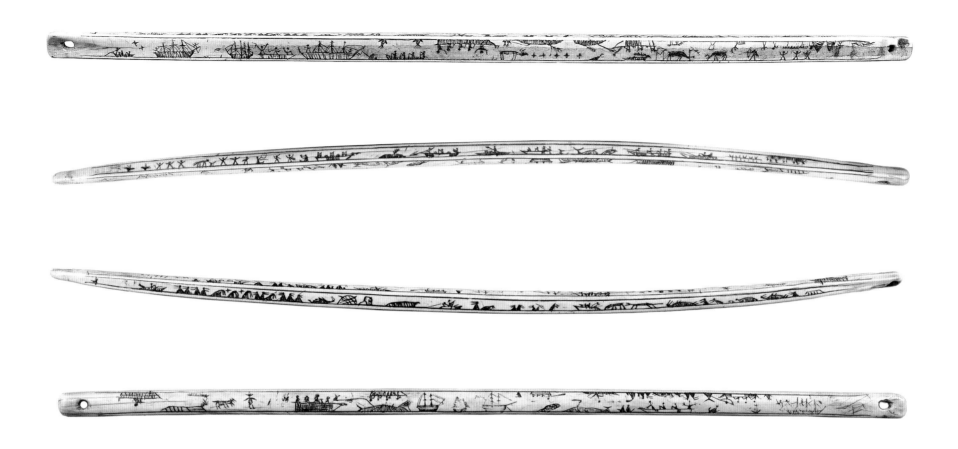

41/ Piṫiksiaq DRILL BOW
Cape Nome
Collected by Edward W. Nelson, accessioned 1880
National Museum of Natural History E45333
Walrus ivory; Length 42.5 cm (16.7 in)

TOP: Artist 1 engraved skin boats paddling out to three whaling ships, a harpooner striking a bowhead whale, and figures hunting caribou.

UPPER MIDDLE: Artist 2 engraved figures drumming, dancing, smoking a pipe, and hunting whales in skin boats and kayaks.

LOWER MIDDLE: Artist 2 also engraved imagery on this side including walrus sunning on the beach, kayaks hunting walrus, and myth-like creatures.

BOTTOM: Artists 1, 2 and 3 engraved this side with three different styles of skin boats and bowhead whales. The repeated subject matter suggests this drill bow was used to teach carvers how to engrave on ivory.

Sinaġuyak *James Omiak, 2012:*

I'm from Diomede; it's where I learned how to carve. As kids down there, we had to learn. I learned from my father, he mostly made billikens or cigarette holders. Then some man always made bracelets; I went to his house and watched how to carve. When I got home, I started carving [see Fig. 42 for an example of an ivory bracelet from Little Diomede and p. 2 for ivory billikens made by Tommy Soolook of Little Diomede].

Jack Frankson Jr., 2012:

I became inspired to start carving when my dad told me to shape a whalebone vertebra to make it look like a face and it turned out pretty good. I've been watching my dad since I was little, helping him sand, like my brother is right now. Once you get into it, it's not that difficult. You just keep doing it. After you make something and sell it, you just want to make something else and sell it too. You can even make gifts [see carved masks made from whalebone vertebrae shown in Fig. 7].

Levi Tetpon, 2012:

I learned to carve when I was about nine, ten years old. Everyone was about that age when we started. It was my job to finish my dad's carving, to put the polish on it, White Diamond, and to do the inking. When my dad was teaching me how to carve, if I made something like a leg out of proportion, he would say, would you run around with a leg like that? My parents were crafts people. They worked bone, they carved, they sewed, and they did fur. That's how they supported the family [see a husband and wife carving and sewing together to make crafts for sale in Fig. 3].

Sylvester Ayek, 2012:

I learned to carve mostly by watching the older people, older men, carving in the clubhouses. As boys, we were always in the clubhouse; where all the carving and tool-making and implement construction, *qayaq* construction, took place. The clubhouses were just a little bigger than this room [see Fig. 26 of a young boy watching his grandfather carve ivory].

42/ Tayaat BRACELET (Bering Strait Inupiaq)
Little Diomede
Collected by William S. Schock, accessioned 2016
Carrie M. McLain Memorial Museum 2016.26.3
Ivory and baleen; Diameter 7.6 cm (3 in)

43/ Pinaugun FILE (Bering Strait Inupiaq)
Bering Strait
Collected by Howard and Mary Knodel, accessioned 2007
Carrie M. McLain Memorial Museum 2007.10.1182
Wood and metal; Length 30.5 cm (12 in)

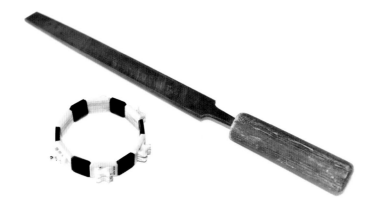

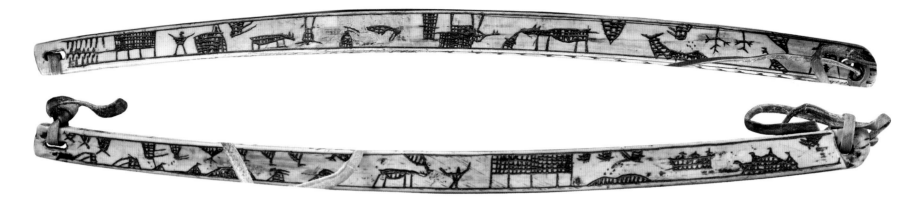

44/ Pitiksiaq DRILL BOW
Diomede Islands
Collected by Edward W. Nelson, accessioned 1882
National Museum of Natural History E49163
Walrus ivory, sealskin; Length 31 cm (12.2 in)

TOP: Barbed and pronged lines related to the Birnirk culture appear on the left and right ends. Scattered in between are walrus, tents, figures, and a polar bear eating a seal.

BOTTOM: Raised houses, traditionally covered with walrus skins, appear in the center next to a figure waving his arms in front of a polar bear. Walrus, geese, and a skin boat pursuing a bowhead whale are on either side of the village scene.

45/ Pitiksiaq DRILL BOW
Nome
Collected by William M. Fitzhugh, accessioned 1936
National Museum of the American Indian 19/3412
Walrus ivory, sealskin; Length 46.5 cm (18.3 in)

TOP: Artist 1 used straight outlines and vertical fill lines to create a scene with seals, caribou, and skin boats hunting walrus and bowhead whales.

BOTTOM: Artist 1 engraved a pair of kayaks hunting walrus on the bottom right. Artist 2 created the village scenes with straight outlines and tight cross hatch fill lines. Artist 3 engraved the skin boats and whale in the center with wavy outlines and loose cross-hatch fill lines.

Suluk *Francis Alvanna, 2012:*

I learned to carve through my dad, in the *qagri*, men's house, community house. I was four, five years old; made polar bears, seals. When we first started, we learn how to use a file. We file on a walrus tooth, take all the brown stuff off, and make a keychain. I would etch on it, a seal or walrus etching. As you grow older, you carve more and you make something else. You used to go through the *qagri* and everybody carved in one place, like they do here in the carving shop in Nome, tell stories [see the metal file shown in Fig. 43].

Thomas Barr, 2012:

Growing up here in Nome and at Kotzebue, my dad had a carving space wherever we lived. When we were living in Kotzebue, he taught me how to make my first carvings; they were seals. Then I made figurines and key chains. I remember when I was in the fourth grade I made my first sale, a walrus tooth seal. I still remember how much money I made off of it, twelve dollars [the small ivory seal shown in Fig. 47 is also made from a walrus tooth].

Aŋmaluq *Vince Pikonganna, 2012:*

I learned to carve by trial and error, on my own. Mostly I watched in the clubhouse, how my Elders carved. They called it a *qagri*, clubhouse. I never carved there, only my dad did. Everybody had their own spot, in that *qagri*. At King Island they had three clubhouses when I was growing up down there. I didn't try to carve until 1957 or 1958, trying to make a

seal, which probably took me two days to finish, a small one, maybe two inches, maybe one inch. But I went to the store and sold it and got a candy for it. That encouraged me, encouraged me to continue my carving [King Island carvers like Vince Pikonganna often started out making small seals like the one shown in Fig. 47].

Ken Lisbourne, 2012:

I learned to carve in school from an Iñupiaq teacher at Point Hope. The first thing I carved was an ivory polar bear. I took it to the store and sold it for $2.50, which was a lot of money. Charlie McDaniels used to come to Point Hope every year in two planes and fill them up with dried sealskin, baleen, ivory bracelets, and carvings [see Fig. 112 of a carved polar bear and Fig. 42 of an ivory bracelet].

46/ Sanalġun CHISEL (Bering Strait Inupiaq)
Bering Strait
Collected by Howard and Mary Knodel, accessioned 2007
Carrie M. McLain Memorial Museum 2007.10.1180
Wood and metal; Length 12 cm (4.7 in)

47/ Nassiŋuaq PRETEND SEAL (Qawiaraq Inupiaq)
Nome
Donated by Clara Mielke-Richards, accessioned 1979
Carrie M. McLain Memorial Museum 1979.1.22
Ivory with baleen eyes; Length 5.5 cm (2.2 in)

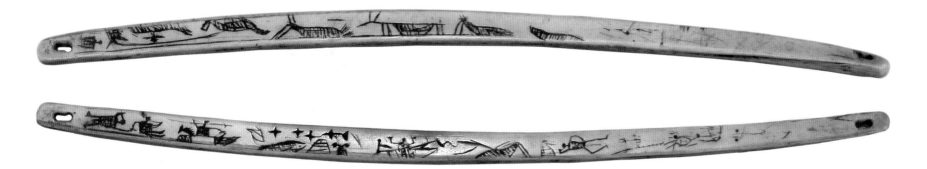

48/ Pitiksiaq DRILL BOW
Alaska
Collected by Edward W. Nelson, accessioned 1991
National Museum of Natural History ET16050
Walrus ivory; Length 24 cm (9.4 in)

TOP: This side features walrus with extra-long tusks and a polar bear with a large stomach in the center.

BOTTOM: Two figures smoke pipes on the left and a pair of hunters in kayaks pursue geese and walrus in the center.

49/ Pitiksiaq DRILL BOW
Alaska
Collected by Lucien M. Turner, accessioned 1876
National Museum of Natural History E24533
Walrus ivory, sealskin; Length 32.3 cm (12.7 in)

TOP: Two whaling ships are anchored off the coast while a skin boat approaches a walrus attacking a figure on the beach. The right end features two wolves, a caribou, and a goose next to diagonal rows of barbed bands and a star.

BOTTOM: A wolf chases caribou towards a hunter hiding behind a hill. A skin boat has harpooned a bowhead whale that now drags three sealskin floats. Two diagonal rows of barbed bands and a star are on the right end.

Natchiq *Jon Ipalook, 2012:*

My biological father is really into carving himself too so I get to learn a lot. A lot of his techniques you will see in my ivory and baleen bracelets. But a lot of the different animals and bigger projects I've learned from my uncles Simon Koonook and Henry Koonook. Carving is where I feel the most comfortable. Kind of brings me back to the places I've been, the people I've worked with; just being able to reconnect. [see Fig. 4 of Jon Ipalook sharing how to use the drill bow].

Ilonraaq *John Pullock, 2012:*

When we were young, we used to begin carving with walrus teeth. File it, smooth it out, polish it, and put a hole in it for a keychain. Those used to sell for one dollar, no matter how big they were, way back then, to tourists. I don't try to sell a carving downtown because they sell a lot cheaper. After that, my older cousin started showing me how to make seals, and I did. I started to copy what the older people carve. They don't show us but if we do something wrong, they tell us, so you fix that. They don't go, "You carve this way, or you do that." We carve by ourselves out of the way. My son learned how to carve from his uncles, sometimes he watches me. He also learned his carving at Nome-Beltz when they had a cultural class [see the carved ivory seal in Fig. 47 and the ivory carving workshop held at Nome-Beltz High School in Fig. 5].

Roy Sockpick, 2012:

I started carving when I was around sixteen. My grandpa Teddy Sockpick Sr. was a carver; he used to make a living only through his carvings. I still use his flat file. I used to have an *ulimaun* (adze) of Teddy's with a driftwood handle and chisel blade; it worked well to rough out bone [see the metal file shown in Fig. 43 and an adze used to rough out ivory and bone shown in Fig. 50].

John Heffle, 2012:

I learned to carve when I was eight or nine years old. My uncles would always come by when they came to Fairbanks to do Native artwork. My uncles, my aunts, my mom, everybody was doing their own little thing and I would get right in there; my house was like a house of art.

50/ Qayunn ADZE (Bering Strait Inupiaq)
Bering Strait
Collected by William A. Woenne Jr., accessioned 2005
Carrie M. McLain Memorial Museum 2005.1.11
Bone, stone, and sealskin; Length 17 cm (6.7 in)

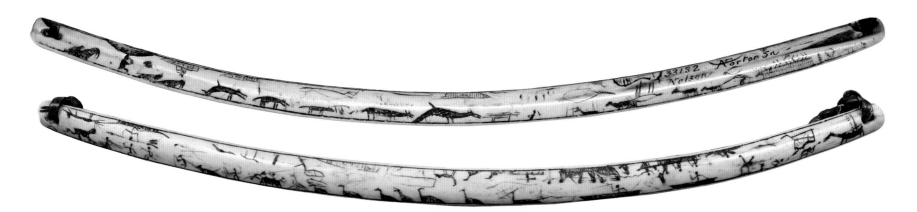

51/ Pitiksiaq DRILL BOW
St. Michael
Collected by Edward W. Nelson, accessioned 1878
National Museum of Natural History E33182
Walrus ivory, sealskin; Length 37.5 cm (14.8 in)

TOP: Two female walrus carry calves on the left end and a herd of caribou, represented by a single rectangular body, appear on the right. A row of myth creatures appears in the center, including *palraiyuk*, with long bodies and sharp teeth, and walrus dogs, with thin bodies and short pointy ears.

BOTTOM: A giant lunges at three running figures on the left end followed by a hunter pulling a seal. Two hunters in kayaks pursue geese in the center. A hunter prepares to spear a bear on the right end.

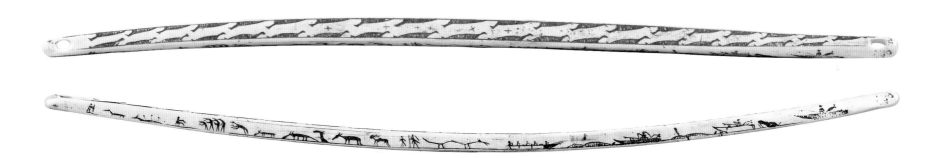

52/ Pitiksiaq DRILL BOW
Kotzebue Sound
Collected by Edward W. Nelson, accessioned 1882
National Museum of Natural History E48523
Walrus ivory; Length 46.6 cm (18.3 in)

TOP: Two rows of seals stretch across the side with crosses in between them that may represent migrating birds.

BOTTOM: A row of myth creatures, including a skin boat with the head of a *tirisiq*, tall creatures with bent necks and outstretched arms, and anthropomorphic wolves and caribou are followed by two figures carrying hunting bags. Hunters in skin boats and kayaks are pursuing bowhead whales and walrus on the right end.

William Simmonds, 2012:

I learned carving from my uncle Samuel Simmonds, around age fourteen or fifteen. I expected to receive a large chunk of ivory when I started. Instead, he gave me small bits and pieces and told me to make something out of them. I thought for a long time and then started with a caribou. My uncle told me I had to stick with my original design and couldn't change it. Uncle Samuel used to say carvings should be kept in the family and community because it's part of our culture [see the caribou head carved on the end of a drill bow in Fig. 63 and the caribou herd engraved on Fig. 54].

Kayvanik *Jerome Saclamana, 2012:*

I used to watch my dad carve ivory. I didn't ask too many questions. I figure when you're watching, you're already imposing. You don't want to impose too much by asking too many questions. I think everybody started off carving a walrus tooth. You just kind of round them out and then they used to sell them as key chains. As a matter of fact, they still do. After that, a seal would be next. Get a pencil and then draw, as much as you can, of a seal. Then my dad or uncle would

say, you've got to cut it this way. They would shade where it needs to be cut off. Then you file it and round it [see Fig. 43 of a metal file used to smooth the edges on ivory and Fig. 47 of a finished ivory seal].

John Heffle, 2012:

Out of respect, hunters wait until the last whale has been taken before going out to hunt walrus. It's cheapest to purchase ivory in the summer when hunters can go get another walrus. When ivory starts running low in the winter it makes it a higher price [see whale and walrus hunts shown on Fig. 53].

Edwin Weyiouanna, 2012:

I started carving when I was eleven years old, thirty-six years ago. Carving with bone and carving by hand. I use a file, hacksaw, three-corner chisel that was made by hand, and silver cream. We used to use a t-shirt for buffing, because it made our carvings shiny. I never used to carve with power tools. At least I got to learn how to carve by hand a long time ago [see cutting ivory with a hacksaw in Fig. 9].

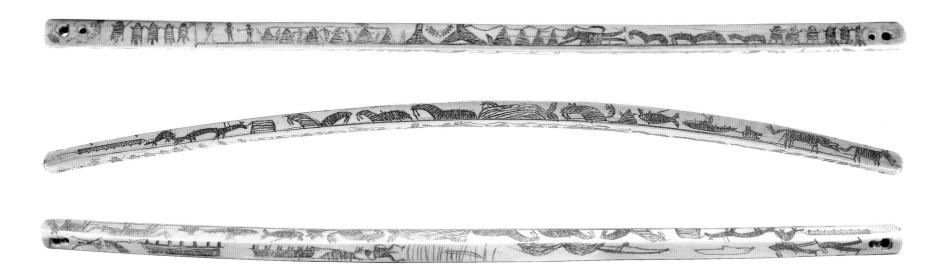

53/ Pitiksiaq DRILL BOW
Kotzebue Sound
Collected by Edward W. Nelson, accessioned 1882
National Museum of Natural History E48524
Walrus ivory; Length 39.2 cm (15.4 in)

TOP: An ermine and row of wolf skins appear on the left end followed by figures in hats, tents, and whale flukes, next to a row of transformational wolf and walrus creatures, and another row of wolf skins.

MIDDLE: A fishnet, two ermine, and a herd of walrus, are followed by a mythological walrus dog with tusks, and a hunter in a kayak harpooning a whale. A wolf chases a caribou on the end.

BOTTOM: Hunters in two skin boats pursue a walrus and a whale, followed by a horizontal figure, two kayaks, and a pair of walrus transformational creatures.

54/ Pitiksiaq DRILL BOW
Pastolik
Collected by Edward W. Nelson, accessioned 1878
National Museum of Natural History E33188
Caribou bone; Length 34.2 cm (13.5 in)

A pair of hunters crawl towards a herd of resting caribou on the left end. Two figures travel with packs and a dog in the center. A raven eyes a dead caribou outside a herd on the right.

Gilford Mongoyak Jr., 2012:

When I started carving, I used a coping saw, hacksaw and vise grips. Nowadays I'm starting to work on my carvings with an electric band saw. We use a Dremel a lot. My hands are getting old. I'm happy for these power tools because they make my work a lot easier. We buy our own ivory when they share their tag. I also use walrus ivory powder, which I color with water paints. Just wet the paint and mix it with the ivory powder [see the use of a vise and hacksaw to cut ivory in Fig. 9].

Henry Koonook, 2010:

Most of my carvings are done with hand tools. I also incorporate modern tools like the Foredom or Dremel. I use a lot of flat files, half-round files, round files, three-quarter files and square files. My favorite tool is an adze. We know it as *ulimaun*. It's a great tool because you can use it to carve wood; you can use it to carve bone. I use it when I carve driftwood masks or when I'm getting ready to carve on a tusk. I use the *ulimaun* to take off all the top layer of the ivory. For the inside I use hacksaws or coping saws. In the old days they used hand tools that look like a chisel with a short blade on it [see Fig. 11 for a variety of hand tools used by carver Henry Koonook].

Aŋmaluq *Vince Pikonganna, 2012:*

I watch old men at King Island carving ivory, very intricate carvings. I don't know how they carved in those days with the tools they had, very limited tools. But they were making some of the most beautiful items I've seen in my life. You just can't go borrow somebody else's tool outright because they may need it, they may want to use it. First you get your own tools. You collect carving tools over the years or you make your own tools [see carvers from King Island using hand tools under a skin boat in Fig. 119].

Albert Matthias, 2012:

My tools I make are from file handles. That's how I started out at first. I had to make my own tools to get the certain details in ivory. When they came out with modern tools, I started using those. I draw on the carvings first, then drill them, and then carve them out with the Dremel tool. It's hard because they're small. I practice carving them out first and then when I get them the way I want, I carve them out and try to avoid the mistakes I made earlier [see carvers using pencils to mark out designs on walrus tusks in Fig. 19].

55/ Pitiksiaq DRILL BOW
Cape Darby
Collected by Edward W. Nelson, accessioned 1880
National Museum of Natural History E44209
Walrus ivory; Length 33.7 cm (13.3 in)

TOP: Artist 1 engraved the five kayaks with raised harpoons pursuing a beluga whale on the left end. Artist 2 appears to have engraved the two kayaks and seal-like figure on the center.

BOTTOM: Artist 3 engraved the six delicate caribou in a realistic style on the left end. Artist 2 engraved the large, rectangular caribou in the center that are being being followed by a hunter wearing an animal tail and holding a firearm.

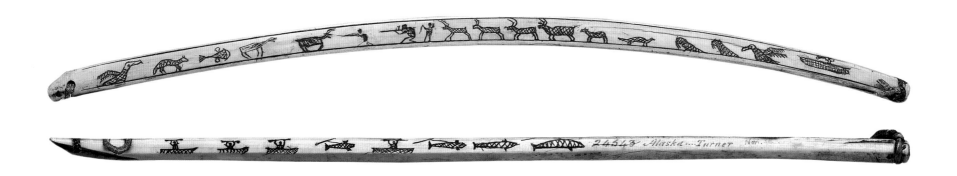

56/ Pitiksiaq DRILL BOW
Norton Sound
Collected by Lucien M. Turner, accessioned 1876
National Museum of Natural History E24543
Walrus ivory, sealskin; Length 41.3 cm (16.3 in)

TOP: Geese, fox, fish, caribou, ermine, and walrus appear on the left and right ends. Hunters with firearms take aim at caribou in the center and a hunter in a kayak appears on the right.

BOTTOM: Four figures raise their kayak paddles to signify a successful hunt of beluga or small gray whales.

Qualayauq *Ross Schaeffer Sr., 2012:*

Our culture's very practical. Dad and these guys had very little education but a lot of learning by watching. So they were real skilled at making anything. That's just natural ability from thousands of years, we made tools. A lot of tools, to provide you with the power to get that animal,  they did that little art, inside those tools. Reflecting the animal or the markings in such a way that reflects their spiritual connection to that animal [see Figs. 46, 50, and 59 for traditional tools made from wood, bone, ivory, and other natural materials].

Nayokpuk *Brian Sockpick, 2012:*

 I started really etching in high school after I took an art class at Shishmaref High. They have Elders that show us how to carve; a lot of good carvers down there. I do a lot of scrimshaw on tusks. I use my dad's engraver from a sharpened drill bit. It's not electric but like a pencil. My dad had a different style of etching. Like some of the reindeer on these drill bows look almost like his. There are different styles of etching. I like to do etchings big, like 3-D. My etchings are more modern [see the engraver shown in Fig. 59 and different styles of caribou etched on Figs. 55, 56, and 58].

Gary Sockpick, 2012:

My favorite etcher I made in the Friendship Center. I found this real old file, designed it, and made it fit my hand just right, real comfortable. Once I get started etching, it won't take me that long. Filing and sanding is harder than etching.  Etching is just like drawing on paper with a tool. The darker I want it, the harder I press. When I'm done, I just smear the etching with ink, let it dry, and take it off. Wherever I etched, the ink will stay. I combine my Uncle Brian's etching style, my Dad's, and my Grandpa Teddy's style. That one's my style now [see Fig. 59 for an engraver and Fig. 10 of Gary Sockpick removing the extra ink from a design he etched on ivory].

Thomas Barr, 2012:

 I think I am an intermediate etcher. I have made etchings for pins or pendants and maybe a little bit for my bracelets but probably not enough to make a story. I use my Dremel tool with a certain bit to etch. There are maybe two bits that I use. I have to have a real steady hand because I don't want to mess up and it has to look real neat [a steady hand would certainly be needed to engrave the narrow bands of barbed lines shown on Figs. 57-58].

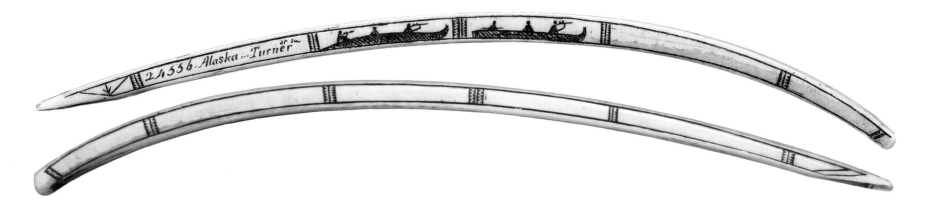

57/ Pitiksiaq DRILL BOW
Norton Sound
Collected by Lucien M. Turner, accessioned 1876
National Museum of Natural History E24556
Walrus ivory, sealskin; Length 34.8 cm (13.7 in)

TOP: Bands of barbed lines frame hunters with firearms in two Alutiiq-style kayaks with three hatches and a bifid or two-part bow. Kayaks with three hatches were used by Russian traders and explorers from the Aleutians to southern Norton Sound.

BOTTOM: Bands of barbed lines decorate the side.

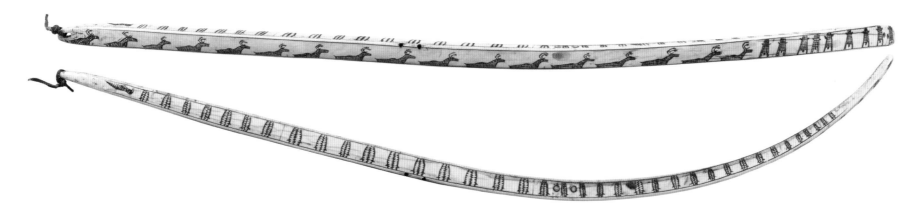

58/ Pitiksiaq DRILL BOW
Norton Sound
Collected by Lucien M. Turner, accessioned 1876
National Museum of Natural History E24540
Walrus ivory, sealskin; Length 58.2 cm (23 in)

TOP: A herd of swimming caribou are followed by a row of stretched animal skins.

BOTTOM: A single walrus is followed by bands of barbed lines.

Anuġi *Whitlam Adams, 2012:*

I was born on the *North Star* ship somewhere between Point Hope and Barrow. I learned how to carve ivory from my father. My carving shop used to be upstairs with big windows but now it's downstairs where I can see people passing by. I use a handmade etching tool with a metal scriber, electric, so when I turn it on I can make etchings and my hands don't shake [see Fig. 150 for ships etched on a drill bow from Point Barrow].

Earl Michael Aiken, 2012:

I'm a retired whaler. I've been etching a long time. I have a scriber and finger bands that go over to protect my fingers. I take baleen art seriously. I have etches, scenes of whaling and caribou hunters. I like to talk about Eskimo stories. They usually use skin boats and high-powered rifles nowadays to catch polar bears and caribou. Mushers put sealskin, caribou meat, and seal meat in sleds. The mushers will pile them up and deliver them to Barrow [see the engraver shown in Fig. 59 and scenes of hunting whales, walrus, and polar bears on a drill bow from Point Barrow in Fig. 62].

Enoch Evak, 2012:

The first thing I ever did was copy something from a drawing. My brother and I were home from school and he had this paper and pencil wondering what to do with it. My dad came around and my brother asked him if he could draw him something and he drew him a dog. Then my brother asked my dad to draw me one. My dad said no, copy this one. So I copied that dog and I've been copying ever since. That's why I can etch like this on baleen [see dogs etched on Figs. 69 and 131].

Eben Hopson, 2012:

I etch on baleen. I use a metal scriber. I started out by watching my dad who makes baleen boats. I asked my dad if I can try to draw on baleen and he said yes. He gave me a picture of a polar bear. He gave me a piece of baleen, square or rectangle. Then I just put the picture over the baleen and taped it. I did the outline and then I just started etching, doing the details after the outline. I made my polar bear all white. That's how I got started [see Figs. 62, 110, and 111 with etched polar bears].

59/ Piksiuun ENGRAVER WITH A HOOKED TIP (Bering Strait Inupiaq)
Seward Peninsula
Collected by Wilfred A. McDaniel, accessioned 2001
Carrie M. McLain Memorial Museum 2001.5.6
Bone, metal, and sealskin; Length 8.5 cm (3.3 in)

60/ Kiinagzaun WHETSTONE (Bering Strait Inupiaq)
Seward Peninsula
Collected by Wilfred A. McDaniel, accessioned 2001
Carrie M. McLain Memorial Museum 2001.5.114
Stone; Length 12 cm (4.7 in)

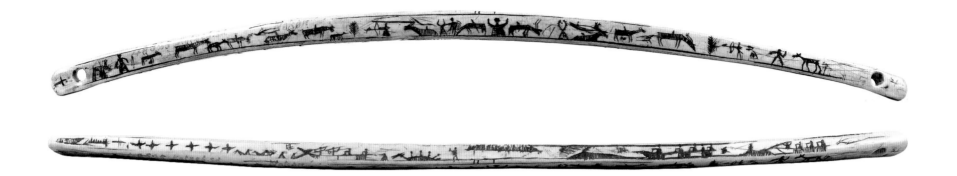

61/ Pitiksiaq DRILL BOW
Kotzebue Sound
Collected by Edward W. Nelson, accessioned 1882
National Museum of Natural History E48525
Walrus ivory; Length 36 cm (14.2 in)

TOP: Bow hunters hide behind trees and take aim at caribou grazing on the tundra.

BOTTOM: Migrating birds appear in front of hunters in skin boats following walrus and bowhead whales. A skin boat with the head of a mythological *tirisiq* can be seen in the center.

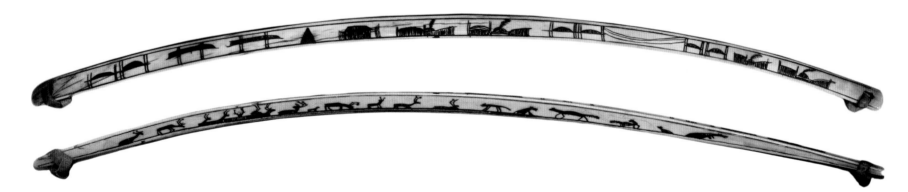

62/ Pitiksiaq DRILL BOW
Point Barrow
Collected by Joseph E. Standley, accessioned 1916
National Museum of the American Indian 5/5598
Walrus ivory, sealskin; Length 42.8 cm (16.9 in)

TOP: A winter village is illustrated with sod houses puffing out smoke, caches piled high, and skin boats stored on racks. A conical skin tent and four-paneled canvas tent are shown next to the sod houses and may represent the temporary lodging of visitors.

BOTTOM: A herd of caribou swim across the water while several hungry wolves wait on the other side. A myth creature known as a walrus dog, with a slender body and pointy ears, appears on the right end.

Joseph Akaran, 2012:

These drill bows take a lot of concentration; the way they made the lines on something so hard. The tools they used to make the lines are kind of neat. Whatever they used it had to be hard. You can probably take a needle and scratch on it but it takes some scratching to do. These drill bows look polished up, being so fine. I wouldn't mind etching some animals on carvings that I do. I am still trying to figure out how I am going to do it. Usually I draw a design with a pencil on a piece of paper and then try to copy it on ivory. I just erase the mistakes I make until I get down to the fine work [an engraver with a sharp bit was needed to make the long, straight lines and rows of barbed bands shown in Figs. 63-65].

Kayvanik *Jerome Saclamana, 2012:*

Carvers used cigarette or tobacco ash for engraving fill in the past. I use India ink. I used to see my uncles lick their thumbs and dip them into the ashtray and rub them on the engravings. Some would add grease of some kind to make it shiny [see Fig. 10 for the use of India ink to darken engravings on ivory].

Levi Tetpon, 2012:

These old carvings are done differently because they were done by hand, with the bow drill. The scrimshaw is not the same anymore, like they used a different point. It has a different touch. Even my dad would say no, to using a drill bow, because at his time there were ways of working easier. Dwight Milligrock from Diomede, that was his selling point, to use the old drill bow [see carvers from Little Diomede using drill bows in Figs. 1 and 26].

Natchiq *Jon Ipalook, 2012:*

I was taking time with another artist and he made a very powerful point stating that you can't rush your pieces, whether it be ivory, baleen, bone, or whatnot. The piece has a tendency to speak to you in its own way. So as you are contemplating what to do with it, sometimes you just have to  set it down and let it find its own way. That's where I find a lot of my creativity comes from, having the option to respect the piece, not in a manner of rushing it or trying to get it done. It just seems to come out a lot better if you take your time and appreciate that piece [Jon Ipalook takes time to visit with other carvers in Fig. 7].

63/ Pitiksiaq DRILL BOW
Point Hope
Collected by Edward W. Nelson, accessioned 1882
National Museum of Natural History E63805
Caribou bone; Length 33.9 cm (13.3 in)

This drill bow features a carved caribou head on the end with an inset blue bead for an eye. A herd of caribou with a calf at the front is engraved along the side.

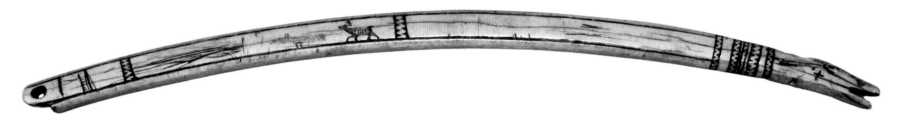

64/ Pitiksiaq DRILL BOW
Unalakleet
Collected by Edward W. Nelson, accessioned 1878
National Museum of Natural History E33191
Walrus ivory; Length 32.1 cm (12.6 in)

The right end of this drill bow features a carved wolf head engraved with whiskers on the snout, a cross or star on each cheek, and five barbed bands around the neck. The faint outline of a wolf followed by a single caribou appears in the center between bands of barbed lines.

65/ Pitiksiaq DRILL BOW
St. Michael
Collected by William H. Emory, accessioned 1920
National Museum of Natural History E313717
Walrus ivory; Length 27.8 cm (10.9 in)

A wolf head with whiskers on the snout and two barbed bands around the neck is carved on the left end of this drill bow. A row of wolves is shown engraved across the side.

Aŋmaluq *Vince Pikonganna, 2012:*

I learned how to carve by watching my Elders do carving at King Island. If I wanted to learn how to make a cribbage board, I just go to the man that is doing a cribbage board. I watch how he does it, from start to finish. It takes days to make a cribbage board way back when, it still does today. I make pretty much anything out of ivory, from rings to earrings, to domino sets. Cribbage boards to *qayaqs*, figurines, letter openers to forks. I make dice out of ivory and inlaid baleen. I like to challenge myself, my mind. When I see something I am interested in, I try it. I may not be perfect the first time but I fix it up here and there as I continue my carving [see a carver working on a cribbage board in Fig. 70 and the completed cribbage board in Fig. 66].

Suluk *Francis Alvanna, 2012:*

When the bus came down to East End, we would go help and watch the carvings for the carvers. These carvers are big; they don't have time to wait for buyers. So we watched the tourists in case somebody slips a carving into a pocket. Then we learned something from those people, tourists. When you hear "beautiful," pointing at the carving, they are not buying [see Figs. 67-69 of drill bows made to sell to tourists].

Ilonraaq *John Pullock, 2012:*

They used to carve in the clubhouse on East End. They had a long table for tourists that used to be filled with carvings and down on the end, a place for slippers to sell. You put your carving on the table and you put your name on it. This guy would look at the carving and put your name down in a little book. Tourists didn't take our information; they just bought the carvings. That's how I used to make money, when we moved here, to Nome [see slippers and ivory carvings for sale in Nome in Fig. 154].

66/ Kaatawik CRIBBAGE BOARD (Bering Strait Inupiaq)
Nome
Donated by Lorna Lawson, accessioned 2017
Carrie M. McLain Memorial Museum 2017.7.1
Walrus ivory; Length 35 cm (13.8 in)

67/ Pitiksiaq DRILL BOW
Alaska
Fred Harvey Collection, accessioned 1917
National Museum of the American Indian 6/2376
Walrus ivory, sealskin; Length 32.5 cm (12.8 in)

A bowhead whale is followed by walrus and hunters in a skin boat. Bow hunters take aim at caribou in the water and on the land. A different style of walrus appears on the right end. A row of nucleated circles is etched underneath the pictorial imagery.

68/ Pitiksiaq DRILL BOW
Alaska
Fred Harvey Collection, accessioned 1917
National Museum of the American Indian 6/2378
Walrus ivory, sealskin; Length 37.9 cm (14.9 in)

A row of swimming walrus on the left are followed by hunters with spears and a polar bear eating a seal. A hunter harpoons a walrus in the center. A dog sled and a row of geese appear on the right.

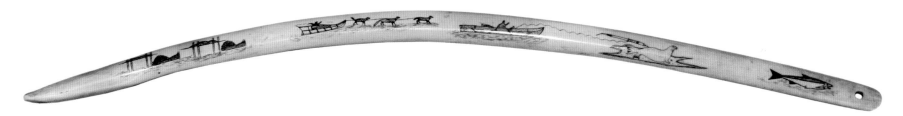

69/ Pitiksiaq DRILL BOW
Alaska
Collected by Victor J. Evans, accessioned 1931
National Museum of Natural History E360421
Walrus ivory; Length 57.6 cm (22.7 in)

Individual scenes are engraved in a realistic style on this drill bow. From left to right are: a pair of winter sod houses and caches, a dog sled, a hunter in a kayak harpooning a bearded seal, and a salmon.

70/ A carver in Nome uses a drill bow to create holes for a walrus ivory cribbage board engraved with animals.
The carver has posed for the studio portrait in a waterproof gutskin parka typically worn when traveling or hunting on the water.
Photograph by H. G. Kaiser, Nome, AK. 1912. Carrie M. McLain Memorial Museum, 2013.1.32.

2

Records of Hunts

Aŋmaluq *Vince Pikonganna, 2012:*

We used to watch men on King Island go down, go out to the ice, go hunting. Five, ten, fifteen miles out depending on the weather of course. Weather played a big part in everybody's life when you live in the village. Weather was the boss. They have to have someone in the village that knows about the weather. A lot of people seek his advice. Of course, you learn a thing or two over the years from hunting. You learn how to tell the weather. But today the weather is so chaotic. You can't tell spring from summer. The winds have gotten stronger and the seasons are getting shorter. Even the ice is getting thinner [see hunters pursuing seals, walrus, and whales through leads in the ice on Figs. 71 and 72].

Henry Koonook, 2010:

Tulugaq (raven) is also my *aanɡuaq* (charm), something that guides me, protects me. The reason for that is because when I was young, I was learning how to hunt the seal. We had just moved back into the village and out there on the ice, there's thin ice. I used to be scared to walk on that thin ice but that's why we have this waking stick called an *aiyauppiaq*, harpoon, or steel rod on one end and a hook on the other end that helps you test the thickness of the ice.

I'm hunting seals that day and out in the distance I see a black spot on the ice. In my mind, that's a seal. So I am going to walk as close as I can to it before I shoot it. But it never happens for a few days. Each time I got close enough, just when I am getting ready to pull the trigger, this seal would take off flying. It was a raven, *tulugaq.*

I told my grandfather about this and he said son, that *tulugaq,* he's teaching you how to walk on that thin ice. He's letting you go farther and farther. He's watching you and guiding you to a safe place. And as long as I maintain a positive attitude about this, everything will be okay. He said that's your *aanɡuaq,* that's your charm. Remember that and keep it right here [see Fig. 72 of hunting seals on the ice, Fig. 75 of a raven following a group of seal hunters, and Fig. 90 of a hunting charm].

Suluk *Francis Alvanna, 2012:*

My brother-in-law, my oldest sister's husband, taught me how to hunt in the moving ice; I was sixteen, seventeen years old. They made me sealskin pants, mukluks, everything the hunters use. In the wintertime we hunt seals, *natchiq,* in King Island. We use the harpoon for *ugruk* (bearded seals) and the gun for both *aiviq* (walrus) and bearded seals [see hunting walrus on the ice in Figs. 71 and 72 and a hunter in a kayak using a firearm in Fig. 57].

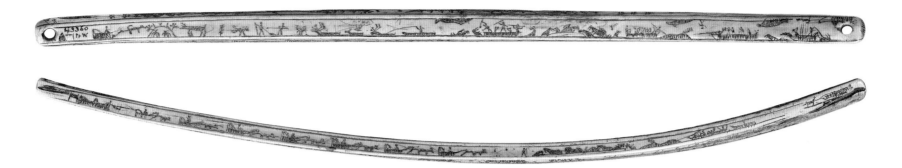

71/ Pitiksiaq DRILL BOW
Wales
Collected by Edward W. Nelson, accessioned 1880
National Museum of Natural History E43360
Walrus ivory; Length 44.4 cm (17.5 in)

TOP: On the left, a dog sled takes flight above a *qagri* with small figures on the outside and a pair of shaman-like figures on the inside. In the center, hunters take aim at caribou, drag seals, and follow caribou swimming in the water. On the right, walrus raise up to attack hunters in a skin boat. The end depicts a pair of skin boats harpooning a bowhead whale.

BOTTOM: Dogs pull Chukchi-style basket sleds with curved frames, walrus haul out on the ice, and hunters in a skin boat harpoon a bowhead whale.

72/ Pitiksiaq DRILL BOW
Point Hope
Collected by Edward W. Nelson, accessioned 1882
National Museum of Natural History E63802
Walrus ivory, sealskin; Length 16.3 cm (17.5 in)

TOP: A hunting crew in a skin boat pursues walrus on the ice and in the water. Whale flukes appear in the center followed by a hunter who crawls over the ice towards two seals at a breathing hole. A hunter in a kayak pursues a flock of geese on the right end.

BOTTOM: A hunter drags a seal on the left. Hunting crews in skin boats harpoon walrus and bowhead whales across the center and right end.

Eliqutaq *Wilfred Anowlic, 2012:*

The east wind broke up the shore ice around midnight early Saturday, May 10. My son-in-law Kourak, my grandson, and Harry Muktoyuk, went hunting on my boat. My engineer mechanic is my son-in-law. My grandson is our sharp shooter. He shoots and I harpoon. My crew and I went southeast of Nome over 20 miles, didn't see any walrus. Some other boats before us got eight walrus. Hunters were just lucky that day.

When we arrived over 20 miles from Nome, the current was so fast that the ice was in smaller pieces of cake ice. We couldn't find any big cake of ice to land my boat on. We stopped and ate dinner in my boat. After dinner we headed up near Golovin east of Cape Nome. Hunting for *ugruk* and ring seals, but no luck, we arrived home before 4 A.M.

After 6 hours of sleep, we went back out on Sunday, this time towards Sledge Island. There's still shore ice, finally got a ring seal, a fat one. We saw a ribbon seal on her seal hole with two babies, geese, white Arctic fox. I had a feeling a polar bear was around somewhere. Arctic foxes always follow polar bears when traveling down to King Island and other villages. We saw pintail ducks, puffins, murres, Eider ducks, some snow geese, brants; we were too busy hunting for seals [see the harpoon head shown in Fig. 73, hunters in kayaks pursuing geese and ducks in Figs. 74-75, and a ribbon seal shown in Fig. 83].

73/ Qalugiaq HARPOON HEAD (Bering Strait Inupiaq)
Nome
Discovered at the Snake River Sandspit, accessioned 2006
Carrie M. McLain Memorial Museum 2006.1.314
Bone, slate; Length 9.5 cm (3.7 in)

Aŋmaluq *Vince Pikonganna, 2012:*

Seals, *ugruk*, walrus, were the main staples of King Island people, their primary food. This time of year, April, crabbing. They are crabbing now at Diomede. They are getting crabs on sinker line. We used to do that when I was a teenager, down in east end over here. In March we would stay up overnight, out in the ice, and do crabbing. We would make many holes and get some lines in there. You have to be careful because the holes are pretty big [see ice fishing shown in Fig. 75].

Suluk *Francis Alvanna, 2012:*

I represent King Island, on the Eskimo Walrus Commission. I tag ivory. I don't know why some of the walrus hunters here, they don't want their ivory to be tagged. There's no limit. They won't finish them. You know when they close the fishing, somebody said, the Bible says, the more fish you catch, the more fish will come next year. Somebody said that. Same way with hunting out there [see large herds of walrus shown on Figs. 71, 72, 74, and 77].

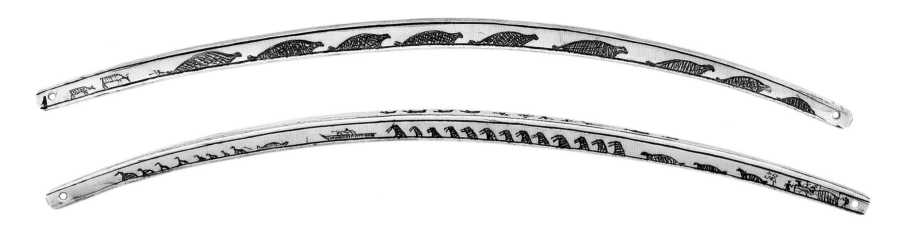

74/ Pitiksiaq DRILL BOW
Cape Nome
Collected by Edward W. Nelson, accessioned 1880
National Museum of Natural History E45346
Walrus ivory; Length 31.9 cm (12.6 in)

TOP: A hunter lies on the ground and aims a firearm at a pair of caribou. A row of bearded seals stretch across the remaining space.

BOTTOM: A row of geese swim in the water and a kayaker hunts a seal. Rows of walrus and seals are followed by a sod house on the right end.

75/ Pitiksiaq DRILL BOW
Sledge Island
Collected by Edward W. Nelson, accessioned 1880
National Museum of Natural History E45016
Walrus ivory; Length 39.6 cm (15.6 in)

TOP: A winter village scene is shown with figures ice fishing and dragging seals trailed by a raven. Figures in kayaks hunt geese with bird spears on the right end.

BOTTOM: Warfare is illustrated on the right end with a spear-wielding giant, a bear, a figure with a tail, and sexual activity.

Henry Koonook, 2010:

I wanted to make a sealskin float this winter, but I didn't get a chance because I didn't get enough male seals, that's what you use to make the float out of. There's no sewing involved. I start from the head part, and work my way into the carcass of the seal with a knife. Then I have to tie a rope around the head and have someone hold the tail, so I can pull the carcass out. Once I do that, I turn the skin inside out and start fleshing the blubber off the skin. Next, I'll take the skin down to the ice and stick it in the ocean and soak it in that water for a few hours, about every 15 to 20 minutes, pull it out, rub it on the snow, turn it inside out, and rub the snow on the fur side, both sides. Then, I'll take it home and hang it up and use my ulu that my mom gave me and scrape all the water off. Once it's dry enough, I'll set it on the floor and let it sit while I carve a piece where you can blow, that one goes on the belly button. I carve a piece of wood for the plug. There's a hole there and the grooves on the plug fit into the belly button. You turn the skin inside out, and the membrane that's connected to this, you tie it together with string, sinew. A wooden handle goes on the part where the head is, strapped down with sealskin. And the harpoon head, which has a rope, is connected to the flippers. If you take care of a float, you can use them for as long as five years or even more [see sealskin floats attached to harpoon lines shown on Figs. 77-78].

Flora Matthias, 2012:

What I really want to learn how to do is poke seal. Start from the head, peel their skin back, all the way to the bottom. You can't cut the skin anywhere. Even down to the flippers. When I went into the hospital I had to stay in Anchorage for a while. I bumped into this lady from Hooper Bay. She did poke seals. My mom said her mom stored salmonberries in them. They still do in Hooper Bay. When you take the berries out from the seal poke, the berries are like when you just picked them. That's one of the reasons I want to try it. When mom went down for a funeral, they had salmonberries and she said, "it's wintertime and the berries taste like you guys just picked them" [see the sealskin poke shown in Fig. 76].

76/ Awata.vak SEAL POKE (Bering Strait Inupiaq)
Bering Strait
Collected by Howard and Mary Knodel, accessioned 2007
Carrie M. McLain Memorial Museum 2007.10.1324
Sealskin with a wood handle and bone nozzle;
Length 79 cm (31.1 in)

77/ Pitiksiaq DRILL BOW
Cape Nome
Collected by Edward W. Nelson,
accessioned 1880
National Museum of Natural History E44367
Walrus ivory; Length 31.7 cm (12.5 in)

TOP: Figures are busily engaged in spring activities including hunting geese and bowhead whales. Seal hunters creep over the ice while walrus fight above. A person pulls a kayak on a sled, hunters butcher a whale and drag a seal, and people drum and dance inside a *qagri*.

MIDDLE: A row of skin boats on racks appears next to a winter village with sod houses and caches.

BOTTOM: A great walrus hunt is shown with kayaks and skin boats approaching walrus swimming in the water and crowded onto the ice.

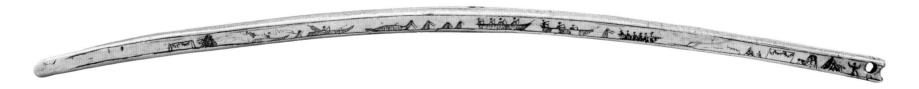

78/ Pitiksiaq DRILL BOW
Cape Nome
Collected by Edward W. Nelson, accessioned 1880
National Museum of Natural History E44400
Walrus ivory; Length 33.9 cm (13.3 in)

Summer camp scenes with tents and fish racks are engraved on both ends. The center depicts hunters in kayaks and skin boats going after walrus in the open water.

Sylvester Ayek, 2012:

A lot of our time is spent helping, being hunters and gatherers. Going out to help hunters bring in seals, for instance. We helped drag them to the village, especially when they bring home whole bearded seals, which are real big seals. Many boys would get together and pull the seals up to the respective clubhouse. They butcher bearded seals in the clubhouse, not on the ice. Once in a while they will butcher them on the ice when it warms up. When it's twenty below zero, they bring the seals home and take them into the clubhouse to butcher [see hunters dragging seals across the ice shown on Figs. 80-81].

Eliqutaq *Wilfred Anowlic*, 2012:

Last year we went out boating four or five times with my hunting crew and brought home four to five *ugruk*, bearded seals, on each trip. We shared the meat and blubber with my Elders and family. I need to do better next year, bring more meat and blubber home. My crew and I hunted overnight. We took naps while we were hunting on my boat. For the first time, I didn't have to drive my boat. My son-in-law is my motor mechanic this year. I teach my grandson how to hunt and cut meat and teach him how to tell the weather, telling him stories.

We didn't have any luck hunting walrus, other hunters just happened to be lucky to find walrus last year. Some years the walrus hunt is bad, next year we hope to have a good walrus hunting season.

I cut all the *ugruk* meat and put it in my freezer, made three pockets of blubber oil, aged flippers, and dried meat. Picked *sura* (willow) greens to store in pocket. I cooked the seal oil with blubber to make it clear like Wesson oil. I learned all this from my mother and King Island lady relatives, how to prepare Native food. I also make *aqutaq*, Eskimo ice cream, with blackberries and blueberries mixed with salmonberries for dessert [see hunting crews in skin boats pursuing walrus and whales shown on Figs. 77, 78, and 81].

Baker Ningealook, 2012:

To pull *ugruk* by the heads, you put the rope under the eye socket in the fleshy cheek area and pull it around the jaw, making a knot to drag the *ugruk* [see Fig. 79 of a seal drag used with rope to pull a seal across the ice].

79/ Uqsiutaq SEAL DRAG (North Slope Iñupiaq)
Wales
Collected by William T. Lopp and Ellen Lopp, accessioned 2019
Carrie M. McLain Memorial Museum 2019.8.52
Walrus ivory; Length 7 cm (2.8 in)

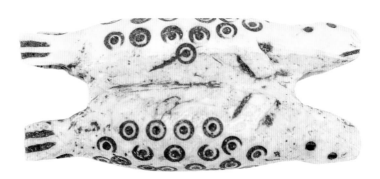

OUR STORIES ETCHED IN IVORY

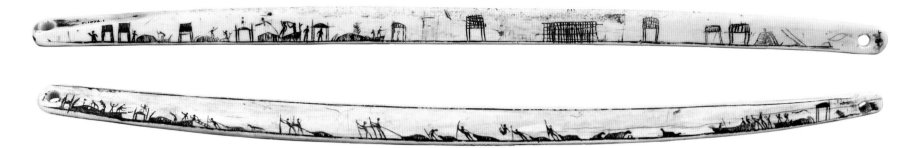

80/ Pitiksiaq DRILL BOW
Alaska
Collected by Edward W. Nelson, accessioned 1991
National Museum of Natural History ET1076-0
Walrus ivory; Length 30.2 cm (11.9 in)

TOP: Artist 1 created the small straight figures and houses in the busy village scene on the left. Artist 2 appears to have tried to fill in the blank space on the right with a house and group of caches engraved with rough outlines and cross hatching.

BOTTOM: Artist 1 created another village scene with figures on top of sod houses, dragging seals, and launching a skin boat.

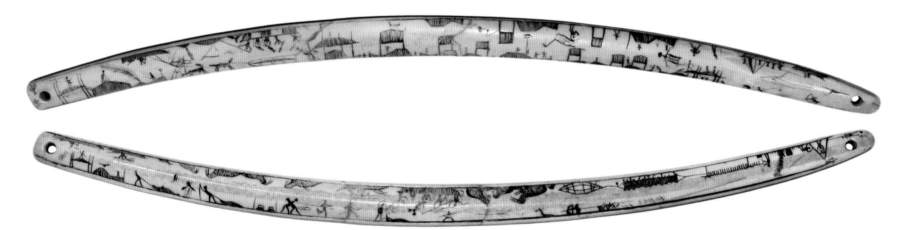

81/ Pitiksiaq DRILL BOW
Alaska
Acquired by MAI through an exchange with David Currie in 1972
National Museum of the American Indian 24/6479
Walrus ivory; Length 31 cm (12.2 in)

TOP: Dogs are pulling a basket sled to a sod house on the left. In the center is a winter village marked by a pole with a wolf-like animal at the top next to the central *qagri*. Above, a whaling crew raises sealskin floats and paddles to signify a successful strike.

BOTTOM: Hunters drag seals across the ice. A pair of hunting bags rest next to two figures wrestling. Hunters in a kayak and skin boat harpoon walrus above while a bow hunter shoots geese below. A figure hangs fish on a rack next to a net stretched out with weights to dry in the sun.

Aŋmaluq *Vince Pikonganna, 2012*:

They never wasted anything in those days, they ate everything. They were very picky about how they divided amongst the crew and the boat captain. Everybody gets a share of course. Once a seal's landed on the shore it belongs to the women. Women can give it away; they can take it home and give it to whoever they want to. Man's job was done. When they got a seal, they would cut it out on the ice, out there, and get rid of the inedible parts, stomach and so on, so it wouldn't spoil so much. When the hunting's done, they take it home and it was now the women's turn to do whatever they wanted to do with it [see hunters dragging seals back to a village on Figs. 80, 81, 83 and 86].

Henry Koonook, 2010:

My wooden stool is called a *nukirvautaq* and it's used for seal hunting. On the inside of the stool it has a retrieving hook and another retrieving hook sits on top of it. I can also use this stool to help save my life. I can take the stool, tie a rope around it, connect it to my walking stick, and turn it into a paddle if I have to. When I'm walking on flat ice I can see in the distance, but when I stand on the stool, I can see that much farther. When I am getting ready to shoot, I use it to sit my rifle on. I use it to drink my coffee on. It's a multiple tool. It is made out of driftwood and it's carved with my favorite tool, an *ulimaun* [see Figs. 83-84 for hunters using walking sticks as they drag seals across the ice and Fig. 82 of a retrieving hook].

Gary Sockpick, 2012:

One time we were walrus hunting and we bumped into these walrus. They must have been on this ice for a long time because they were on ice like a martini glass, way up there. The ice lifted up somehow. They jumped off, there was a bunch of them, and we shot the three biggest ones. Those other ones had to jump down a long ways. First time I ever saw that.

When walrus are hauling out on ice for a long time, their skin is real tough like sandpaper; even with the sharpest knives it's real hard to cut that leather, their skin. But when walrus are in the water, soaking wet, it's a little easier [see butchering a walrus on the ice shown in Figs. 40 and 84 and the hunting knife in Fig. 85].

82/ liłhak SEAL RETRIEVING HOOK (Bering Strait Inupiaq)
Seward Peninsula
Collected by Wilfred A. McDaniel, accessioned 2001
Carrie M. McLain Memorial Museum 2001.5.137
Wood, metal, sealskin; Length 28 cm (11 in)

OUR STORIES ETCHED IN IVORY

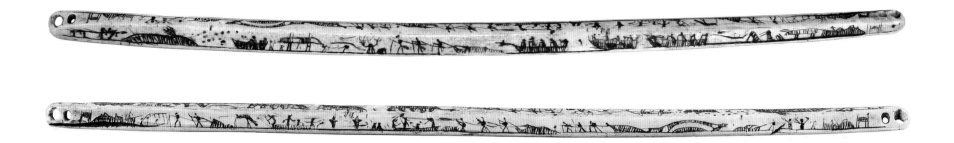

83/ Pitiksiaq DRILL BOW
Kotzebue Sound
Collected by Edward W. Nelson, accessioned 1882
National Museum of Natural History E48521
Walrus ivory; Length 42.2 cm (16.6 in)

TOP: Skin boats hunt bowhead whales and walrus on the ends. Three hunters wear animal tails and drag a large bearded seal in the center.

BOTTOM: Sod houses and caches appear on the ends. Crews in skin boats hunt walrus and caribou. Two groups of hunters work together to drag bearded seals and are followed by a large ribbon seal.

84/ Pitiksiaq DRILL BOW
Sledge Island
Collected by Edward W. Nelson, accessioned 1880
National Museum of Natural History E45022
Walrus ivory; Length 36 cm (14.2 in)

TOP: Scattered across this side are crews in skin boats hunting walrus and hunters in kayaks pursuing geese. On the right, a hunter prepares to throw a harpoon at a seal from behind a snow blind and figures butcher a walrus on the ice.

BOTTOM: Images on this side include figures in skin boats hunting whales, kayaks, walrus, migrating geese, and hunters dragging seals back to a sod house. A pair of mythological walrus dogs attack a figure on the left and two transformational seal figures appear on the right.

Joseph Kunnuk Sr., 2012:

I started hunting when I was eleven, went out walrus hunting with my grandpa. It's exciting. It's lots of work. It's not easy. Back in the 1970s, Sylvester Ayek and I used to take young kids, just out of high school, hunting. You teach them out there, while we're hunting walrus, how to cut the heads off, how to cut the meat. It's not easy work to teach someone out there but we have sharp knives [see hunters cutting up a walrus on the ice in Figs. 40 and 84 and a hunting knife in Fig. 85].

Aŋmaluq *Vince Pikonganna, 2012:*

First they do *ugruk* hunting and then they try to get walrus, mostly the middle of May and beginning of June they would start to get walrus. Everything's changed so much, you can't be sure today. Even the walrus are beginning to go up earlier and earlier each year. We have to travel quite a ways out for walrus hunting, twenty, thirty miles out from Nome; maybe towards King Island or past Sledge Island and go south from there. However many walrus you get, the captain and the motor get a share. The motor is the one that's doing the work, for us to travel. Everybody gets an equal share. Just because I am the captain, I don't get any more than somebody else's share. Because I own the boat and motor, I get the motor share [see hunting crews traveling out after walrus in Figs. 86-87 and dividing up walrus tusks in Fig. 6].

Eliqutaq *Wilfred Anowlic, 2013:*

We had lots of ice this year; it helped us to have a good spring season hunt. My hunting crew of three and myself went hunting and brought home a load of walrus meat, intestines, kidneys, livers, and flippers and made walrus blubber oil. We shared the meat with our Elders first. I have been having a feast, eating walrus for five days. I didn't eat walrus meat for eight years. My Elders are very happy, walrus meat for winter.

Before I was born, our Elders had it harder. The natives hunted with harpoons and today we hunt with rifles and harpoons and bring more meat home. I fill up my freezer with meat and flippers for winter.

West winds are taking the ice farther out. The ice will come back again, one more time. Once the weather calms down, we can hopefully hunt bull walrus [see walrus hunts shown in Figs. 86-87 and cutting up walrus meat inside a home on Fig. 124].

85/ Sawik KNIFE   Kiinailitaq SHEATH (Bering Strait Inupiaq)
Wales
Acquired by Walter C. Shields, accessioned 2016
Carrie M. McLain Memorial Museum 2016.28.2
Metal blade with bone handle wrapped in sealskin,
reindeer skin sheath with woven initials "W.C.S"; Length 21.5 cm (8.5 in)

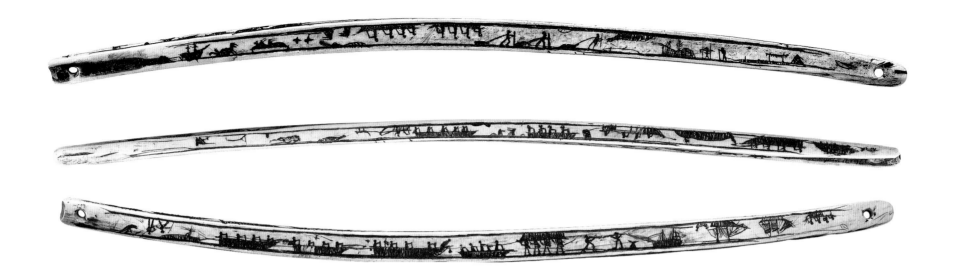

86/ Pitiksiaq DRILL BOW
Unalakleet
Collected by Edward W. Nelson,
accessioned 1897
National Museum of Natural History E176171
Walrus ivory; Length 39.8 cm (15.7 in)

TOP: A ship appears on the left followed by crews in two skin boats hunting walrus in the water and on the ice. Three hunters drag seals to a village on the right.

MIDDLE: A dog sled on the left is followed by skin boats with hunters harpooning walrus and bowhead whales.

BOTTOM: Skin boats are tied together and pulling a bowhead whale on the left. Figures carry a skin boat upside down in the center and a skin boat on the right end rows out to meet three ships.

87/ Pitiksiaq DRILL BOW
Cape Darby
Collected by Edward W. Nelson, accessioned 1880
National Museum of Natural History E44208
Walrus ivory; Length 32 cm (12.6 in)

Hunters in kayaks and a skin boat head towards a herd of walrus on the left. On the right, villagers stand on tops of sod houses to catch a glimpse of the hunters. The large number of skin boats and paddles still hanging on racks suggest this is the beginning of the spring hunting season.

Natchiq *Jon Ipalook, 2012:*

Umaktuq, just being out on the ice in your whaling boats, *umiat.* Last year was my grandmother's last time, doing the crew on her own, funding the hunt, and doing the feeding. She stays in town and does a lot of the cooking, sets it out on the ice, the lead, wherever it may be. She's nearing her late eighties. She needs some time to just relax so she passed the crew on to one of my uncles [see whaling boats out on the ice in Figs. 72, 92, and 94].

Henry Koonook, 2010:

When I get the fifth whale for my father, I'm going to put in *tuutaq,* labrets. I will do that because I asked my grandfather if it was okay for us to still use them and he said yes. Then he told me when I'm going to make the holes, to have one of my uncles make the holes for me. I don't do it myself, I don't let my dad do it; one of my uncles has to make the holes. So when the time comes maybe I will have *tuutaq.* Something I have always wanted [see Figs. 88-89 for examples of labrets].

Eben Hopson, 2012:

Either a family crew goes out whaling or two people and their friends go out whaling. Last year my uncle's crew caught a super big whale; the flipper was 6'4" and it was taller than all of them. I'm either going to go out whaling when I am thirteen or fourteen [see Fig. 91 for flippers (pectoral fins) shown on bowhead whales].

Alzred 'Steve' Oomittuk, 2010:

My mom's older brother is a whaling captain and I'm his co-captain. We do the sharing the way it's always been done. We have eight shares of a whale; this is how a whale has been marked and cut up for hundreds of years. Everybody gets a share. A meat hook for whale has prongs because the meat, or *inutuk,* of whale is real tender. They hook it and drag it away. In their skin boat they have their knives, *unaaqs* (harpoons), and *niksiks* (hooks) for cutting up a whale [see Figs. 92 and 127 of hunters cutting up a whale].

88/ Tuutaq LABRET (Bering Strait Inupiaq), Bering Strait
Collected by Caroline Coons, accessioned 1985
Carrie M. McLain Memorial Museum 1985.3.29
Stone; Length 5 cm (2 in)

89/ Tuutaq LABRET (Bering Strait Inupiaq), Wales
Collected by William T. Lopp and Ellen Lopp, accessioned 2013
Carrie M. McLain Memorial Museum 2013.11.79
Walrus ivory, bead; Length 2.5 cm (1 in)

90/ Aaġnuaq CHARM, AMULET (Bering Strait Inupiaq), Wales
Collected by William T. Lopp and Ellen Lopp, accessioned 2013
Carrie M. McLain Memorial Museum 2013.11.16
Walrus ivory, bead; Length 4 cm (1.6 in)

91/ Pitiksiaq DRILL BOW
Point Barrow
Collected by Patrick H. Ray and John Murdoch, accessioned 1883
National Museum of Natural History E89425
Walrus ivory; Length 38 cm (15 in)

A row of ten bowhead whales appears in the center and may indicate the hunting success of a great *umialik,* whaling captain.

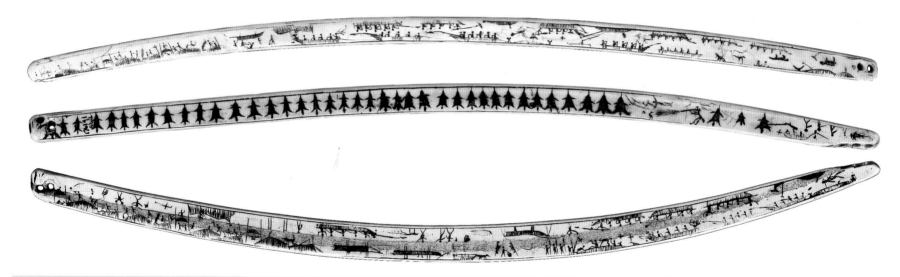

92/ Pitiksiaq DRILL BOW
Sledge Island
Collected by Edward W. Nelson, accessioned 1897
National Museum of Natural History E176191
Walrus ivory; Length 44 cm (17.3 in)

TOP: The village scene on the left features figures visiting, sliding off a roof, and playing on the beach. Whaling crews appear to the right with three skin boats linked together to bring in a harpooned whale marked with the flag of the crew.

MIDDLE: A row of wolf skins stretches across the side. On the right, a hunter fires at a small animal. Another firearm is engraved on the right end.

BOTTOM: On the left, people walk across sod houses and climb on caches. Two skin boats are up on racks on the beach. A person carries a bucket to what appears to be two dogs sacrificed and placed ceremoniously on spikes in a custom related to Siberian Yupik villages. On the right, skin boats are pulling a bowhead whale to shore where another whale is being butchered.

Alzred 'Steve' Oomittuk, 2010:

They always said that once you catch your five whales, you're *umialik*, a whaling captain, for the rest of your life, whether you put a boat in the water or not. When you catch your five whales, you get that status, you're a great *umialik*.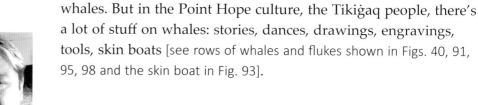

This whole area was a burial ground for Point Hope, for the Tikiġaq, the whale hunters of Point Hope. We've been hunting the whale for about two thousand years. Ipiutak is about 2,500 years ago. They had that five hundred year gap. They are trying to figure out how the Ipiutak people became the Tikiġaq people. There's no evidence of the Ipiutak people hunting the whale. They don't have evidence of Ipiutak people having big boats, the *umiat*. They have evidence of them having *qayaqs*, the small boats, but no big boats for hunting whales. Their carvings and engravings don't show harpooning whales or pulling up whales. But in the Point Hope culture, the Tikiġaq people, there's a lot of stuff on whales: stories, dances, drawings, engravings, tools, skin boats [see rows of whales and flukes shown in Figs. 40, 91, 95, 98 and the skin boat in Fig. 93].

Henry Koonook, 2010:

 A whale will sink, so before you harpoon it you have to watch the blowhole. As soon as he lets air out, you will hear him take a deep breath and that's when you strike it. There's one called a *usifautchiaq*, it's a bowhead whale with a big head and a slim body. They're males and those whales sink. A lot of times they sink because their heads are so big. But if you catch it when it's taking a deep breath it won't sink [see Figs. 92, 94 and 102 for a harpooner striking a bowhead whale].

93/ Umiaq SKIN BOAT "Model" (Bering Strait Inupiaq)
Nome
Collected by Curtis Jacobs Sr., accessioned 2006
Carrie M. McLain Memorial Museum 2006.20.3
Sealskin, wood; Length 94 cm (37 in)

94/ Pitiksiaq DRILL BOW
Alaska
Collected by John J. McLean, accessioned 1882
National Museum of Natural History E67904
Walrus ivory; Length 31.9 cm (12.6 in)

On the left, a hunter drags a seal across the ice. A row of skin boats ends in a harpooner striking a whale. A hunter snares a seal in the center. On the right, figures work at a summer camp with tents and a fish rack. A row of vertical lines is on the end.

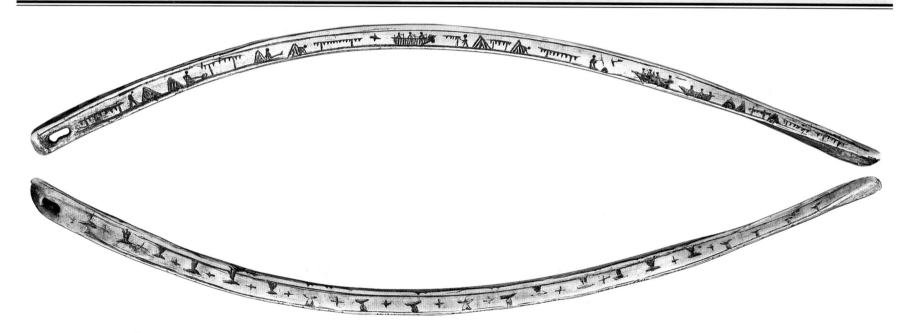

95/ Pitiksiaq DRILL BOW
Diomede Islands
Collected by Edward W. Nelson, accessioned 1882
National Museum of Natural History E63621
Walrus ivory; Length 22.9 cm (9 in)

TOP: A summer camp scene depicts fish racks, people coming out of tents, and travelers in skin boats.

BOTTOM: A long row of whale flukes is interspersed with cross marks that may represent the spring arrival of migratory birds.

Damian Tom, 2012:

I used to teach students at the old school building how to make nets. You need a net gauge, needle, and line. My short gauge I made quickly from a pallet but my long gauge is carved from driftwood. My long needle belonged to my stepfather Richard Tom. I use 21 braided line for salmon and 72 braided for beluga.

In 2006, I caught a California gray whale in one of my nets; it took a bunch of people to shoot it. Sometimes I will sit down and spend 10-12 hours making nets. I don't say I'm making nets, I say this is my survival [see nets for catching fish and marine mammals shown in Figs. 40, 53, 81, 98, and 121 and the netting needle and gauge shown in Figs. 96 and 97].

Aŋmaluq *Vince Pikonganna, 2012:*

Thousands of years ago, a man in the village of Qawiaraq wanted to help people get more fish. Thinking, tired of thinking, he went into the trees and looked at a spider making a web. Pretty soon it caught one fly and then caught another fly. It gave him the idea of how to make a fishnet [see fish shown on Figs. 34 and 99 and fish drying on racks shown on Figs. 38, 39, 121, and 131].

96/ Qilaun NETTING NEEDLE (Bering Strait Inupiaq)
Bering Strait
Collected by Howard and Mary Knodel, accessioned 2007
Carrie M. McLain Memorial Museum 2007.10.144
Bone; Length 13 cm (5.1 in)

97/ Qaaġauntutiaaq NET GAUGE (Bering Strait Inupiaq)
Bering Strait
Collected by Howard and Mary Knodel, accessioned 2007
Carrie M. McLain Memorial Museum 2007.10.398
Bone, ivory; Length 14 cm (5.5 in)

OUR STORIES ETCHED IN IVORY

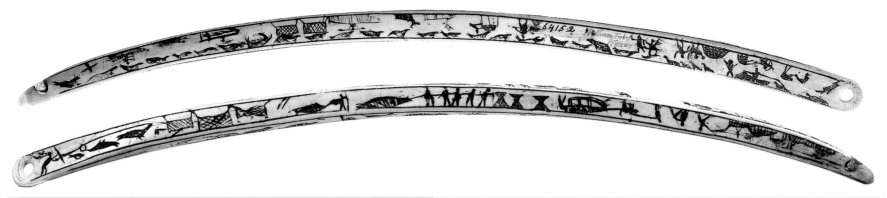

98/ Pitiksiaq DRILL BOW
Hotham Inlet
Collected by Edward W. Nelson, accessioned 1882
National Museum of Natural History E64152
Walrus ivory, sealskin; Length 35 cm (13.8 in)

TOP: Two nets are set under the ice to catch a long row of seals. On the right, two figures travel on snowshoes and a hunter in a kayak spears a goose.

BOTTOM: Hunters catch seals with nets and snares under the ice. A group of figures drag seals across the center. Three whale flukes appear next to a dog sled carrying a walrus to a village on the right.

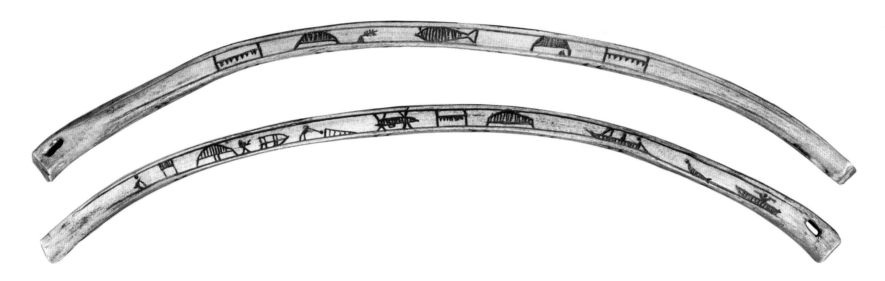

99/ Pitiksiaq DRILL BOW
Pastolik
Collected by Edward W. Nelson, accessioned 1878
National Museum of Natural History E33189
Caribou bone; Length 31.8 cm (12.5 in)

TOP: A fish appears in the center with a tent and fish rack on either side.

BOTTOM: Figures work at a summer camp with tents, a kayak on a rack, and a fish rack. Hunters in a skin boat and kayak pursue a seal on the right.

Gary Sockpick, 2012:

One time we got stranded up at Cape Espenberg before the ice spread out. We had a tarp over our boat but it was real loud, just flapping in the wind. The only shotgun we had was Brandon's 410 and it was too weak so I switched to a 223 and started getting lots of geese. They're real tame when they have nests. Those Emperors will try to hide their crown, their head, underneath their wing and try to hide their white part. You can almost touch them on their nest when they're doing that. So I was cooking those geese I was getting. We were boiling them one piece at a time [see hunting geese in the water shown on Figs. 101-102 and geese on the tundra shown on Fig. 128].

Sinaġuyak James Omiak, 2012:

When they used bolas, the ducks always fell down. The bolas are what they call *kinuqituun*, at Diomede. When we were kids, we had these, out of homemade walrus teeth [see the bola in Fig. 100; geese and ducks were also hunted with bird spears as shown on Fig. 101].

Joseph Kunnuk Sr., 2012:

Summertime you can't go hungry down there on King Island. Eat birds. Walrus meat, seal, and *ugruk,* dried meat. We had lots of fun climbing. Sometimes they put the rope around me to go down and get eggs. Murre eggs. It happened to me

when I was eleven or twelve years old. My dad and his friend went up on top of the Island to go down the cliffs. They threw me down, they told me not to look down. It's lots of fun, picking the eggs [see migrating geese arriving for the summer shown on Figs. 84 and 122].

Eliqutaq *Wilfred Anowlic, 2012:*

Just about the near the end of June is the time to go egg hunting at Sledge Island, Bluff, and King Island, for murres, puffins, and sea gulls. Best scrambled eggs in the world.

Edwin Weyiouanna, 2012:

They tied lots of these weights on a string. When they threw them under the ducks, this thing goes in a circle and they would always get caught on their duck wings. They used baleen for the string that goes on there a long time ago. These weights get lots of ducks [see the bola shown in Fig. 100].

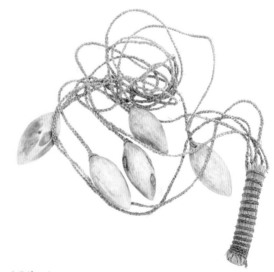

100/ Qilavitaun BOLA (Bering Strait Inupiaq)
Bering Strait
Collected by William A. Woenne Jr., accessioned 2005
Carrie M. McLain Memorial Museum 2005.1.64
Ivory, grass, sinew; Length 18 cm (7.1 in)

101/ Pitiksiaq DRILL BOW
Diomede Islands
Collected by Edward W. Nelson, accessioned 1882
National Museum of Natural History E63623
Walrus ivory, sealskin; Length 33.4 cm (13.1 in)

TOP: People in skin boats and kayaks are hunting walrus with harpoons and waterfowl with bird spears. A polar bear trails a skin boat in the center.

BOTTOM: A pair of crosses and row of geese are followed by bands of barbed lines. The center depicts a bowhead whale, followed by walrus, geese, and two ships.

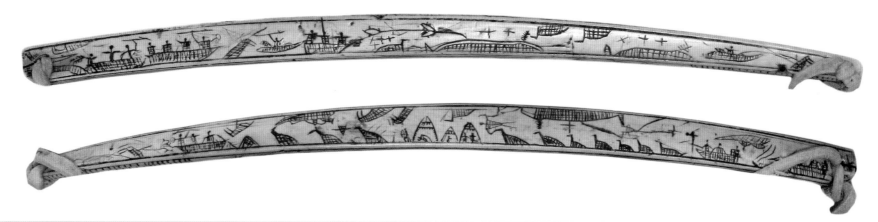

102/ Pitiksiaq DRILL BOW
Alaska
Collected by Edward W. Nelson, accessioned 1991
National Museum of Natural History ET16060
Walrus ivory, sealskin; Length 34.1 cm (13.4 in)

TOP: Hunters in skin boats and kayaks are harpooning walrus and bowhead whales.

BOTTOM: Figures in skin boats and kayaks are hunting geese, walrus, and a bowhead whale. Three conical tents with figures appear in the center next to a horizontal figure holding a harpoon or ice tester.

RECORDS OF HUNTS

William Simmonds, 2012:

My brothers and I used to trap a lot. A good year would be almost one hundred Arctic fox. For wolverine, we would have to go further inland towards the mountains. My mother made many, many fur parkas. I still have some of the traps and stretcher frames that belonged to my uncles [see the wolverine fur ruff shown on the parka in Fig. 103 and the animal skins that have been stretched and dried shown on Figs. 58, 104, 105, 106 and 114].

Qualayauq *Ross Schaeffer Sr., 2012:*

I've been teaching my grandson how to trap lynx. Last year we got twenty and he got five so we made a parka out of lynx for him. This year I'm going to make a parka for myself. We leave the fur inside, that way it keeps you real warm [wolves and beavers are also trapped for clothing, see Figs. 53, 92, 104, and 105].

Flora Matthias, 2012:

When I was growing up, when we were living in Kotlik, my brothers used to take us out snaring, rabbits and ptarmigans. We set out snares in the willows. I remember parts of that. My sister and I went out to go check his traps one time. We walked. I think it was better a long time ago because there was a lot to do.

I took two of my kids out rabbit hunting and I could not spot those rabbits. They were in the willows. Then when I finally spotted one, I stopped the snowmachine. My kids thought I was going to shoot it. I stood on the seat and watched it hop away. They were saying, mom, how come you never shoot it? I said, "It's beautiful!" That's something I remember and my kids remember and they always bring that up [hunters also set snares for ground squirrels, fox, and caribou as shown in Figs. 127 and 136].

103/ Atkuk PARKA (St. Lawrence Island Yupik)
Savoonga
Made and donated by Angela Kingeekuk Larson, accessioned 2018
Carrie M. McLain Memorial Museum 2018.21.1
Sealskin, polar bear, wolf, wolverine, leather;
Length 112 cm (44 in)

104/ Pitiksiaq DRILL BOW
St. Michael
Collected by Edward W. Nelson, accessioned 1878
National Museum of Natural History E33180
Walrus ivory, sealskin; Length 38.8 cm (15.3 in)

On the left, a wolf chases a caribou outside a sod house and hunters in skin boats are harpooning walrus. A hunter drags a seal to a village in the center where people are climbing on top of a sod house and cache and tending a cook pot. Five wolf skins are stretched out on the right.

105/ Pitiksiaq DRILL BOW
Hotham Inlet
Collected by Edward W. Nelson, accessioned 1882
National Museum of Natural History E64151
Walrus ivory; Length 39.2 cm (15.4 in)

A long row of ducks or geese are followed by a band of crossed lines and a row of nine stretched beaver skins.

106/ Pitiksiaq DRILL BOW
Nubviukhchugaluk
Collected by Edward W. Nelson, accessioned 1880
National Museum of Natural History E43932
Walrus ivory, sealskin; Length 36.8 cm (14.5 in)

A long row of caribou skins extends across the side.

Edwin Weyiouanna, 2012:

We have a reindeer herder in Shishmaref, Fred Nayokpuk. He has permission from Brevig Mission to get reindeer. The caribou herd took away the majority of reindeer from the State of Alaska and our district many years ago, 1970s and early 1980s. You can tell if they're reindeer or caribou, shorter legs or longer legs. Their faces are different, longer or shorter noses. You eat reindeer fried, in the oven, frozen, or the leg part with seal oil [see Figs. 108 and 109 for images of caribou and Figs. 124 and 153 for images of reindeer].

Qualayauq *Ross Schaeffer Sr., 2012:*

We hunt larger bulls in the fall time. We wait for the caribou to cross and then go after them in the boat. Shoot the caribou with a .22 and then drag them to shore; they float [see hunting caribou with bow and arrows in Figs. 108-109, with firearms in Figs. 55, 56, and 113, and crossing the water in Fig. 71].

Baker Ningealook, 2012:

I used to hear stories about George Ozenna. He drove a herd of reindeer from Wales to the stranded whalers in Barrow during the winter. My father used to herd reindeer. We had several sod houses along the coast where we stayed when herding reindeer. Those were beautiful days [see the reindeer collar in Fig. 107 and herders riding reindeer shown on Fig. 124].

Gilford Mongoyak Jr., 2012:

The story is that reindeer herders used wolf scares to keep the wolves away from their reindeer, or rather, when they herd their reindeer in the corral. When the string is long, wolf scares make a lot of noise [see wolf stalking caribou and reindeer shown in Figs. 104, 109, 110, and 153].

107/ Ulikitaq COLLAR (Qawiaraq Inupiaq)
Seward Peninsula
Collected by Howard and Mary Knodel, accessioned 2007
Carrie M. McLain Memorial Museum 2007.10.1329
Wood, yarn, sealskin, inscribed "Penny River Reindeer Herd, March 3, 1917;" Length 43 cm (16.9 in)

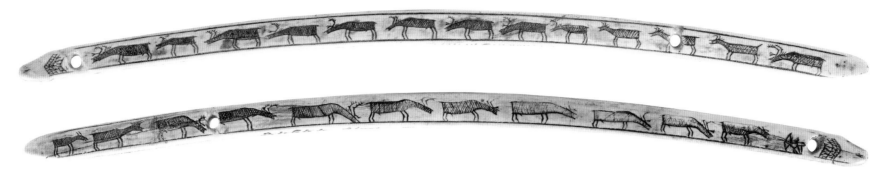

108/ Pitiksiaq DRILL BOW
Norton Sound
Collected by Lucien M. Turner, accessioned 1876
National Museum of Natural History E24554
Walrus ivory; Length 36 cm (14.2 in)

TOP: This drill bow features a carved caribou head on the end with a row of barbed bands engraved on each side of the neck. Caribou are depicted with bent legs and long necks.

BOTTOM: A caribou herd grazes on the tundra followed by a bow hunter poised to shoot on the right end.

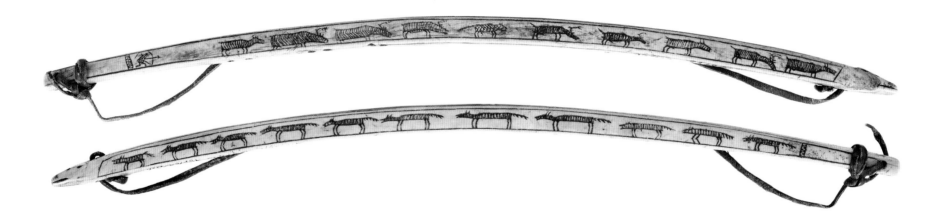

109/ Pitiksiaq DRILL BOW
Kigiktauik
Collected by Edward W. Nelson, accessioned 1878
National Museum of Natural History E33186
Walrus ivory, sealskin; Length 40.1 cm (15.8 in)

TOP: This drill bow includes a carved caribou head with detailed facial features. A bow hunter is shown pursuing a herd of caribou with a prowling wolf in the center.

BOTTOM: A row of sharp-toothed wolves, an aggressive predator of caribou, stretch across the side.

Suluk *Francis Alvanna, 2012:*

December, January, and February, when the north wind blows for two weeks at a time, it drives those polar bears close to King Island. That's when they get polar bear out there [see the polar bears on Figs. 110-111 and the carved polar bear in Fig. 112].

Gary Sockpick, 2012:

When I was younger, my dad used to go polar bear hunting around here. He has the record for the most in one day, six of them; they were all eating on one carcass. My dad used to have a dog team and a storage of seals for the dogs. The bears used to go pick on the seals during nighttime. Dad got a couple of them nighttime bears. He showed me how to skin them.

One time we were walrus hunting in Kotzebue Sound and we bumped into this big male polar bear in the open water. When I first saw it, I saw it a long ways away. I thought it was a walrus.

I tried to scare it down and almost hit it with a .22 magnum but it didn't go down. I got the binoculars and looked, holy cow, that's a polar bear. So we went to it. We looked for maybe four and a half hours, just following it. Polar bears swim, climb on ice, run for a while, and then dive under ice [see a polar bear eating a seal shown on Fig. 44 and polar bears going after walrus shown on Figs. 110-111].

Aŋmaluq *Vince Pikonganna, 2012:*

I've been part of the Alaska Nanuuq Commission for many years. There are lots of polar bears around Little Diomede and King Island. You first shoot and then spear a polar bear if you run out of bullets. You have to watch out for the left paw. If men are hunting in a boat, whoever sees the bear first, it belongs to that person. On the ice, whoever kills the bear, it belongs to that person. On King Island, we had a Polar Bear Dance to release the spirit. The polar bear hide was hung on the roof and the polar bear skull was hung above the dancing floor inside the *qagri* [see a hunter spearing a polar bear on Fig. 39 and a hunter with a firearm taking aim at a pair of polar bears on Fig. 62].

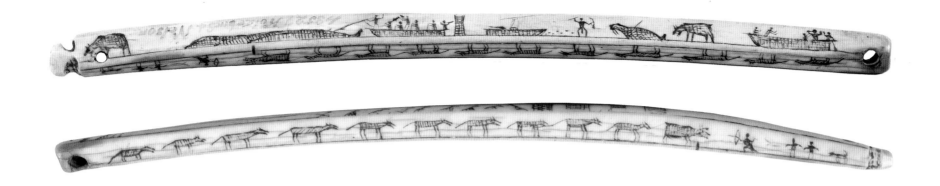

110/ Pitiksiaq DRILL BOW
St. Michael
Collected by Edward W. Nelson, accessioned 1882
National Museum of Natural History E48527
Walrus ivory; Length 26.4 cm (10.4 in)

TOP: A polar bear is followed by a bowhead whale that has been harpooned. The whaling crew is preparing to throw a sealskin float to create drag and mark the line. On the right, a hunter with a kayak has just harpooned a walrus that is being approached by a hungry polar bear.

BOTTOM: A row of hungry wolves stalk a caribou that is headed towards a waiting bow hunter. Two figures and a dog appear on the right end.

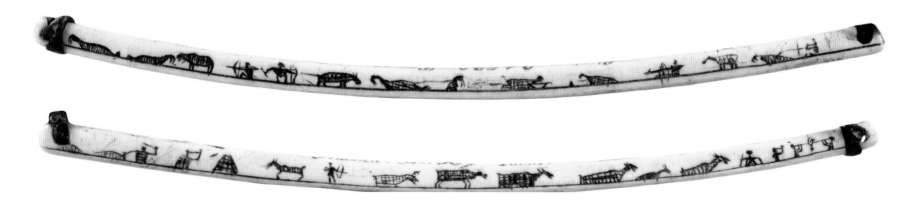

111/ Pitiksiaq DRILL BOW
Norton Sound
Collected by Edward W. Nelson, accessioned 1876
National Museum of Natural History E24539
Walrus ivory, sealskin; Length 29.3 cm (11.5 in)

TOP: Two bow hunters prepare to shoot polar bears that are stalking walrus. In the center, a hunter crawls across the ice to reach a seal at a breathing hole. Additional hunting is happening on the right end.

BOTTOM: Figures are smoking pipes at both ends. A bow hunter takes aim at a row of caribou in the center.

Henry Koonook, 2010:

We were out on the edge of the ice with a boat and we had the tent, maybe five minutes walk, behind us. My nephew Gus and his brother, Bob Lee and a boy named Tyler, were together in the tent warming up. Then my nephew was going to go use the bathroom. So he opens the flap of the tent. About a foot away, is a polar bear's head. Without thinking, he just shuts the flap. His brother whispers, what's out there? There's a polar bear out there. So instead of panicking, they stayed calm. His brother Bob Lee had two knives in each hand. We have a fork that we use to grab the seal blubber to put into the wood stove, and my nephew takes that and ties it on to a piece of wood, for a spear.

They're in the tent, and they're listening to this bear, and all they could hear was the bear breathing heavily. The bear finds beluga blubber on the ice. So he munches on that. There's a seal carcass a little ways over on this side, so he munches on that. Then he takes off behind the tent. I guess my nephews thought that was their chance to run down towards us, to let us know about this bear.

So they grab the smallest boy, put him between them, and all three of them start running, as fast as they could. Before they reach us, we hear somebody crying. We look back and that's my nephew that shot the bear, running ahead of his brother and the other younger boy. He's crying. He comes and tells us what happened and without saying anything else, he jumps on his four-wheeler and grabs his 300 Weatherby and goes after this polar bear. He caught that polar bear. One of our crewmembers went along with him and helped him get the bear. It was a real experience for him [polar bears track marine mammals across the ice as seen in Figs. 62, 110, and 111 while brown bears typically stalk caribou and reindeer herds on the tundra as seen in Figs. 113-114].

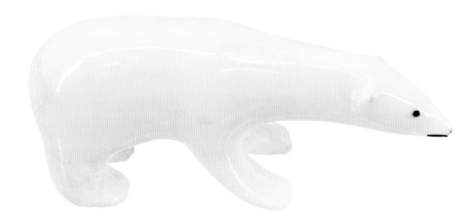

112/ Sanaugaq CARVING (Bering Strait Inupiaq)
Nome
Acquired by the Nome Historical Museum, accessioned 1968
Carrie M. McLain Memorial Museum 1968.2.5
Ivory; Length 7.5 cm (3 in)

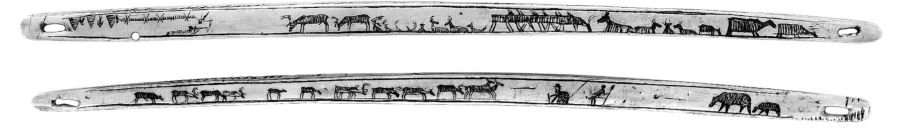

113/ Pitiksiaq DRILL BOW
Cape Nome
Collected by Edward W. Nelson, accessioned 1880
National Museum of Natural History E45345
Walrus ivory; Length 31 cm (12.2 in)

TOP: A hunter lies on the ground and aims his firearm at a herd of caribou resting and grazing on the tundra. A summer fish camp appears above the hunter.

BOTTOM: A Westerner, identified by a beard and hat, kneels down in front of a caribou herd. Next to him, a hunter readies a spear and faces a pair of bears.

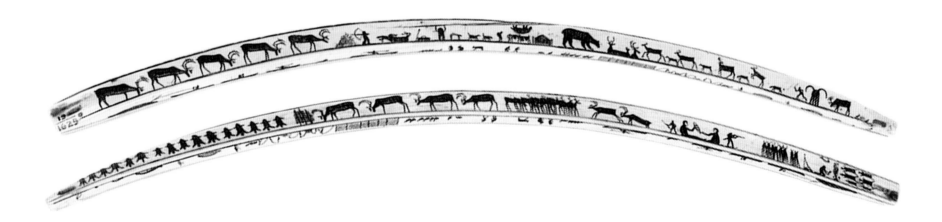

114/ Pitiksiaq DRILL BOW
Kotzebue Sound
Purchased by MAI from an unknown source in 1937
National Museum of the American Indian 19/1629
Walrus ivory; Length 43 cm (16.9 in)

TOP: A bow hunter uses a blind to take aim at a row of caribou. A summer camp scene with a tent and fish rack is followed by a bear stalking a herd of caribou and their calves.

BOTTOM: A row of animal skins are followed by a herd of grazing caribou. A pair of drummers appear on the right and are followed by additional animal skins.

Aŋmaluq *Vince Pikonganna, 2012:*

In those days, they used to have goggles, out of ivory, or bone, or wood. They have goggles. And they do the work. They take the glare off the ice. When you're traveling long distance, you cannot afford to get snow blind, you can't. You have to keep looking around, just don't look at the snow too long. And to top it off, you won't even know when it's happening [see snow goggles shown in Fig. 115].

Joseph Kunnuk Sr., 2012:

The light color on the skin boats are brand new skins. The skin's just been dried out and put on. Sometimes they paint over the skin, use it again. They ran out of oil paint one time and my grandpa mixed it with seal oil. The skin was kind of sticky when it was not dried up right [see Figs. 77, 81, 92, and 116 for skin boats illustrated with light and dark walrus skins].

Edwin Weyiouanna, 2012:

I have a lot of mom's sinew that I saved; the Eskimo thread, from the back leg of a reindeer or caribou. When they take the leg off a caribou, they take off all the meat and clean it out. That's their sinew, their muscle that they use. It tears; it comes apart, like thread. It's a lot stronger than a lot of thread, they don't get old and they last [see hunters cutting up caribou shown on Fig. 127].

Qualayauq *Ross Schaeffer Sr., 2012:*

A lot of the Eskimos had conical lodges in the spring made of fur, *tuttu* (caribou) hides, with the fur inside. In the old days. They were all gone by the time I came over here; they were using canvas tents by that time [see Figs. 116-118 for examples of lodges or tents made from animal skins].

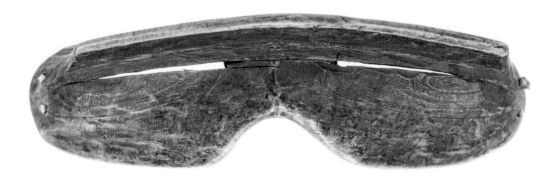

115/ Mazaqsiutik SUNGLASSES (Bering Strait Inupiaq)
Wales
Collected by William T. Lopp and Ellen Lopp, accessioned 2019
Carrie M. McLain Memorial Museum 2019.8.53
Wood; Length 11.5 cm (4.5 in)

116/ Pitiksiaq DRILL BOW
Nubviukhchugaluk
Collected by Edward W. Nelson, accessioned 1880
National Museum of Natural History E43931
Walrus ivory; Length 30.7 cm (12.1 in)

TOP: Artist 1 engraved hunters standing on top of a small whale, figures dancing next to a summer camp, and hunters in kayaks pursuing walrus. A horizontal figure floats in mid-air next to hunters in a skin boat harpooning a bowhead whale. A row of geese swim across the top. A polar bear sniffs the air next to a tent on the right end.

BOTTOM: Artist 2 added his own style of imagery in the center and on the right with hunters pursuing walrus, a bowhead whale, and a caribou. Images made by Artist 2 are larger than those of Artist 1 and darkened with loose cross hatching.

117/ Pitiksiaq DRILL BOW
Norton Sound
Collected by Lucien M. Turner, accessioned 1876
National Museum of Natural History E24538
Caribou bone; Length 32.3 cm (12.7 in)

Crossed lines are engraved on the left end. In the center, figures with broad torsos are dancing and riding a dog sled next to a row of tents positioned between two trees and three swimming geese.

118/ Pitiksiaq DRILL BOW
Norton Sound
Collected by Lucien M. Turner, accessioned 1876
National Museum of Natural History E24545
Walrus ivory; Length 29.2 cm (11.5 in)

A village scene is shown with figures hanging clothes up to dry, cooking over a campfire, and hunting walrus on the beach.

119/ Ivory carvers from King Island are working under an upturned *umiaq* on the beach at Nome (from left): Charles Mayac, Louis Seeganna, Edward Penatac, and Ayek. The name of the carver on the right is currently unknown. A bentwood toolbox, drill bow, and other carving tools can be seen in the foreground.
Photograph by Steve McCutcheon, Nome, AK. c. 1940.
Anchorage Museum of History and Art, Library and Archives, B1990-014-5-AKNative-2-1.

OUR STORIES ETCHED IN IVORY

3

Stories of Community

Qualayauq *Ross Schaeffer Sr., 2012:*

When the first Christians came up here, they went to a big dance across the bay in 1898, and they had a Wolf Dance. The shamans did such things that it scared the missionaries. They walked all the way back to Kotzebue. The missionaries declared all Native dancing shamanism. It stopped all Native dancing for years. Except for a few, what we call, Catholic, or renegade people. They wanted to preserve it, and did preserve it, that's why dancing is still alive today. No other reason. Because they were rebels compared to the Quakers. It was only until about twenty years ago, that the Friends Church finally acknowledged that Eskimo dancing wasn't shamanism. It was a way of showing our culture. They finally said, we will accept it, we will tolerate it, but we will not practice it. It's even changed more now, where their kids are dancing, which is good. So it took a long time. Once you declare it as an evil thing, it took a long time to convince folks that it's not [see dances shown on Figs. 121-122].

Sinaġuyak *James Omiak, 2012:*

There was the Wolf Dance down in Diomede when we were kids. The Wolf Dance comes from Qawiaraq. In the story, the man goes hunting on Qawiaraq and the eagle takes him to the South Hill Mountain. The eagle talked to him, if you go home, you make a drum; it sounds like my heart. When you go home, you make a drum, a wooden drum, and hit it. I heard that story in Diomede but that's from Qawiaraq. King Islanders still have the Wolf Dance but we lost our dancing long ago, when the missionaries started coming. In Wales and Shishmaref, they lost their dancing, at that time, and when there were Catholics at Diomede, King Island, and even St. Lawrence Island. They still dance up north [see Fig. 39 of dancing on a drill bow from Little Diomede, Fig. 120 of dancing mitts used in the Wolf Dance, and Figs. 125-126 of a drum and stick].

120/ Aqłitik DANCING MITTS (Bering Strait Inupiaq)
Bering Strait
Collected by Howard and Mary Knodel, accessioned 2007
Carrie M. McLain Memorial Museum 2007.10.1053
Sealskin, ivory, polar bear fur; Length 29 cm (11.4 in)

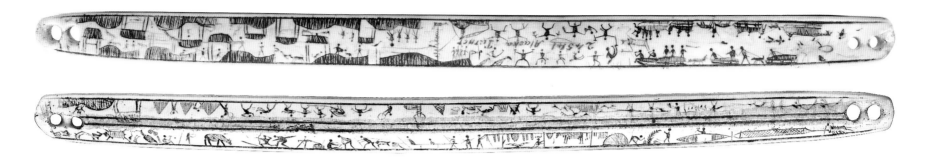

121/ Pitiksiaq DRILL BOW
Norton Sound
Collected by Lucien M. Turner, accessioned 1876
National Museum of Natural History E24541
Walrus ivory; Length 32 cm (12.6 in)

TOP: A community participates in a celebration that may represent a Feast to the Dead with visitors arriving on sleds and dancers performing welcoming songs outside of a *qagri*. The *qagri* is framed by two posts with carved caribou and goose emblems on the ends.

BOTTOM: (upper scene) A summer camp is shown with dancers and drummers, figures crawling out of a tent, ravens eating a dead caribou, and three weasel-like myth creatures with barbed backs on the right end. (lower scene) A pair of antlers and a stretched caribou skin are followed by a pair of figures using a spear and bow to hunt a bear, a crew straining to pull a skin boat onto shore, and a figure hanging fish next to sealskins and a caribou skin on a rack. The right end shows a camp with figures cooking and carrying a kayak up from the beach, where a net is stretched out to be dried and tended.

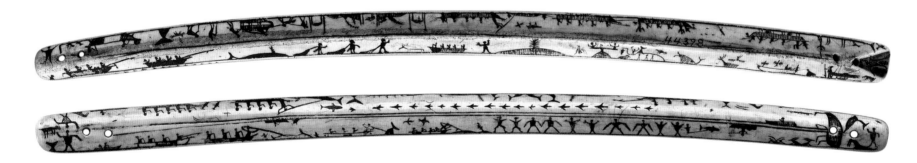

122/ Pitiksiaq DRILL BOW
Cape Nome
Collected by Edward W. Nelson, accessioned 1880
National Museum of Natural History E44398
Walrus ivory; Length 46 cm (18.1 in)

TOP: (upper scene) A skin boat and whale fluke on the left are followed by two Elders using walking sticks and two people moving a heavy sled to a village. Hunters harpoon a whale on the right while another crew prepares to launch their skin boat. (lower scene) Whaling crews pursue bowhead whales, hunters drag seals, and figures dance inside a *qagri* next to a myth creature with a long neck.

BOTTOM: (upper scene) Crews in skin boats hunt whales while geese fly overhead. (lower scene) Three bowhead whales have been harpooned, figures are dancing, and a hunter in a kayak has harpooned a beluga whale. A pair of giants appear on the left end and an insect creature with antennas is on the right end.

Sylvester Ayek, 2012:

There were three clubhouses on King Island when we were growing up [Aguliit, Nutaat, and Qagriuraaġmiut]. There were more, before our time. I suppose you can call the people who go to different clubhouses, clans. But I wouldn't use that though. A clan, that's something you would see from a place like St. Lawrence Island and Indian nation, down southeast, they use a clan system. And King Island, a lot of it was family, extended family members.

All three of them had their own dance groups. The way they danced, was not very different, but using different songs and dances to share with the other groups. We grew up together in our teens, in our clubhouse. We were there learning the songs that they use. We mostly came up with dance motions, to simpler songs, that they used for bench dancing, for instance. Sometimes, we would go to a different clubhouse to listen to different songs and dances. That's how they spend the nights, from about early winter until it gets warm. That stretches out about maybe three or four months [see the walrus dance mask from King Island shown in Fig. 123 and figures dancing inside a clubhouse or *qagri* shown on Figs. 40, 122, 124, 137, and 140].

Joseph Akaran, 2012:

We have the potlatch every year between March and April. That's when pretty much all the town goes. That's a tradition here. They held a potlatch, about last month or so, over at Stebbins. Some of the people from St. Michael, Kotlik, a few other places, went over to Stebbins. They had another potlatch at Kotlik one week after that. My mom went. She said it was just jam-packed. They talk about new dancers, new people. People from other places getting together, just having a good old time [see visitors arriving at a village by dog sled for feasting and dancing shown in Figs. 121 and 127].

123/ Kiinauq MASK (Bering Strait Inupiaq)
King Island
Collected by Howard and Mary Knodel, accessioned 2015
Carrie M. McLain Memorial Museum 2015.15.132
Wood, walrus ivory, sealskin; Length 28 cm (11 in)

124/ Pitiksiaq DRILL BOW
Cape Nome
Collected by Edward W. Nelson, accessioned 1880
National Museum of Natural History E44467
Walrus ivory; Length 34.5 cm (13.6 in)

TOP: Three reindeer herders are riding on the backs of reindeer and directing the herd to a bow hunter on the right end.

MIDDLE: A scene of warfare is shown with invaders carrying spears and guns, attacking people, entering houses, and engaging in sexual activity. The small groups of dots may represent swarms of mosquitoes.

BOTTOM: A busy village scene is shown with figures dancing inside *qagrit*, cutting up walrus, hanging boots up to dry, tending fires, driving a dog sled, and launching skin boats on the beach.

Alzred 'Steve' Oomittuk, 2010:

Our community revolves around whales. You catch a whale, you have the whaling feast, things follow. Thanksgiving and Christmas, you give out more whale. When you don't catch a whale, you can't have your whaling ceremonies. It's part of who we are. It's our identity.

There was a death, during the whaling feast time, and it's supposed to be a time of joy. One of our whaling captains died, an old man. We thought they weren't going to Eskimo dance because there was a death in the community. Sometimes they don't. One of the Elders stood up and said, this is a ceremony that has to continue. This is our way of life, the cycle of life, as people of Tikiġaq. We live in the cycle of life. The whale being the center of everything. The importance of continuing what has passed from generation to generation. Our deaths, in the community, we might be in sorrow, but we need to continue these things. This is a whaling ceremony that has to continue. We will have the Eskimo dance. We will continue. Same with the old custom dances, they must be performed. We have to continue with the cycle of life. Even though we are feeling bad about what happened, we need to finish this ceremony. When we are done, we can mourn.

It was the last day of the Christmas weeklong celebration. So we had the old custom dances and then we had *winook,* the masquerade dance, you go to houses and you dress up. Then it was over [see Figs. 125-126 of a drum and stick used in Inupiaq dancing, Fig. 127 of cutting up a whale and hosting a celebration, and Fig. 72 of a whale hunt shown on a drill bow from Point Hope].

125/ Sauyaq DRUM (Bering Strait Inupiaq)
Bering Strait
Donated by the Sitnasuak Native Corporation, accessioned 2008
Carrie M. McLain Memorial Museum 2008.10.38
Wood, gutskin, cotton thread; Length 54.6 cm (21.5 in)

126/ Mumiq DRUM STICK (Bering Strait Inupiaq)
Wales
Collected by William T. Lopp and Ellen Lopp, accessioned 2015
Carrie M. McLain Memorial Museum 2015.4.84
Walrus ivory; Length 56 cm (22 in)

127/ Pitiksiaq DRILL BOW
Cape Darby
Collected by Edward W. Nelson, accessioned 1882
National Museum of Natural History E48115
Walrus ivory; Length 34.5 cm (13.6 in)

TOP: People work together to pull a bowhead whale onto the shore. In the center, figures use knives and meat hooks to cut blubber and meat into squares and pass them on down the line.

MIDDLE: A winter whaling celebration such as Kivgiq appears to be happening with drummers, dancers wearing bird headdresses and rattle mittens, and visitors arriving and watching the festivities on their sleds.

BOTTOM: Hunters on both ends force a caribou herd into a row of snares where a bow hunter is waiting to dispatch the entangled animals. A hunter cuts up a killed caribou on the left end.

Sinaġuyak *James Omiak, 2012:*

Siberians used to come across and fight Qawiaraq people with bows and arrows. There's one story of a mother who escaped by using grass to breathe underwater but the baby drowned. Some people have heard the baby crying when berry picking. The Siberians came over, long ago, to Teller. They had a war, a long time ago. Some people have found Siberian arrowheads. They said there were lots of human skeletons around there. They say that white people came around and collected all those skeletons, and took them someplace [see figures wearing Siberian armor made from bone plates (slats) shown on Figs. 21 and 128].

Sylvester Ayek, *2012:*

Villagers come into another village and kill as many men as possible. King Island was one of the very difficult places to invade. There's a war song, warrior's song, that we know today. There are no dance motions to it, they just sang it. Telling the other villagers, that there's no place to hide on our Island, because it's so small. The Islanders knew every rock and cranny all around the Island. All of those rocks have names, every one of them, even the smallest ones [see warfare shown on Figs. 75 and 124].

Baker Ningealook, *2012:*

It looks like this carver didn't know how to show a sod house being underground. Normally you would only see the mound of the living quarters. The entrance is underground with a log roof and blends into the landscape. They wanted to be hidden from warring people, particularly the Siberians, who would come over to fight [see sod houses shown on Fig. 129 and Siberians on Fig. 128].

Jack Frankson Jr., *2012:*

There used to be people who go to your village, take your things. People that will go and kill you and take your food, take your clothes, take your tents, take your whole camp. That's how my mom said it was back then. So my mom's grandma had a rifle. She had it with her at all times. When she went hunting, she would leave one of the dogs with my mom and the rest of her family because there was no father figure. No protection. My grandma had to look after them herself. She had to do all the hunting, all the sewing to make the clothes, all the shelter building, all the fishing [see giants attacking people in camps and boats shown on Figs. 51, 129, and 137].

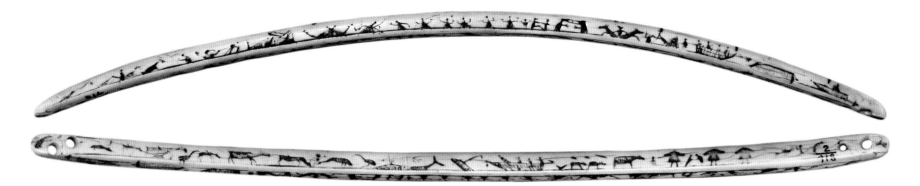

128/ Pitiksiaq DRILL BOW
Cape Darby
Collected by Edward W. Nelson and acquired by George Heye through an exchange with the U.S. National Museum in 1908 (original number NMNH E44212)
National Museum of the American Indian 2/418
Walrus ivory; Length 37.4 cm (14.7 in)

TOP: Three people on the left struggle to drag myth creatures, two *kokogiak* with curved bodies extend their legs, and a row of triangular figures dance with raised arms. Two pairs of attached creatures strain to separate from one another and a transformational wolf figure stands between two walrus dogs. A skin boat and kayak appear on the right end.

BOTTOM: Caribou and geese are grazing on the left next to a bowhead whale lunging out of the water after being harpooned. A polar bear stands with her two cubs on the right and are followed by three figures wearing coats of Siberian slat armor.

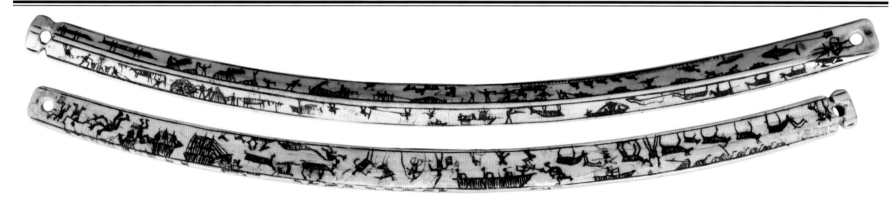

129/ Pitiksiaq DRILL BOW
Norton Sound
Collected by Edward W. Nelson, accessioned 1879
National Museum of Natural History E38886
Walrus ivory; Length 33 cm (13 in)

TOP: (upper scene) A village scene on the left is followed by hunters dragging a bearded seal, kayaks pursuing geese, and hunters crawling over the ice to reach seals. (lower scene) People tend a campfire, hang up animal skins, and hunt bears. A supernatural figure appears on the right end.

BOTTOM: Giants attack figures on the left and in the center where a skin boat uses a harpoon to fend off another giant. Additional imagery includes two whaling ships, ravens picking at a dead caribou, a figure carrying a bucket, a hunter in a kayak spearing geese, and a row of caribou.

Sylvester Ayek, 2012:

We played a lot of Native games on King Island. One in particular, that was participated in by many, is what we call Eskimo baseball. Another one for mostly men was sort of like hockey. There were two goals that each team would try to get to. Then, sometimes when we don't have a ball, the men would make a walrus-hide ball, and those are hard when they hit you [see the sealskin game ball in Fig. 130, playing with a game ball on Fig. 131, and the two-foot high kick played with a suspended ball on Figs. 40, 132, and 133].

Baker Ningealook, 2012:

We used to go sledding on seal hides when we were young. We put weights on the top edges when the hides were drying and you would have two flaps for handles. They worked real well except the extra oil would get on your clothes and we'd smell like blubber walking into the house [see hunting seals and dragging them home on Fig. 131].

Aŋmaluq *Vince Pikonganna, 2012:*

We had to make our own toys growing up on King Island. My favorite toy was a little harpoon. Women would throw out bits of inedible blubber and the boys would use the pieces for target practice. We had fun playing and making our own toys, making our own sleds. If we can't make our own toys, we had big brothers or uncles who made them for us.

We used to go sledding on the side of the Island. Young boys and girls would receive a polar bear skin to clean and would take it to the side of the Island. All the kids would get on the skin and slide, back and forth, all day long [see dancing and playing games on Figs. 131-132 and polar bears on Figs. 39 and 111].

130/ Aangqaq BALL (St. Lawrence Island Yupik)
Gambell
Collected by David and Mitzi Shinen, accessioned 2015
Carrie M. McLain Memorial Museum 2015.3.14
Sealskin, felt, beads; Diameter 13 cm (5.1 in)

131/ Pitiksiaq DRILL BOW
Sledge Island
Collected by Edward W. Nelson,
accessioned 1880
National Museum of Natural History E45021
Walrus ivory; Length 33.4 cm (13.1 in)

TOP: A busy village scene is shown with figures dancing on sod houses, hanging boots up to dry, and playing ball games. Above, a bow hunter takes aim at a caribou.

MIDDLE: Hunters drag seals back to sod houses on each end. In the center, figures tend a campfire and hang fish on racks.

BOTTOM: Sod houses appear at each end. A dog drags home a seal, four people strain to pull a large bearded seal, and a skin boat heads out to a group still hunting seals on the ice.

132/ Pitiksiaq DRILL BOW
St. Michael
Collected by Edward W. Nelson, accessioned 1878
National Museum of Natural History E33179
Walrus ivory, sealskin; Length 35.5 cm (14 in)

On the left, a skin boat, kayak, and ship head towards some walrus. On the right, figures dance and participate in a game of one or two-foot high kick to try and touch the suspended ball.

Sylvester Ayek, 2012:

It was a totally different upbringing for the people, on the Island. I am amazed that we didn't get hurt that often, living in a dangerous place like King Island. Of course there were a few serious accidents. They always recovered, the ones who got hurt real bad. There were some people who had, a healing touch. They worked on the ones that got hurt. They just had a natural ability to shorten the pain from accidents. They know just what to do.

Of course, there were mentors, sort of counselors that were good at making or creating peace, with the people who were emotionally disturbed. So there was a lot of help, good, healthy help. It was a good, healthy place to grow up.

The shamans were before our time. There were shamans when the missionaries came in and introduced Christianity. But then, they were converted into the Christian faith. Sometimes I wonder what these missionaries shared with the villagers, to be accepted, that much. Because before missionaries came around, there were, in some villages, hostile feelings towards outsiders. Even people from different villages were treated differently [see the shaman shown on Fig. 133 and figures or myth creatures from different villages confronting each other shown on Fig. 134].

Aŋmaluq *Vince Pikonganna, 2012:*

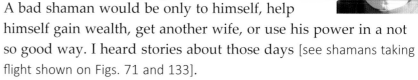

This drill bow (Fig. 133) looks like it belongs to a shaman. The shaman right there, he's going to fly. There were good and bad shamans in those days. The good shamans were to help the village of course, hunting, weather, foreseeing the future. A bad shaman would be only to himself, help himself gain wealth, get another wife, or use his power in a not so good way. I heard stories about those days [see shamans taking flight shown on Figs. 71 and 133].

Kayvanik *Jerome Saclamana, 2012:*

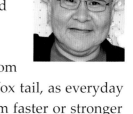

This shows a shaman with his drum and a guy flying (Fig. 133). The dancers may be from the Inviting in Dance during the Messenger Feast in Barrow. The right drummer with his head lifted up is singing. They're wearing headdresses of some sort. They used to wear a feather tucked horizontally behind the ear to cover the face from the sun. Some people used to use a tail, like a fox tail, as everyday garment wear, they thought it might make them faster or stronger [see bird headdresses shown in Figs. 127 and 133 and figures wearing tails shown on Figs. 83 and 133].

OUR STORIES ETCHED IN IVORY

133/ Pitiksiaq DRILL BOW
Kotzebue Sound
Collected by Edward W. Nelson, accessioned 1882
National Museum of Natural History E48522
Walrus ivory; Length 37.7 cm (14.8 in)

TOP: Two vertical lines separate three scenes: the left scene illustrates a figure wearing a hunting bag, a drummer and shaman-like figure being expelled from a *qagri*, a bowhead whale and walrus, and two dancers; the center scene appears to show a scene from Kivgiq with drummers, dancers wearing loon headdresses, and a figure doing the two-foot high kick; the right scene includes bearded seals, a bowhead whale, and a skin boat.

BOTTOM: A row of thirteen hunters are holding ice picks and pulling bearded seals.

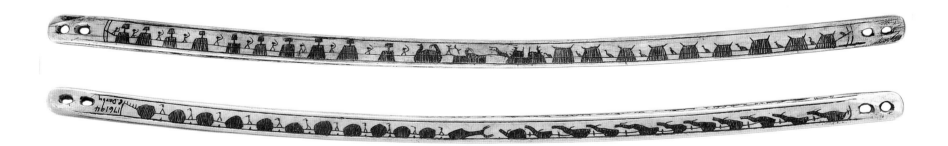

134/ Pitiksiaq DRILL BOW
Cape Darby
Collected by Edward W. Nelson, accessioned 1897
National Museum of Natural History E176194
Walrus ivory; Length 38 cm (15 in)

TOP: Figures carry knives and march across a rope strung between fort-like structures to confront a mythological *palraiyuk* with long jaws and sharp teeth who is guarding a series of forts with bird creatures.

BOTTOM: Figures walk across a rope stretched between a series of round houses or forts to face a row of mythological *tirisiq* with extended necks and wavy horns.

Jack Frankson Jr., 2012:

My mom's grandmother, she used to tell me a lot of stories. Like there used to be shamans, witch doctors. One time she said there were little people trying to break into their tent, she called them *innukins*. Basically they're just like small people, real tough. She says they could take down caribou by themselves even though they were so small, or fight a bear, using just their strength. Even though they're really small, they could probably take down a normal size person pretty easily. They're kind of like little Eskimo hunters. But they have nothing to do with us [see giants or myth figures outside tents shown on Figs. 40 and 137].

Alzred 'Steve' Oomittuk, 2010:

They talk about the old days, the *ulinaaq* who lived at the moon, who was a keeper of the animals. He lived in Point Hope and then he did something in disgrace, so he moved to the moon. He was a shaman. Shamans always talk about how they go into these trances and they would meet at the moon, on a full moon. On a full moon you were able to ask, under the skylight, for the gift of an animal, when wood was scarce and it was cold and it was winter and there was no daylight and food was scarce because you didn't catch enough during the spring or summer to feed you all through the winter. The woman would ask on a full moon, she could see the moon through the skylight, she would ask, with a real wooden bowl, we call them *puggutaq,* for a gift of an animal [see wood bowl in Fig. 135 and people or shamans transforming into animals on Figs 136, 137, and 140].

135/ Puggutaq BOWL, DISH (North Slope Iñupiaq)
Bering Strait
Collected by Caroline Coons, accessioned 1985
Carrie M. McLain Memorial Museum 1985.3.18
Wood; Length 38 cm (15 in)

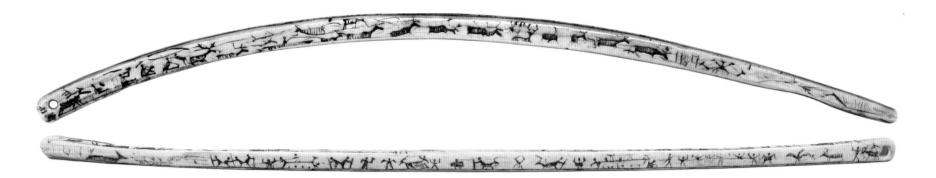

136/ Pitiksiaq DRILL BOW
Cape Darby
Collected by Edward W. Nelson, accessioned 1882
National Museum of Natural History E48116
Walrus ivory; Length 34.6 cm (13.6 in)

TOP: People smoke pipes and appear to fall into a transformative state on the left end. In the center, a hunter uses a kayak to drive caribou across the water towards a series of snares with a mound of caribou bones and antlers on the other side.

BOTTOM: Several pairs of figures are attached at the waist while other figures are transforming into caribou. Rectangular *qagrit* or dance screens are surrounded by dancers in various poses.

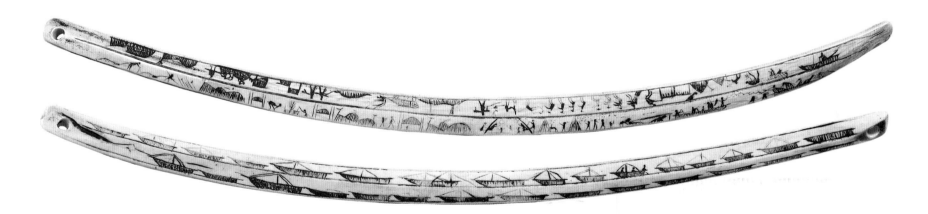

137/ Pitiksiaq DRILL BOW
Cape Nome
Collected by Edward W. Nelson, accessioned 1880
National Museum of Natural History E44464
Walrus ivory; Length 41.8 cm (16.5 in)

TOP: (upper scene) A pair of hunters drag a bearded seal to a village on the left. A line of dancers perform a transformational song. Giants attack a fish camp on the right end. (lower scene) Hunters drag seals to a village where a figure tends a cook pot, and people dance and drum inside a *qagri*. A hunting crew harpoons walrus on the right.

BOTTOM: (upper scene) A row of skin boats, some under sail, travel across the water. A lone skin boat on the right carries three people. (lower scene) Another row of skin boats extends across the side.

Kenny Tikik, 2012:

Allen Lane's father said one time while he was in Point Hope laying on the tundra, he was five or six years old, he was going to sleep, real nice out, sunshine day. While he was sleeping, he says a shadow went over and he noticed that a real big eagle was coming down to him and it grabbed him and he started moving around and the eagle started going back up again, big as a Twin Otter. That's how my dad used to say Allen's dad got caught by one of those hunting out on the ice, on the lead. He said a big eagle went and got him. Where he was at, there were tracks right by the lead, three shells, 30-30 shells, and like thirty feet apart were the wingtips of an eagle hitting the snow. He said that's where the eagle's wings brushed the snow. I heard stories where a big eagle like that would grab a *qayaq* and a hunter at the same time, just grab them and fly away. *Tiġimaqpuk*, big eagle [see Fig. 138 of a hunter taking aim at a giant eagle].

Qualayauq *Ross Schaeffer Sr., 2012:*

These are the most interesting things, these serpents with the wavy bodies. I've seen pictures of them and I always wondered, what kind of creature was out there at one time. Because they usually show what they've seen. So there must have been something out there a long time ago [see myth creatures shown on Figs. 134, 139, and 140].

138/ BOOKMARK
Nome
Collected by Nels and Charlotte Swanberg, accessioned 2011
Carrie M. McLain Memorial Museum 2011.11.32
Walrus ivory; Length 10.2 cm (4 in)

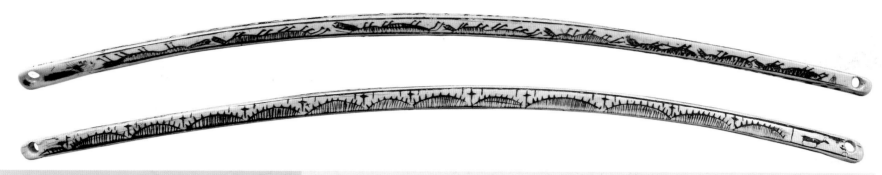

139/ Pitiksiaq DRILL BOW
Alaska
Collected by Edward W. Nelson, accessioned 1991
National Museum of Natural History ET1076-1
Walrus ivory; Length 39.2 cm (15.4 in)

TOP: A row of mythological *kokogiak* rest on their curved backs, wiggle thin legs, and raise heads filled with jagged teeth.

BOTTOM: Crosses or birds appear above a row of myth creatures, possibly another style of *kokogiak*, with spines along their backs. A caribou appears on the right end.

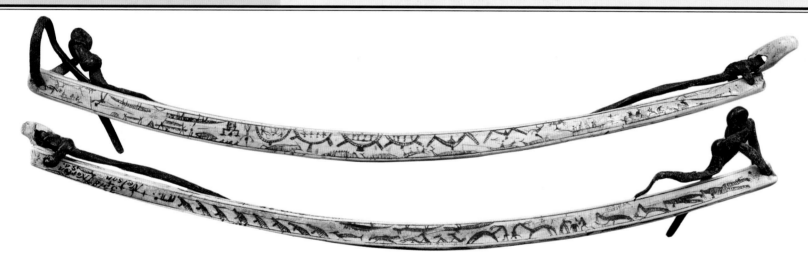

140/ Pitiksiaq DRILL BOW
St. Michael
Collected by Edward W. Nelson, accessioned 1878
National Museum of Natural History E33187
Walrus ivory, sealskin; Length 45 cm (17.7 in)

TOP: People work at a summer camp, a *kokogiak* with a curved body rises up to grab a small whale that has been harpooned, and a brave hunter stands on an ice floe spearing a herd of enraged walrus. Above, two crocodile-like creatures face each other with long pincer-like bodies filled with teeth. In the center, three giants prowl outside a row of arches or *qagrit* with figures dancing and drumming inside.

BOTTOM: A row of transformational seal figures are followed by a skin boat with a crew of three mythological walrus dogs, a pair of *tirisiq* with long necks and curved horns tearing a human figure apart, another walrus dog beheading a human, and four transformational walrus figures with fingers and legs. Above, a *palraiyuk* with short legs and crocodile-like jaws stalks two additional myth creatures.

Sinaġuyak *James Omiak, 2012:*

They had a pipe a long time ago, a real thin one, what the old people call *quiniq*. The pipes had a wooden stem and an ivory mouthpiece for puffing, homemade maybe, real small. My father made pipes, small ones to long ones, and cigarette holders, from ivory [see Figs. 141-142 for examples of pipes made from ivory and from wood and lead].

Kenny Tikik, *2012:*

I used to hear stories about when they used to smoke grass. They'd get it up on the mountains. There are two different kinds of grass that look the same. You smoke the wrong one and all your hair will fall out [see Figs. 48, 111, 136, 143, and 144 for people smoking pipes].

141/ Paipak PIPE (Bering Strait Inupiaq)
Wales
Collected by William T. Lopp and Ellen Lopp, accessioned 2013
Carrie M. McLain Memorial Museum 2013.11.40
Walrus ivory; Length 28 cm (11 in)

142/ Kuynga PIPE (St. Lawrence Island Yupik)
Savoonga
Collected by Chuck Coyle, accessioned 2013
Carrie M. McLain Memorial Museum 2013.17.1
Wood with lead, leather pouch with ivory pick and reindeer skin;
Length 22.5 cm (8.9 in)

OUR STORIES ETCHED IN IVORY

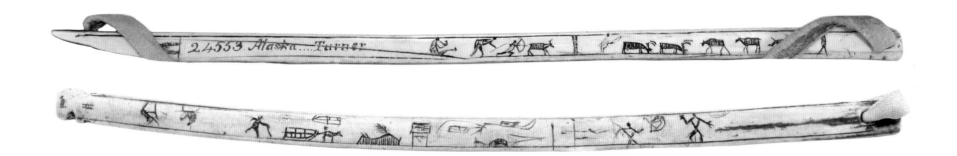

143/ Pitiksiaq DRILL BOW
Norton Sound
Collected by Lucien M. Turner, accessioned 1876
National Museum of Natural History E24553
Walrus ivory, sealskin; Length 35 cm (13.8 in)

TOP: Artist 1 engraved figures smoking a pipe and hunting caribou with a bow on the left side. Artist 2 engraved a row of caribou in a realistic style on the right side.

BOTTOM: Artist 3 engraved the majority of sketch-like motifs on this side including the dog sled, sod house, and figures with triangular torsos.

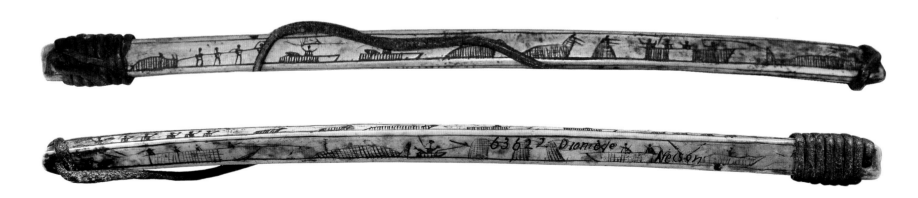

144/ Pitiksiaq DRILL BOW
Diomede Islands
Collected by Edward W. Nelson, accessioned 1882
National Museum of Natural History E63622
Walrus ivory, sealskin; Length 33.5 cm (13.2 in)

TOP: Four figures strain to pull a walrus across the ice. A pair of hunters in kayaks pursue walrus, and a whaling crew celebrates the successful strike of a bowhead whale.

BOTTOM: (upper scene) Six figures smoke pipes on the left end. A row of seals in the center is followed by two hunters in kayaks going after geese. (lower scene) Hunters in skin boats pursue walrus and a bowhead whale in the open water.

Sinaġuyak *James Omiak, 2012:*

My dad's from Big Diomede, he was born down there. We have relatives in Siberia. They went back and forth in summertime with boats from Uelen and Lavrentiya. Lots of people, lots of boats on the beach when they start walrus hunting. On the left side the Russians always come across; they use a sail. The Siberians had wooden whaling boats they received from whalers. Some of them had skin boats like we had on Diomede.

There are no Natives now on Big Diomede. They have been moved to the mainland. They removed everybody from there, to other villages. We found some of our relatives. The younger ones, they wonder who their relatives are and try to find them now. They have a hard time too [see skin boats traveling under sail shown on Figs. 145-148].

Qualayauq *Ross Schaeffer Sr., 2012:*

For about 900 or 1000 years, Kotzebue was a trade center for this whole Arctic region. The reason why is that Kotzebue is in a big bay and we've got a sand bar that protects small boats. So we have thousands of salmon coming by. In the early spring, we have thousands of whitefish,  trout run by, and we have sea mammals, *ugruk*, seals, and belugas coming by. Then upriver, we have all this birch, jade and flint that they come down to trade with, like furs. So Kotzebue was the ideal location for a trade center. Everybody shared in gathering the food during the summer. Once the summer was ended, it became the Kotzebue people's hunting ground. That's the way it was for a long time [see summer travelers arriving on the beach at a neighboring village shown on Figs. 145-146].

Aŋmaluq *Vince Pikonganna, 2012:*

Back then, a hundred years ago they did a lot of trading. In order to trade, you had to create your own trading partner, in the village. You could start whenever, when you are young or when you are in your 20s. The trading places were St. Michael, Wales, Kotzebue, and Teller area. Those were the places of trading, where people gather.

Once you establish a trading partner at each of them, you would request something for next year. If I bring baby sealskins, ten of them, what were you going to bring me? And they would come to a term, this is what I'm going to bring, this is what I'm going to bring, and they would come together next year and then trade. They almost did anything for one another. That's how you obtained things, over time. We saw some things that were not from around here, long ago, that were from far away; that was done by trading. The further it goes, the more expensive it gets [see Figs. 145-146 of summer travel to villages to trade and Figs. 148 and 150 of trading with Western ships].

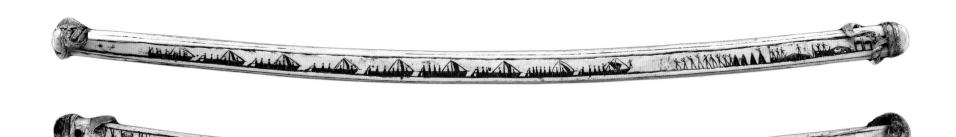

145/ Pitiksiaq DRILL BOW
Cape Nome
Collected by Edward W. Nelson, accessioned 1880
National Museum of Natural History E44399
Walrus ivory, sealskin; Length 43.7 cm (17.2 in)

TOP: Travelers direct a long row of skin boats under sail to a village where waiting figures are standing on the beach and on sod houses to welcome the visitors.

BOTTOM: Figures stand between two tents on the left end. In the center, skin boats hunt walrus on the ice and in the water.

146/ Pitiksiaq DRILL BOW
Sledge Island
Collected by Edward W. Nelson, accessioned 1880
National Museum of Natural History E45017
Walrus ivory; Length 34 cm (13.4 in)

TOP: Four skin boats with raised sails depart a village to travel across the water where they are greeted by waving figures.

BOTTOM: This scene appears unfinished and a continuation of imagery on the top side with villagers waving and standing on a sod house to greet visitors.

Aŋmaluq *Vince Pikonganna, 2012:*

Many days ago a shaman at King Island said there would come a ship and you will hear a bird like a rooster. The villagers laughed, as there was no such thing. Some time later, there comes a ship and the first sound heard was a rooster and they believed him since then.

Shamans used to travel to faraway places, even Seattle. Years ago whaling ships took people from King Island as translators to other villages, even Hawaii [see whaling ships shown on Figs. 147-150].

Qualayauq *Ross Schaeffer, Sr., 2012:*

The Diomede people came here to trade. They didn't like going to Nome but they liked coming to Kotzebue. The Diomede people came here every year until 1967. That's when some guys that were acting smart, young guys, got knives and tore up their skin boats. They never came back after that. Most of us were really good friends with all those folks. Charlie Ayapana is the master carver who came from Diomede; he carved here for years before he finally moved to Nome. He used the bow drill [see summer camps on drill bows from the Diomede Islands in Figs. 39 and 95 and skin boats paddling out to trade with Western ships on Figs. 147-148].

Sinaġuyak *James Omiak, 2012:*

Point Spencer used to be a trading area for Diomede, King Island, Teller, Qawiaraq, Siberians, and Shishmaref people. Sledge Island people probably traded at Port Clarence. Mainland communities traded wolverine, fish and caribou for rawhide rope, seal oil and dried walrus meat [see Fig. 148 of trade between Inupiat and Westerners on a drill bow from Sledge Island].

Suluk *Francis Alvanna, 2012:*

These guys cannot direct the wind but they can adjust the sail, don't forget that. You cannot direct the wind, but you can adjust the sail. The boat we used had a spot to place the mast in the middle of the boat, to tie it on the bottom. But I never saw one. I was too little to see a skin boat with sails [see skin boats with sails on Figs. 147-148].

147/ Pitiksiaq DRILL BOW
Cape Darby
Collected by Edward W. Nelson, accessioned 1880
National Museum of Natural History E44213
Walrus ivory; Length 33.2 cm (13.1 in)

TOP: Hunters in a skin boat and kayak pursue a bowhead whale below a sod house and tent. A ship and a small barge with two figures in hats paddle out to meet three skin boats coming to trade in the center. A hunter in a kayak aims his harpoon at two beluga whales and figures dance inside a *qagri*.

BOTTOM: Four-paneled tents are pitched on the beach and three ships, a small barge, and a kayak are meeting out in the water.

148/ Pitiksiaq DRILL BOW
Sledge Island
Collected by Edward W. Nelson, accessioned 1880
National Museum of Natural History E45020
Walrus ivory; Length 45.1 cm (17.8 in)

TOP: Villagers wave to a group of skin boats paddling out to trade with two whaling ships anchored in the center. Above, hunters in kayaks are pursing geese on the left and a skin boat is harpooning a bowhead whale on the right. Above and center, a large figure in a brimmed hat is leading two figures wearing conical hats tied together in the manner of slaves or prisoners.

BOTTOM: Figures are ice fishing outside a winter village. A lone skin boat appears on the right.

Kachuk *Glenn Ipalook, 2012:*

My great-grandmother was on the Karluk Expedition. She was a good sewer who made clothes for the crew. I've found stone ballasts washed up on the beach that I thought I might use for a baleen boat base. I keep them at home on my coffee table with a piece of whalebone on top and tell people it's a ballast and they wonder what that is [Inupiat carry a long history of trading and working with Westerners as shown on Fig. 150].

Ilonraaq *John Pullock, 2012:*

My grandpa used to talk about "Biaq." When "Biaq" comes, they go sell stuff, trade. Later on I was reading a book and I see "Bear," that's the word. That's the one, *Bear*. The Revenue Cutter *Bear* used to come out to King Island in wintertime. That's when they sell their carvings, they trade. In wintertime, they run out of things, what they buy from mainland, especially sugar. Springtime, sugar is gone, a little bit of flour. So sometimes I see my uncles, and they go by boat, they go across to Wales, to pick up sugar and things like that [the *Bear* was an ice-strengthened auxiliary steam ship with three masts that served in Alaska from 1885-1927 and might be one of the ships shown on Fig. 150].

Aŋmaluq *Vince Pikonganna, 2012:*

We went to Lavrentiya by way of Teller to Wales, Wales to Diomede, wait there a few days and then we all went across, six, seven boats. We just went over there to go see our friends that used to come over, from their side to us. We were going to go to Uelen but it was iced-in. What we call "Uvelyk," Uelemiut. They pretty much speak our dialect. That's where they used to go trading, many years ago, before the border. We wanted to see their carving at Uelen. They have a workshop just like King Island. They're good at carving, very good. They take their time [see skin boats traveling together on Figs. 145-146].

Baker Ningealook, 2012:

Some of the first whalers gave gold coin money to Inupiaq people from Shishmaref. They thought it was worthless because the coins didn't have any holes for buttons so they tossed it overboard before being stopped. I think about those coins out there somewhere. Another time, whalers gave flour to Inupiaq ladies who didn't know how to use it. So they climbed to the top of a hill and threw fistfuls into the air and watched it in the breeze. The first time they used flour it was as a thickener when put into broth [see whaling ships shown on Figs. 149-150].

149/ Pitiksiaq DRILL BOW
Alaska
Collected by Mildred McLean Hazen,
accessioned 1892
National Museum of Natural History E154071
Walrus ivory; Length 31.9 cm (12.6 in)

TOP: Two whaling ships towing skiffs head out after walrus and bowhead whales. The ships appear to be leaving the village on the right that features figures walking on sod houses, climbing on caches, and dragging seals with the help of a dog.

BOTTOM: Large-scale imagery on this side includes a fox, two figures wrestling, and a village with caches, sod houses, and skin boats on racks.

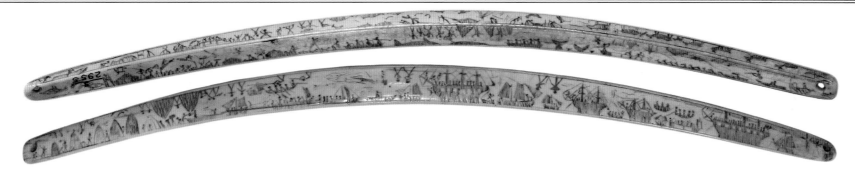

150/ Pitiksiaq DRILL BOW
Point Barrow
Collected by Frank Wood, accessioned 1916
National Museum of the American Indian
5/2955
Walrus ivory; Length 41.2 cm (16.2 in)

TOP: (upper scene) A kayak draws close to a village where figures wrestle, dance on top of a *qagri*, and attack each other with a spear. Hunters drag seals over the ice and take aim at a herd of caribou. (lower scene) Figures toss each other up in the air and peer down through the skylight on top of a *qagri* to watch the dancing and drumming below. Three dogs gather on the beach to watch skin boats head out to hunt whales. On the right end, a kayaker prods a herd of caribou across the water to a waiting bow hunter.

BOTTOM: On the left is an active beach scene that might depict Port Clarence with figures setting up tents and packing trade items into a skin boat. To the right are three anchored whaling ships and a three-masted schooner, possibly the U.S. Revenue Cutter *Bear*. Between the ships are skiffs carrying whalers as well as skin boats and kayaks paddling out to barter for trade goods.

Joseph Akaran, 2012:

Some of these drill bows have steamboats on them. Around St. Michael, we used to have a lot of steamboats; there's still a little bit of rubble in the canal about eight or nine miles out from here. You can take a boat and go through the canal to a place called Steamboats, that's what we call it. I guess they didn't follow the river right and landed up on shore and there they sit [see paddle steamer shown on Fig. 152].

Suluk *Francis Alvanna, 2012:*

That father-in-law of mine, John Kiminock Sr., was born on a whaling ship, up by the Beaufort Sea. The name of the whaling ship was *Belvedere*. That's what it said on his birth certificate. After I found a picture of the ship, I was going to try and make one [see the whaling ships on Figs. 152-153 and the boat made from ivory and bone in Fig. 151].

Anaqulutuq *Othniel Anaqulutuq "Art" Oomittuk Jr., 2010:*

If you read Tom Lowenstein's book *Ultimate Americans*, he talks about Anaqulutuq, which is my Eskimo name. He refers to Anaqulutuq as a cartographer, somebody who makes maps. So he drew these maps of the layout of the land for the commercial whalers because they got tired of eating fish and seafood, they wanted something that comes from the land. And this bow drill right here (Fig. 153) reminds me of something like that, where you see the ships, but you also see the land animals [see scenes on water and land shown on Fig. 153].

151/ Umiaqpak SHIP "Model" (Bering Strait Inupiaq)
Nome
Collected by Carrie M. McLain, accessioned 1967
Carrie M. McLain Memorial Museum 1967.1.58
Walrus ivory, bone, thread; Length 18 cm (7.1 in)

OUR STORIES ETCHED IN IVORY

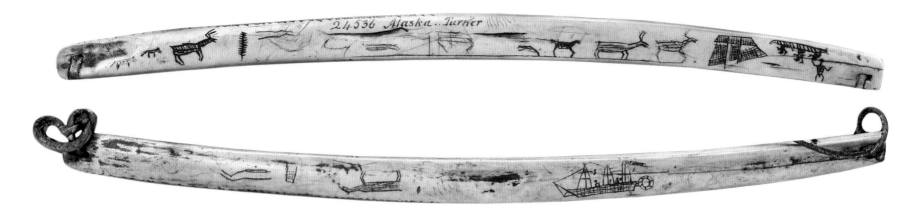

152/ Pitiksiaq DRILL BOW
Norton Sound
Collected by Lucien M. Turner, accessioned 1876
National Museum of Natural History E24536
Walrus ivory, sealskin; Length 37 cm (14.6 in)

TOP: Two wolves on the left chase a herd of caribou scattered across the side. A whaling ship and a three-person kayak with dancing figures appear on the end.

BOTTOM: A single caribou is engraved on the left. A large paddle steamer with a crew onboard appears on the right.

153/ Pitiksiaq DRILL BOW
Cape Nome
Collected by Edward W. Nelson, accessioned 1880
National Museum of Natural History E44366
Walrus ivory; Length 33.6 cm (13.2 in)

TOP: A figure runs on snowshoes to catch up with a hunter taking aim at a wolf stalking a herd of caribou or reindeer. Two Westerners wearing hats stand next to a four-paneled tent. Four whaling ships appear to the right of the camp.

BOTTOM: On the left, a row of tents with a raised flag in the center appears next to a whaling ship and may represent an Inupiaq summer camp at Port Clarence. Below the camp, a dog trails a figure carrying a pack to his camp where a hunter takes aim at a bear. In the center, two whaling ships sail along the coast and a hunter lies on the ground to shoot a caribou. The right end illustrates more caribou or reindeer.

154/ An upturned skin boat provides a windbreak for an ivory carver using a drill bow on the Nome beach around 1940. Sealskin slippers, salt and pepper shakers, and an ivory ink stand for sale are displayed on top of a crate. Carrie M. McLain Memorial Museum, 97.8.1.

appendices

155/ An Inupiaq carver holds a pipe and an ivory carving shaped like a polar bear as he returns the gaze of a photographer on the Snake River Sandspit in Nome. Next to the carver, a fashionably-dressed woman holds up her purse and handkerchief suggesting she is about to purchase the carving and wrap it up to take home. c. 1905.
Carrie M. McLain Memorial Museum, NMP-80-3-131.

OUR STORIES ETCHED IN IVORY

Appendix 1

Engraved Drill Bows with Collector Information in the Smithsonian National Museum of Natural History (NMNH) and National Museum of the American Indian (NMAI)

Collector	Dates of acquisition	Collector notes, recorded locations of acquisition, and catalogue numbers	Number of drill bows	Source
William H. Dall	1866-1868	Assembled a large collection of ethnological and natural history material for the Smithsonian as a member of the Western Union Telegraph Expedition. Observed carvers using engraved drill bows. *Port Clarence* (E46054)	1	NMNH Accession Number: 9536 Dall 1870:237
Lucien M. Turner	1874-1877	Assembled a large ethnological collection while stationed at St. Michael as an officer with the U.S. Signal Corps. Made the first sizeable collection of engraved ivory carvings for the Smithsonian. *St. Michael* (E129223) *Norton Sound* (E24533, E24536, E24537, E24538, E24539, E24540, E24541, E24543, E24545, E24546, E24547, E24548, E24549, E24550, E24551, E24552, E24553, E24554 E24556, E24557)	21	NMNH Accession Numbers: 76A0010 19248 Hoffman 1897:774-775, 785-786
Edward W. Nelson	1877-1881	Acquired over 10,000 objects for the Smithsonian while stationed at St. Michael as an officer with the U.S. Signal Corps. Single largest collection of engraved drill bows. *Point Hope* (E63802, E63803, E63804, E63805) *Kotzebue Sound* (E38782, E48518, E48519, E48520, E48521, E48522, E48523, E48524, E48525, E48526) *Hotham Inlet* (E64151, E64152, E64153) *Cape Prince of Wales* (E43360) *Diomede Islands* (E49163, E63621, E63622, E63623) *Sledge Island* (E45016, E45017, E45018, E45020, E45021, E45022, E45025, E176191)	81	NMNH Accession Numbers: 8133 78A00080 80A00050 82A00003 31796 999999 NMAI catalogue records Nelson 1899:84-85, Pl. XXXVI

Collector	Dates of acquisition	Collector notes, recorded locations of acquisition, and catalogue numbers	Number of drill bows	Source
		Cape Nome (E44366, E44367, E44398, E44399, E44400, E44464, E44465, E44467, E44618, E45330, E45332, E45333, E45345, E45346)		
		Golovin Bay (E176172)		
		Cape Darby (E44206, E44207, E44208, E44209, E44210, E44213, E48115, E48116, E176194, 2/418 [originally E44212])		
		Kigiktauik (E33178, E33183, E33186)		
		Nubviukhchugaluk (E43931, E43932)		
		Shaktoolik (E38521, E38522, E43810)		
		Unalakleet (E33191, E33192, E176171)		
		St. Michael (E33179, E33180, E33182, E33184, E33187, E33190, E48527)		
		Pastolik (E33188, E33189)		
		Norton Sound (E38781, E38886)		
		Alaska (ET1076-0, ET1076-1, ET16050, ET16060)		
John G. Brady	1878-1909	Presbyterian minister and lawyer who co-founded the Sheldon Jackson School in 1878. Served as the Governor of the District of Alaska from 1897 to 1906. *Alaska* (E274548)	1	NMNH Accession Number: 54171
Patrick H. Ray and John Murdoch	1881-1883	Members of the International Polar Expedition to Point Barrow. Collected a range of implements with pictorial engravings from North Alaska communities. *Point Barrow* (E89420, E89421, E89424, E89425)	4	NMNH Accession Number: 13712 Murdoch 1892:175-180, Figs. 153-154

Collector	Dates of acquisition	Collector notes, recorded locations of acquisition, and catalogue numbers	Number of drill bows	Source
Mildred McLean Hazen and John McLean	1882-1884	McLean Hazen was the daughter of Washington McLean, owner of the *Cincinnati Enquirer*, and wife of General William B. Hazen. She was a prominent figure in the Democratic party and socialite in Washington, D.C. Her son John McLean died at the age of twenty-two in 1898. *Sitka* (E75461/E75462) *Alaska* (E67904, E154071)	3	NMNH Accession Numbers: 15716 25748 Rutherford B. Hayes Presidential Library & Museums, Mildred McLean Hazen Dewey, GA-52
John Hackman and Heinrich Koenig Joseph E. Standley	1889-1905	Hackman and his brother-in-law Koenig operated a shore-based whaling station at Point Hope from 1889 to 1905. The pair acquired ethnographic material that they sold to collector George Heye and curio dealers, such as Joseph E. Standley, who owned and operated the Ye Olde Curiosity Shop in Seattle, WA. In 1916, George Heye purchased three engraved drill bows from Standley that probably originated with Hackman and Koenig. *Point Barrow* (5/4337, 5/5597, 5/5598) *Point Hope* (4488)	4	NMAI catalogue records
Victor Justice Evans	1900-1930	Established a patent business and amassed a large collection of Native American objects that he lent and eventually bequeathed to the Smithsonian. *Alaska* (E360421, E360422)	2	NMNH Accession Number: 113605
Suzanne Rognon Bernardi Jeffery	1901-1906	School teacher at Wales from 1901-1906. *Cape Prince of Wales* (6/7885)	1	NMAI catalogue records

Collector	Dates of acquisition	Collector notes, recorded locations of acquisition, and catalogue numbers	Number of drill bows	Source
Miner Bruce	1904	Manager of the Teller Reindeer Station from 1892-1893 where he assembled an extensive collection from Port Clarence. Set up trading post in Kotzebue Sound and sold ethnographic material to major museums. *Point Barrow* (2142)	1	NMAI catalogue records
Floyd Fellows	1908	*Icy Cape* (E398234)	1	NMNH Accession Number: 231572
U.S. Department of the Interior	-1910	Interior Department, Bureau of Education. *Port Clarence* (E260132)	1	NMNH Accession Number: 5115
Frank Wood	- 1916	Collector and curator of the Old Dartmouth Historical Society in New Bedford, MA. *Point Barrow* (5/2955)	1	NMAI catalogue records
Fred Harvey	- 1917	Entrepreneur who served as a leader in promoting tourism in the American Southwest. Stimulated the commercialization and revitalization of Native arts in the Southwest. *Alaska* (6/2376, 6/2378)	2	NMAI Catalogue records Howard and Pardue (1996)
Museum of the American Indian	- 1919	Museum founder George Heye acquired the majority of objects for the MAI through in-person exchanges, purchases from traders, and sponsored field expeditions. *Little Diomede* (9/4635) *Alaska* (10/6592, 19/1629)	3	NMAI catalogue records
Francis Sayre	c. 1920	Law professor who acquired archaeological and ethnographic material from Alaska, Siberia, and Canada. *Diomede Islands* (A380771) *Point Hope* (E379814)	2	NMNH Accession Number: 153865

OUR STORIES ETCHED IN IVORY

Collector	Dates of acquisition	Collector notes, recorded locations of acquisition, and catalogue numbers	Number of drill bows	Source
William M. Fitzhugh	- 1929	San Francisco collector. *Nome* (19/3412)	1	NMAI catalogue records
Judge Nathan Bijur	- 1930	Supreme Court Justice from New York who specialized in corporate law. *Point Hope* (20/8880)	1	NMAI catalogue records *Jewish Daily Bulletin*, July 10, 1930, p.2
Ira S. Reed	- 1936	Artifact collector and auctioneer in Sellersville, PA. *Cape Nome* (19/5046)	1	NMAI catalogue records
David Currie	- 1972	*Alaska* (24/6479)	1	NMAI catalogue records
Preston R. Bassett	- 1982	Engineer and inventor of instruments for aviation whose interests included early technology and collecting antiques. *Alaska* (E422574)	1	NMNH Accession Number: 349794 Amherst College, History of the Basset Planetarium, https://www.amherst.edu/museums/bassett/history
	TOTAL		134	

Learn more about these collectors and the objects they acquired through the NMNH and NMAI collections databases:

Smithsonian National Museum of Natural History: Anthropology Collections Search
https://collections.nmnh.si.edu/search/anth/

Smithsonian National Museum of the American Indian: Collections Search
https://americanindian.si.edu/explore/collections/search

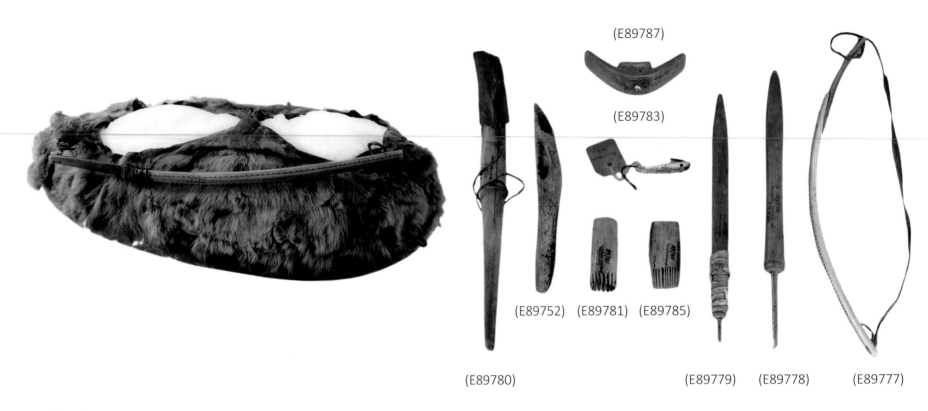

(E89787)

(E89783)

(E89752) (E89781) (E89785)

(E89780) (E89779) (E89778) (E89777)

156/ IKŁIĠVIK TOOL BAG (North Slope Iñupiaq)
Point Barrow
Collected by Patrick H. Ray and John Murdoch, accessioned 1884
National Museum of Natural History E89776
Wolverine skin, ivory, antler, sealskin; Length 51.5 cm (20.3 in)

The carver Nunatañmiun Ilûbw'ga sold this tool bag (E89776) made from four wolverine heads to Patrick H. Ray and John Murdoch while they were stationed at Point Barrow from 1881 to 1883 (Murdoch 1892:187-189). The clasp is made from a short piece of sealskin strung through the nostrils of the two wolverine heads on the sides. The bag is carried by an ivory handle engraved with barbed lines that has been lengthened with a section of caribou antler. The tool bag was purchased with ten items inside including: a drill bow (E89777), a mouthpiece (E89787), two wood drills (E89778 and E89779), a large crooked knife with a sheath (E89780), a flint flaker (E89784 missing), a comb for deerskins (E89781), a hair comb made of antler (E89785), a fishhook (E89783), and a harpoon head (E89752).

OUR STORIES ETCHED IN IVORY

Appendix 2

Hand Tools and Materials used in Carving Ivory

aġra	ash, used to darken engravings *(Bering Strait Inupiaq)*
agiun	flat file *(North Slope Iñupiaq)*
aglaun	pencil, pen *(Bering Strait Inupiaq)*
aliq	a rawhide thong of bearded sealskin *(Bering Strait Inupiaq)*
ayupqat	toolbox *(Bering Strait Inupiaq)*
itiŋnaq	jade, used for drill bits or mouthpiece sockets *(Bering Strait Inupiaq)*
iwalu	thread, sinew *(Bering Strait Inupiaq)*
iġitaq	ocher, reddish rock to stain wood or ivory *(Bering Strait Iñupiaq)*
kiggitit	vise *(Bering Strait Inupiaq)*
kigiak	nail *(Bering Strait Inupiaq)*
kiinagzaun	whetstone, knife sharpener *(Bering Strait Inupiaq)*
kiḷiġvak tuugaaŋi	mammoth tusks *(North Slope Iñupiaq)*
kilituq	strip of animal skin to be used for rope *(Bering Strait Inupiaq)*
kiŋmiaq	mouthpiece used with a drill bow *(Bering Strait Inupiaq)*
maasiun	a chisel with a rounded end used to remove the core of a walrus tusk *(Bering Strait Inupiaq)*
miłghaq	carving knife, curved knife *(Qawiaraq Iñupiaq)*
niuqtuun	drill bow *(North Slope Iñupiaq)*
niuun	wood drill *(Bering Strait Inupiaq)*
niuutit	wood drills with varied bits *(Bering Strait Inupiaq)*
paulaq	soot [used to darken engravings] *(Bering Strait Inupiaq)*
piksiuun	engraver with a hooked tip *(Bering Strait Inupiaq)*
pinaugun	file *(Bering Strait Inupiaq)*
piññuqtaq	pocket knife *(North Slope Iñupiaq)*
pitiksiaq	drill bow *(Bering Strait Inupiaq, King Island)*
puttun	awl *(North Slope Iñupiaq)*
qaiqsaun	sandpaper *(Bering Strait Inupiaq)*
qayuun	adze with narrow blade for chipping bone or ivory *(Bering Strait Inupiaq)*
sanalġun	tool for carving or woodwork; chisel *(Bering Strait Inupiaq)*
sanauġun	carving knife with bent, curved tip *(Bering Strait Inupiaq)*
satquaq	drill bow *(Bering Strait Inupiaq, Little Diomede)*
sauniq	bone *(Bering Strait Inupiaq)*
siḷḷiñ	whetstone, knife sharpener *(North Slope Iñupiaq)*
suŋauraat	beads *(Bering Strait Inupiaq)*
suqqaq	baleen *(Bering Strait Inupiaq)*
tivraq	driftwood *(North Slope Iñupiaq)*
tuniqtaq	soapstone [used for a mouthpiece socket] *(North Slope Iñupiaq)*
tuugaaq	new ivory; walrus tusk *(Bering Strait Inupiaq)*
tuugaaqłuk	old ivory *(Bering Strait Inupiaq)*
tuugarriqun	large rasp, file for use in carving ivory *(North Slope Iñupiaq)*
ulimaun	adze *(North Slope Iñupiaq)*
uluginauyuq	coping saw *(Bering Strait Inupiaq)*
uluun	saw *(North Slope Iñupiaq)*
unaqsit	driftwood *(Bering Strait Inupiaq)*
uyaġak	stone or rock [used for a mouthpiece socket] *(Bering Strait Inupiaq)*

Source: Kaplan (1994); MacLean (2012); Omiak (2012a); Pikonganna (2012); Tiulana (2012)

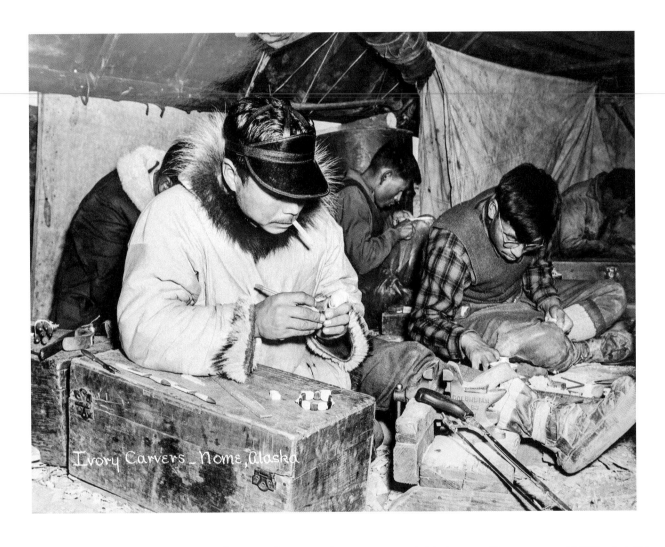

Ivory Carvers _ Nome, Alaska

157/ A carver pencils a design on a small piece of ivory under an upturned skin boat at Nome around 1930. A drill bow, mouthpiece, and set of drills can be seen on the toolbox to the left. A variety of pieces are being fashioned for the curio trade including a bracelet, pickle fork, and engraved letter openers.
Carrie M. McLain Memorial Museum, 2002.17.1.

OUR STORIES ETCHED IN IVORY

Material Culture Objects Engraved with Pictorial Imagery from the Collections of the Smithsonian National Museum of Natural History (NMNH), National Museum of the American Indian (NMAI), and Carrie M. McLain Memorial Museum

Adze QAYUUN "adze with narrow blade for chipping bone or ivory" (Bering Strait Inupiaq)

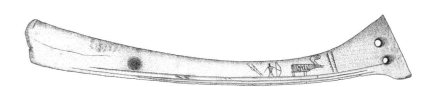

158/ Adze QAYUUN
Wales, Kurigitavik site
Collected by National Geographic Society, accessioned 1936
National Museum of Natural History A393714
Antler; Length 31 cm (12.2 in)

159/ Adze QAYUUN
This adze handle features a bow hunter taking aim at a caribou. A pair of barbed lines are etched across the end. The sparse and sketchy imagery relates to the early Birnirk-Thule culture at Wales (see Fig. 13).

Pen and ink drawing of NMNH A393714
National Anthropological Archives, Smithsonian Institution
Henry B. Collins Papers, Box 110

Arrow Shaft Straightener UUSUUTIT "piece of wood used for straightening arrow shaft" (North Slope Iñupiaq)

160/ Arrow Shaft Straightener UUSUUTIT
Sledge Island
Collected by Edward W. Nelson, accessioned 1880
National Museum of Natural History E45109
Walrus ivory; Length 17.8 cm (7 in)

Images of caribou grazing and resting cover this arrow straightener carved in the shape of a caribou at rest. Arrow straighteners were some of the first engraved carvings acquired by European explorers to the Arctic (see Bockstoce 1977:24, 31-32).

161/ Arrow Shaft Straightener UUSUUTIT
Port Clarence
Collected by U.S. Department of the Interior, accessioned 1910
National Museum of Natural History E260154
Walrus ivory; Length 14.5 cm (5.75 in)

Figures carrying staffs and wearing four-cornered hats in the style of Sámi reindeer herders are engraved on the side of this arrow straightener.

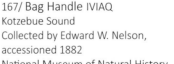

162/ Artwork IKSIAQTUQ
Norton Sound
Collected by Lucien M. Turner,
accessioned 1876
National Museum of Natural History E24563
Walrus ivory; Length 10.5 cm (4.1 in)

This piece of ivory from an old tool has been repurposed for sale and decorated with scenes of summer fish camp and winter dog sleds. The dog sled on the left features a curved frame in the style of a Chukchi sled while the sled on the right resembles a traditional Inupiaq basket sled.

163/ Artwork IKSIAQTUQ
St. Michael
Collected by Lucien M. Turner,
accessioned 1887
National Museum of Natural History
E129277
Walrus ivory; Length 11 cm (4.3 in)

The artist of the carving on the left also engraved this piece that illustrates Westerners in hats moving supplies from a canvas tent to a waiting skiff on the left. This prolific artist also engraved a number of drill bows (see Figs. 40 and 81 and Chan 2013:356-362).

Awl PUTTUN "awl, tool for making holes" (Bering Strait Inupiaq)

164/ Awl PUTTUN
Bering Strait
Collected by Howard and Mary Knodel,
accessioned 2007
Carrie M. McLain Memorial Museum
2007.10.1056
Bone; Length 20 cm (7.9 in)

This awl features a row of engraved caribou with a figure and two cross-like designs in the center. The imagery relates to the early Birnirk-Thule culture (see pp. 30-32 and similar cross designs on Fig. 202).

165/ Awl PUTTUN
Unalakleet
Collected by Edward W. Nelson,
accessioned 1878
National Museum of Natural History
E33177
Walrus ivory; Length 23 cm (9 in)

A row of engraved caribou stretch across the side of this awl that features a carved caribou head on the end (see Fig. 64 of a drill bow from Unalakleet and Figs. 108-109 of caribou heads on the ends of drill bows).

Bag Handle IVIAQ "handle as on a pail, pot, or pan" (Bering Strait Inupiaq)

166/ Bag Handle IVIAQ
Kotzebue Sound
Collected by Edward W. Nelson,
accessioned 1882
National Museum of Natural History E48529
Walrus ivory, blue bead; Length 39.5 cm
(15.6 in)

This bag handle features a row of caribou skins on the left and a row of wolf pelts on the right. A blue bead is inset into the right end (see blue beads inset into drill bows on Figs. 21 and 63).

167/ Bag Handle IVIAQ
Kotzebue Sound
Collected by Edward W. Nelson,
accessioned 1882
National Museum of Natural History
E48531
Walrus ivory; Length 36.5 cm (14.4 in)

This bag handle depicts hunters pursuing bears, geese, and a whale. The beveled edges reference the older Punuk-Thule culture and are similar to a style of wavy bag handle from Point Barrow (see Chan 2013:246-247; Murdoch 1892: 190).

Boat Hook NIKSIKPAK "anchor, large hook" (North Slope Iñupiaq)

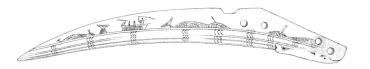

168/ Boat Hook NIKSIKPAK
Alaska
National Museum of Natural
History AT5952
Walrus ivory;
Length 31.6 cm (12.4 in)

Hunters in a skin boat are pursuing bowhead whales across the side of this boat hook. Rows of pronged lines are engraved along the bottom. The imagery relates to the Birnirk-Thule culture and is similar to a boat hook from Little Diomede (see Chan 2013:243-245).

169/ Boat Hook NIKSIKPAK
Pen and ink drawing of NMNH AT5952
National Anthropological Archives,
Smithsonian Institution
Henry B. Collins Papers, Box 110

Bucket Handle IPU "handle for carrying water bucket" (North Slope Iñupiaq)

170/ Bucket Handle IPU
Point Hope
Collected by Edward W. Nelson,
accessioned 1882
National Museum of Natural History E63808
Walrus ivory, blue bead;
Length 18 cm (7.1 in)

Engraved bands with ladder lines frame a row of caribou on this bucket handle. One blue bead remains in the center.

171/ Bucket Handle IPU
Point Hope
Collected by Edward W. Nelson,
accessioned 1882
National Museum of Natural History
E63801
Walrus ivory; Length 25.5 cm (10 in)

Two bowhead whales face a row of whale flukes on this bucket handle. A whale fluke has been carved in the center (see Fig. 36 of a drill bow from Point Hope with a similar carved whale fluke).

Crooked Knife SANAUĜUN "carving knife with bent, curved tip" (Bering Strait Inupiaq)

172/ Crooked Knife SANAUĜUN
St. Michael
Collected by Edward W. Nelson,
accessioned 1880
National Museum of Natural History E45488
Bone, sealskin, metal;
Length 22.4 cm (8.8 in)

Three whaling ships are engraved on the handle of this knife. The series of holes on the left suggest the bone might have been previously used for a different tool.

173/ Crooked Knife SANAUĜUN
Kotzebue Sound
Collected by Samuel Prescott Fay,
accessioned 1951
National Museum of the American Indian
21/8949
Bone, metal; Length 28.5 cm (11.2 in)

This knife handle features a bow hunter aiming at a goose, dog sled, and a row of double pronged lines. The irregular outlines and abstract motifs relate to the Birnirk-Thule culture (see Table 2, Figs. 13-14).

Drill Bow PITIKSIAQ "traditional tool for making fire and drilling holes" (Bering Strait Inupiaq)

174/ Drill Bow PITIKSIAQ
Kotzebue Sound
Collected by Edward W. Nelson,
accessioned 1882
National Museum of Natural History E48520
Walrus ivory; Length 44 cm (17.3 in)

Bowhead whales are spouting plumes of water along the top and bottom of this drill bow (see Fig. 52 of a drill bow with similar rows of facing animals).

175/ Drill Bow PITIKSIAQ
Sledge Island
Collected by Edward W. Nelson,
accessioned 1880
National Museum of Natural History E45025
Walrus ivory; Length 40.3 cm (15.9 in)

This drill bow features scattered imagery of figures ice fishing, dragging seals, and driving dog sleds. The thin, wispy-like quality of the figures relate to other drill bows from Sledge Island (see Figs. 131, 145, 148).

Gorget MANUĠUN "bib, wide necklace" (North Slope Iñupiaq)

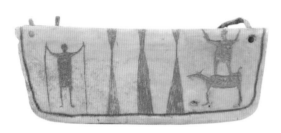

176/ Gorget MANUĠUN
Point Barrow
Collected by Patrick H. Ray and John Murdoch, accessioned 1883
National Museum of Natural History E56517
Walrus ivory, sealskin; Length 10.4 cm (4.1 in)

This dance gorget was repurposed from an old snow shovel, engraved with lines, figures, and a reindeer, and darkened with red ocher. The large figures with raised arms relate to the hero Kikamigo painted on older wood dance gorgets from Point Barrow (see Murdoch 1892:363, 370-372; Phillips-Chan 2020b:165-166).

Hair Comb ILLAIYUTIT "comb" (Bering Strait Inupiaq)

177/ Hair Comb ILLAIYUTIT
Point Hope
Collected by Dr. John Harley Stamp,
accessioned 1918
National Museum of the American Indian 7/7604
Bone; Length 7.5 cm (3 in)

A single whale fluke is engraved on the center of this comb. Sparse and centralized motifs are also found on bone wrist guards from the Punuk-Thule culture (see Fig. 16).

178/ Hair Comb ILLAIYUTIT
Bering Strait
Collected by Judge Nathan Bijur, accessioned 1946
National Museum of the American Indian 20/8902
Bone; Length 9.2 cm (3.6 in)

This comb features a carved caribou at the top and is engraved with a barbed line, dots, and two figures engaged in sexual activity.

179/ Hair Comb ILLAIYUTIT
Point Barrow
Purchased from Joseph E. Standley,
accessioned 1916
National Museum of the American Indian 5/3937
Bone; Length 28.5 cm (11.2 in)

This comb is more recent than the two on the left and was probably made to sell. Dog sleds and sod houses are engraved along the edges while the center features two women with elaborate hairstyles that appear to illustrate the use of hair combs.

OUR STORIES ETCHED IN IVORY

Harpoon Rest NAULIGAQAĠVIK "harpoon rest or oar rest" (North Slope Iñupiaq)

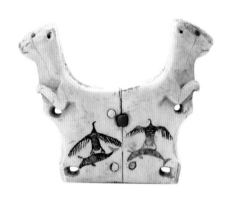

180/ Harpoon Rest NAULIGAQAĠVIK
Wales
Collected by Edward W. Nelson,
accessioned 1882
National Museum of Natural History E48169
Walrus ivory, blue bead; Length 15 cm (5.9 in)

This harpoon rest is carved with two weasel-like animals on the sides and engraved with two giant eagles (*tiŋmiaqpait*) carrying bowhead whales. A blue bead is inset into the center (read Kenny Tikik's story about a giant eagle on p. 144).

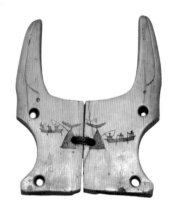

181/ Harpoon Rest NAULIGAQAĠVIK
Point Barrow
Purchased by MAI, accessioned 1919
National Museum of the American Indian
9/2527
Walrus ivory, sealskin; Length 11 cm (4.3 in)

The heads of two bowhead whales are carved on the sides of this harpoon rest. The center depicts harpooners in skin boats that are each making a strike on a bowhead whale.

Hunting Tally

182/ Hunting Tally
Point Barrow
Collected by Patrick H. Ray and John Murdoch, accessioned 1883
National Museum of Natural History E89474
Walrus ivory; Length 25.5 cm (10 in)

A carver from Utqiaġvik engraved hunters pursuing caribou and a row of whale flukes on this carving. Although Murdoch expressed uncertainty about the factual nature of the records, engraving rows of flukes or animal skins relates back to the tradition of recording hunting stories or experiences on drill bows (see Murdoch 1892:360-363; pp. 41, this volume).

183/ Hunting Tally
Point Barrow
Collected by Patrick H. Ray and John Murdoch, accessioned 1883
National Museum of Natural History E89487
Walrus ivory; Length 12 cm (4.7 in)

This ivory piece is engraved with figures and caribou. The row of engraved lines at the bottom resemble the tines on bone and ivory combs.

Ice Chisel TUUQPAK "ice chisel, ice chipper" (Bering Strait Inupiaq)

184/ Ice Chisel TUUQPAK
Sledge Island
Collected by Edward W. Nelson,
accessioned 1880
National Museum of Natural History E44692
Walrus ivory; Length 19.5 cm (7.7 in)

Two artists appear to have worked on this ice chisel. Carver 1 seems to have engraved the skin boat and the barbed bands related to the Punuk-Thule culture. Carver 2 appears to have engraved the figures and animals with irregular outlines scattered across the sides.

185/ Ice Chisel TUUQPAK
Icy Cape
Collected by Dr. Floyd F. Fellows,
accessioned 1960
National Museum of Natural History E398266
Walrus ivory; Length 32 cm (12.6 in)

This ice chisel features images of fish, summer camp, hunting a bear and a whale, and a river. The row of isolated motifs relate to a style of pictorial engraving that emerged during the curio trade (see p.37 and Figs. 67-69).

Needle Case KANNUYAKUIK "needle case" (Bering Strait Inupiaq)

186/ Needle Case KANNUYAKUIK
Alaska
Purchased from Joseph E. Standley,
accessioned 1916
National Museum of the American Indian 5/3178
Walrus ivory, sealskin; Length 28 cm (11 in)

Travelers and two dog sleds are engraved on the side of this needle case.

187/ Needle Case KANNUYAKUIK
Alaska
Collected by Victor J. Evans,
accessioned 1931
National Museum of Natural History
E360386
Walrus ivory, sealskin; Length 23 cm (9 in)

This needle case is engraved with a figure driving a dog sled. The ivory thimble with its circular depressions is made to imitate a metal thimble.

Net gauge NIGAQTUTILAAĠUN "net measure, net gauge" (North Slope Iñupiaq)

188/ Net gauge NIGAQTUTILAAĠUN
Nome
Purchased by MAI, accessioned 1928
National Museum of the American Indian
15/8595
Walrus ivory; Length 12 cm (4.7 in)

A busy summer scene at Port Clarence appears to be shown on this net gauge. Imagery includes a reindeer herder, three Chukchi-style yurts, a whaling ship, and a figure wearing a Western-style coat (see Fig. 150).

189/ Net gauge NIGAQTUTILAAĠUN
Norton Sound
Collected by U.S. Department of the Interior,
accessioned 1910
National Museum of Natural History E260110
Walrus ivory; Length 26.7 cm (10.5 in)

Two Sámi herders are shown driving sled reindeer on the blade of this net gauge (see Sámi herders also illustrated on Fig. 190).

Pipe PAIPAK "smoking pipe" (Bering Strait Inupiaq)

190/ Pipe PAIPAK
Norton Sound
Collected by U.S. Department of the Interior,
accessioned 1910
National Museum of Natural History
E260095
Walrus ivory; Length 31.5 cm (12.4 in)

This elaborate pipe is carved with animals across the top and an eagle around the bowl. The side is engraved with rows of barbed bands and a detailed scene of the Teller Reindeer Station with buildings, Sámi and Inupiaq herders, and reindeer in harness.

191/ Pipe PAIPAK
Alaska
Collected by Victor J. Evans,
accessioned 1931
National Museum of Natural History
E360410
Walrus ivory, lead, sinew, wood;
Length 33.3 cm (13.1 in)

This pipe is engraved across the top with crosses made from barbed bands and radiating nucleated circles. The lower portion features busy scenes of figures dancing inside *qagrit*, warfare, and hunting. Almost a dozen pipes by this skilled carver are now in museum collections (Chan 2013:645-649).

Powder Horn IGNIKSRAQAĠVIK "gunpowder horn" (North Slope Iñupiaq)

192/ Powder Horn IGNIKSRAQAĠVIK
St. Michael
Collected by Lucien M. Turner,
accessioned 1887
National Museum of Natural History
E129221
Antler; Length 13.5 cm (5.3 in)

This powder horn features engraved scenes of hunting, summer camp, and buildings with windows that appear to be those of the Alaska Commercial Company at St. Michael (see Fig. 153 of a drill bow that also appears to depict a scene at St. Michael).

193/ Powder Horn IGNIKSRAQAĠVIK
Wales
Collected by William "Tom" Lopp and Ellen Kittredge Lopp, accessioned 2013
Carrie M. McLain Memorial Museum
2013.11.32
Antler, wood; Length 15.5 cm (6.1 in)

Scattered images of hunters dragging seals, whaling, and using firearms to hunt caribou are engraved on this powder horn. Square buildings are engraved on the right end and may represent frame houses used by Tom and Ellen Lopp at Wales.

Tobacco Box TILAAMMAAYUUN "snuff box or small bag" (North Slope Iñupiaq)

194/ Tobacco Box TILAAMMAAYUUN
Alaska
Purchased from the Fred Harvey Company, accessioned 1917
National Museum of the American Indian
6/2388
Walrus ivory, sealskin; Length 6.8 cm (2.7 in)

This tobacco box is decorated with nucleated semi-circles, caribou, wolves, and a row of wolf dancers in the center that may represent visions induced from smoking tobacco (see figures smoking pipes and entering a transformative state on Fig. 136).

195/ Tobacco Box TILAAMMAAYUUN
Alaska
Collected by Sheldon Jackson, accessioned 1921
National Museum of Natural History E316727
Wood, cord; Length 9 cm (3.5 in)

Engraved rows of imagery encircle this tobacco box, including wolves chasing caribou at the top, and geese flying over hunters pursuing walrus at the bottom. The center includes two bands of alternating dark and light crosses.

Trap NIŊITAQ "snare, trap" (North Slope Iñupiaq)

196/ Trap NIŊITAQ
Port Clarence
Collected by U.S. Department of the Interior, accessioned 1910
National Museum of Natural History E260004
Antler, wood, sealskin; Length 11.4 cm (4.5 in)

These spring traps would have been primarily used to hunt wolves. The same artist has decorated both traps with large scale-imagery that includes zigzag lines, nucleated circles, caribou, geese, and houses that have been darkened with dense cross hatching.

197/ Trap NIŊITAQ
Port Clarence
Collected by U.S. Department of the Interior, accessioned 1910
National Museum of Natural History E260006
Antler, wood, sealskin; Length 10.2 cm (4 in)

198/ Ulu ULUAPAK
St. Michael
Collected by Lucien M. Turner,
accessioned 1876
National Museum of Natural History E24378
Bone; Length 16 cm (6.3 in)

A carved seal head is on the end of this ulu handle engraved with figures dragging a bearded seal home.

199/ Ulu ULUAPAK
Kotzebue Sound
Collected by William M. Fitzhugh,
accessioned 1936
National Museum of the American Indian 19/3396
Walrus ivory; Length 16.5 cm (6.5 in)

This ulu handle depicts skin boats hunting bowhead whales. The rectangular-shaped bodies and ladder lines on the left relate this piece to the Birnirk-Thule culture (see Chan 2013:221-227).

200/ Walrus Tusk TUUGAAQ
Kotzebue Sound
Collected by William M. Fitzhugh,
accessioned 1936
National Museum of the American Indian
19/3388
Walrus ivory; Length 25 cm (9.8 in)

This tusk is engraved in an all-over pattern with the central theme of Chukchi herders driving sled deer and moving reindeer to the corral on the right.

201/ Walrus Tusk TUUGAAQ
Nome
Collected by Walter C. Shields,
accessioned 2017
Carrie M. McLain Memorial Museum
2017.5.2
Walrus ivory; Length 65 cm (25.6 in)

This tusk features organized rows of imagery including dogs helping to pull a skin boat, a summer fish camp, figures competing at the two-foot high kick, and dancing on the beach. Motifs are darkened with a rocker fill technique that became popular during the curio trade (see imagery engraved with rocker fill on Figs. 20 and 39).

202/ Wrist Guard MAŊŊIAQ
St. Michael
Collected by Edward W. Nelson,
accessioned 1882
National Museum of Natural History E48388
Bone; Length 6.7 cm (2.6 in)

The figure and caribou with irregular outlines and cross-like motifs on this wrist guard relate to the Birnirk-Thule culture (see the wrist guard shown in Fig. 13 and the awl in Fig. 164).

203/ Wrist Guard MAŊŊIAQ
Norton Sound
Collected by E. W. Keyser,
accessioned 1916
National Museum of Natural History E292233
Bone; Length 9 cm (3.5 in)

A caribou in the center of this wrist guard appears to face a figure waving their arms. Bands of barbed lines encircle the right end. The engraving style reflects the overlap of the Birnirk-Punuk-Thule cultures, such as seen at Wales (see Figs. 16-17).

204/ Eben Hopson describes his polar bear etching inside the Iñupiat Heritage Center at Utqiaġvik. Artists in Utqiaġvik commonly use baleen donated by whaling crews rather than raw walrus ivory that must often be purchased at a high cost.
Photograph by Amy Phillips-Chan, 2012.

Appendix 4

Engraved Characters on Ivory and Bone Drill Bows in the Smithsonian National Museum of Natural History (NMNH) and National Museum of the American Indian (NMAI). Character names are offered in English and Inupiaq/Iñupiaq. The museum catalogue number and location of acquisition are listed under each image. Images have been enlarged to show detail and are not to scale.

Animals

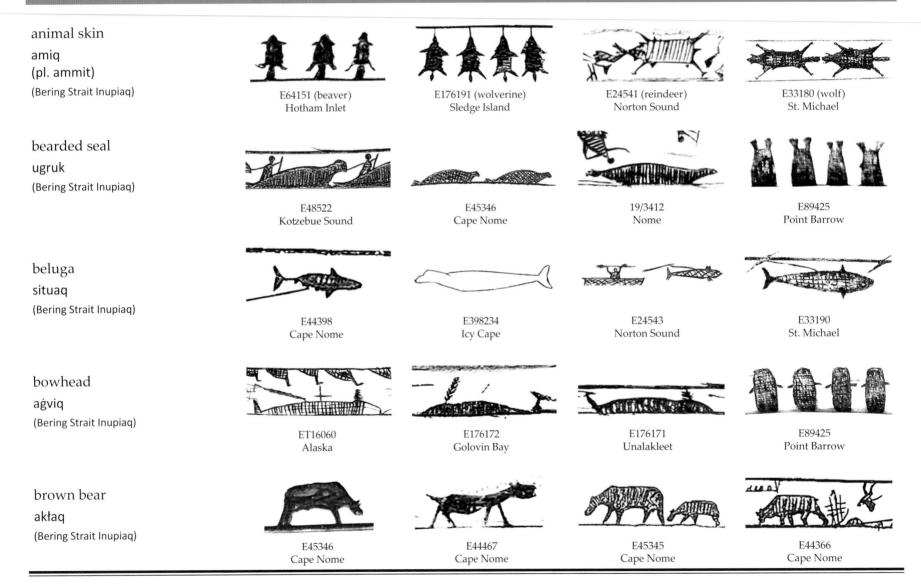

animal skin
amiq
(pl. ammit)
(Bering Strait Inupiaq)

E64151 (beaver)
Hotham Inlet

E176191 (wolverine)
Sledge Island

E24541 (reindeer)
Norton Sound

E33180 (wolf)
St. Michael

bearded seal
ugruk
(Bering Strait Inupiaq)

E48522
Kotzebue Sound

E45346
Cape Nome

19/3412
Nome

E89425
Point Barrow

beluga
situaq
(Bering Strait Inupiaq)

E44398
Cape Nome

E398234
Icy Cape

E24543
Norton Sound

E33190
St. Michael

bowhead
aġviq
(Bering Strait Inupiaq)

ET16060
Alaska

E176172
Golovin Bay

E176171
Unalakleet

E89425
Point Barrow

brown bear
akłaq
(Bering Strait Inupiaq)

E45346
Cape Nome

E44467
Cape Nome

E45345
Cape Nome

E44366
Cape Nome

caribou

tuttu

(Bering Strait Inupiaq)

E44210
Cape Darby

E33186
Kigiktauik

E44209
Cape Darby

E44366
Cape Nome

caribou herd

tuttut siakłaurirut
"The caribou are behind
one another and making a
long line"

(North Slope Iñupiaq)

E44467
Cape Nome

E33182
St. Michael

5/5598
Point Barrow

E45345
Cape Nome

caribou swimming

puvruqtuttut
"to swim with nose above water
(as caribou)"

(North Slope Iñupiaq)

E43360
Cape Prince of Wales

6/2376
Alaska

E44398
Cape Nome

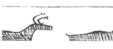

E24540
Norton Sound

dog

qimugin

(Bering Strait Inupiaq)

E45021
Sledge Island

E44467
Cape Nome

E45018
Sledge Island

E44367
Cape Nome

fish

iġaluk

(Bering Strait Inupiaq)

E360421
Alaska

E24550
Norton Sound

E24543
Norton Sound

6/2378
Alaska

flukes

saqpiik

(Bering Strait Inupiaq)

E176172
Golovin Bay

E89424
Point Barrow

E48524
Kotzebue Sound

E24537
Norton Sound

fox

kayuqtuq "red fox"

(Bering Strait Inupiaq)

5/5598
Point Barrow

E24543
Norton Sound

E129222
St. Michael

E154071
Alaska

migrating birds

pigruqtiŋmiat
"to leave on migration
(of birds)"

(North Slope Iñupiaq)

E45022
Sledge Island

E44398
Cape Nome

5/4337
Point Barrow

E43931
Nubviukhchugaluk

polar bear

taguġaq (pl. taguqat)

(Bering Strait Inupiaq)

E49163
Diomede Islands

E398234
Icy Cape

2/418
Cape Darby

E63623
Diomede Islands

porcupine

ilaatquziq

(Bering Strait Inupiaq)

E24552
Norton Sound

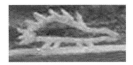

E24557
Norton Sound

raven

tiŋmiaġruaq

(Bering Strait Inupiaq)

E45016
Sledge Island

E38886
Norton Sound

E24541
Norton Sound

E33188
Pastolik

raven flying

tiŋmilaruq
"The bird is flying."

(Bering Strait Inupiaq)

E43360
Cape Prince of Wales

E45022
Sledge Island

E44398
Cape Nome

E45025
Sledge Island

OUR STORIES ETCHED IN IVORY

reindeer

qunŋiq

(pl. qunŋit)

(Bering Strait Inupiaq)

E44467
Cape Nome

E38782
Kotzebue Sound

9/4635
Little Diomede

E44366
Cape Nome

seal

qairaliq

"seal of any kind that migrates north in spring"

(Bering Strait Inupiaq)

E64152
Hotham Inlet

6/7885
Cape Prince of Wales

E44399
Cape Nome

E44209
Cape Darby

walrus

aiviq

(pl. aiġvit)

(Bering Strait Inupiaq)

E43931
Nubviukhchugaluk

24/6479
Alaska

E44367
Cape Nome

E45333
Cape Nome

walrus on ice

nunavak

(usu. pl. nunavait) "walrus on land or on top of the sea ice, out of the water"

(Bering Strait Inupiaq)

E176171
Unalakleet

E43360
Cape Prince of Wales

E33180
St. Michael

E44399
Cape Nome

walrus with calf

izagvalik

"female walrus with baby"

(Bering Strait Inupiaq)

E44399
Cape Nome

E43360
Cape Prince of Wales

E33182
St. Michael

E43931
Nubviukhchugaluk

waterfowl

tiŋmirat (pl.)

"bird, fowl"

(Bering Strait Inupiaq)

E45022
Sledge Island

E38886
Norton Sound

E49163
Diomede Islands

2/418
Cape Darby

weasel

tiġiaq

(Bering Strait Inupiaq)

E24557
Norton Sound

E24543
Norton Sound

E33188
Pastolik

E48524
Kotzebue Sound

wolf

amaġuq

(Bering Strait Inupiaq)

E45025
Sledge Island

E48520
Kotzebue Sound

E67904
Alaska

E33180
St. Michael

Legends

animal transformation

il,immaq- "to metamorphose,
to transform oneself *(of shaman)*"

(North Slope Iñupiaq)

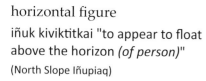

E45022 (seal)
Sledge Island

E33187 (walrus)
St. Michael

E48524 (wolf)
Kotzebue Sound

E48116 (caribou)
Cape Darby

giant

iñukpasuk
"giant, large man"

(North Slope Iñupiaq)

E38886
Norton Sound

E176172
Golovin Bay

E44464
Cape Nome

E44398
Cape Nome

horizontal figure

iñuk kiviktitkai "to appear to float
above the horizon *(of person)*"

(North Slope Iñupiaq)

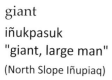

E48519
Kotzebue Sound

E24541
Norton Sound

E44467
Cape Nome

ET16060
Alaska

insect creature

aviŋŋaurayuuq "an insect with a
long snout, snout beetle"
Coleoptera: curulionidae

(North Slope Iñupiaq)

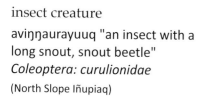

E176194
Cape Darby

E45333
Cape Nome

E129222
St. Michael

E44398
Cape Nome

myth creature

mittayyak
"mythical, frightening animal"
(North Slope Iñupiaq)

E48523
Kotzebue Sound

E44398
Cape Nome

E46054
Port Clarence

E48521
Kotzebue Sound

palraiyuk
(Central Yup'ik)

E176194
Cape Darby

E33187
St. Michael

E33182
St. Michael

E44464
Cape Nome

walrus dog

E33187
St. Michael

2/418
Cape Darby

E33187
St. Michael

E48523
Kotzebue Sound

shaman

aŋatkuq
(Bering Strait Inupiaq)

E48522
Kotzebue Sound

E44398
Cape Nome

E43360
Cape Prince of Wales

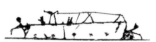
E48116
Cape Darby

tirisiq
"mythical reptile, dinosaur. There is said to be one in Imaruk Basin."
(Bering Strait Inupiaq)

E48521
Kotzebue Sound

E33187
St. Michael

E176194
Cape Darby

Objects

bag for hunting gear
aġġinaq
(Bering Strait Inupiaq)

E24541
Norton Sound

E44210
Cape Darby

E44206
Cape Darby

E33188
Pastolik

belt with tail

pamiuqtaq
"man's belt with
tail in back"
(North Slope Iñupiaq)

E44398
Cape Nome

5/4337
Point Barrow

E44209
Cape Darby

E43360
Cape Prince of Wales

boots

kammak
(pl. kaŋmit)
(Bering Strait Inupiaq)

24/6479
Alaska

E45021
Sledge Island

E44467
Cape Nome

E176191
Sledge Island

building

maptiaq
"house"
(Bering Strait Inupiaq)

E44206
Cape Darby

E48519
Kotzebue Sound

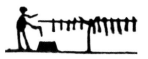

E274548
Alaska

E44366
Cape Nome

bucket

piqtaq
"bentwood bucket sewn with
spruce roots"
(Bering Strait Inupiaq)

E38886
Norton Sound

E176191
Sledge Island

24/6479
Alaska

E44206
Cape Darby

cache

igiġat
"elevated platform, cache"
(Bering Strait Inupiaq)

E33180
St. Michael

E24545
Norton Sound

E44467
Cape Nome

E176191
Sledge Island

canvas tent

palatkaaq
"tent, modern style cloth tent"
(Bering Strait Inupiaq)

E44366
Cape Nome

E44213
Cape Darby

E274548
Alaska

E43932
Nubviukhchugaluk

community house
qagri
"men's house"
(Bering Strait Inupiaq)

E45025
Sledge Island

E48115
Cape Darby

E48519
Kotzebue Sound

E44367
Cape Nome

cooking pot
iggan
(Bering Strait Inupiaq)

E24541
Norton Sound

E24545
Norton Sound

E38886
Norton Sound

E45021
Sledge Island

dog sled
uniat
(Bering Strait Inupiaq)

E43360
Cape Prince of Wales

E44398
Cape Nome

E44467
Cape Nome

E45330
Cape Nome

firearm
saatkaaq "shotgun"
suppun "rifle"
(Bering Strait Inupiaq)

E24543
Norton Sound

E176191
Sledge Island

E44467
Cape Nome

E44206
Cape Darby

harpoon
nauliaq
"harpoon, any type"
(Bering Strait Inupiaq)

E360422
Alaska

E43931
Nubviukhchugaluk

E67904
Alaska

E63802
Point Hope

hat used to represent a
Westerner
nasautaq
"hat, cap"
(North Slope Iñupiaq)

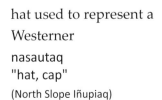

E44213
Cape Darby

E45332
Cape Nome

E176172
Golovin Bay

E44206
Cape Darby

ice chisel

tuuqpak

(Bering Strait Inupiaq)

E48523
Kotzebue Sound

E45021
Sledge Island

E33180
St. Michael

5/4337
Point Barrow

kayak

qayaq

"decked-in skin canoe"

(Bering Strait Inupiaq)

6/7885
Cape Prince of Wales

E24556
Norton Sound

E24547
Norton Sound

E24541
Norton Sound

kayak on rack

qayaq tazik

"wooden rack for storage of a kayak"

(Bering Strait Inupiaq)

E33189
Pastolik

E44367
Cape Nome

net

kuvraq

"fishnet, seal net, beluga net"

(Bering Strait Inupiaq)

E129222
St. Michael

E64152
Hotham Inlet

E176172
Golovin Bay

24/6479
Alaska

oar

ivun

(Bering Strait Inupiaq)

E63623
Diomede Islands

E44208
Cape Darby

E176191
Sledge Island

E43810
Shaktoolik

paddle

paaġutik

"double-bladed kayak paddle"

(Bering Strait Inupiaq)

E48527
St. Michael

E45333
Cape Nome

E44209
Cape Darby

E45345
Cape Nome

OUR STORIES ETCHED IN IVORY

pole with animal emblem

napaqsraq
"pole, post, pillar"
(North Slope Iñupiaq)

E24541
Norton Sound

24/6479
Alaska

E154071
Alaska

rack

innitat (pl.)
"rack for drying meat, fish"
(Bering Strait Inupiaq)

E45021
Sledge Island

E24541
Norton Sound

5/4337
Point Barrow

E33187
St. Michael

sealskin float

awataq
(Bering Strait Inupiaq)

E44367
Cape Nome

E43931
Nubviukhchugaluk

E45333
Cape Nome

E176172
Golovin Bay

ship

umiaqpak
(Bering Strait Inupiaq)

5/2955
Point Barrow

E38886
Norton Sound

E48519
Kotzebue Sound

E154071
Alaska

skin boat

umiaq
(Bering Strait Inupiaq)

E43931
Nubviukhchugaluk

24/6479
Alaska

E33180
St. Michael

E44467
Cape Nome

skin boat on rack

umiam taziit "umiaq on a wooden
rack on which skin boats are
stored, originally made of whale
ribs"
(Bering Strait Inupiaq)

E176191
Sledge Island

E44208
Cape Darby

E44367
Cape Nome

E45020
Sledge Island

snare niaq (Bering Strait Inupiaq)	 E48115 Cape Darby	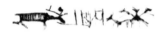 E48116 Cape Darby	 E33190 St. Michael	 E45333 Cape Nome
snowshoes putyuyaak (Bering Strait Inupiaq)	 E44366 Cape Nome	 E64152 Hotham Inlet	 E44206 Cape Darby	
sod house igluuraq "traditional style house covered with sod, snow, or rock" (Bering Strait Inupiaq)	 E176191 Sledge Island	 E33180 St. Michael	 E45021 Sledge Island	 E44399 Cape Nome
spear nauligzaun (Bering Strait Inupiaq)	 E45345 Cape Nome	 E48526 Kotzebue Sound	 E44467 Cape Nome	 E33187 St. Michael
tent tuviq (Bering Strait Inupiaq)	 E24545 Norton Sound	 E43931 Nubviukhchugaluk	 E44399 Cape Nome	 E24538 Norton Sound
whaling charm aaġnuaq "amulet, charm" (North Slope Iñupiaq)	 E176191 Sledge Island	 E176171 Unalakleet	 2/418 Cape Darby	 E67904 Alaska

yurt

mangteghapik
"traditional walrus skin-covered house"
(St. Lawrence Island Yupik)

E360422
Alaska

9/4635
Little Diomede

E38886
Norton Sound

Activities

carrying a skin boat

umiam agra.tuqtuak
"They are hauling or carrying an umiaq."
(Bering Strait Inupiaq)

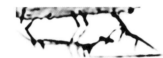

E176172
Golovin Bay

E48115
Cape Darby

E44398
Cape Nome

E176171
Unalakleet

cutting up caribou

pilaaqtatuq
"He cut up meat."
(Bering Strait Inupiaq)

E48115
Cape Darby

E44206
Cape Darby

cutting up whale

aġviuq "
to divide up, butcher a whale into shares"
(North Slope Iñupiaq)

E48115
Cape Darby

E176191
Sledge Island

E44367
Cape Nome

E45022
Sledge Island

dancing

sayuqtut
"They are dancing a motion dance."
(Bering Strait Inupiaq)

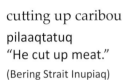

E45346
Cape Nome

9/4635
Little Diomede

E44464
Cape Nome

E48115
Cape Darby

dancing in qagri

aŋayurut "They are dancing, coming into the qagri through the entrance hole."
(Bering Strait Inupiaq)

E176172
Golovin Bay

E44367
Cape Nome

5/2955
Point Barrow

E33187
St. Michael

dragging a seal

uniaqtuq niksamiq

"He is dragging a seal."

(Bering Strait Inupiaq)

ET1076-0
Alaska

24/6479
Alaska

E154071
Alaska

E45016
Sledge Island

---

high kick

aqsraasiaqtut

"They are competing at high-kick."

(Bering Strait Inupiaq)

E48522
Kotzebue Sound

E24541
Norton Sound

E33179
St. Michael

E176172
Golovin Bay

---

hunting bear

taguġaktuq

"He killed a polar bear."

(Bering Strait Inupiaq)

E33182
St. Michael

9/4635
Little Diomede

E24541
Norton Sound

E24539
Norton Sound

---

hunting caribou on land

tuttuniaqtuq

"He is hunting caribou."

(Bering Strait Inupiaq)

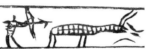

E43931
Nubviukhchugaluk

5/4337
Point Barrow

E45021
Sledge Island

E33190
St. Michael

---

hunting caribou in the water

tuttun narvaqtuqtut

"They are hunting caribou from a kayak in a lake."

(North Slope Iñupiaq)

E45345
Cape Nome

E48116
Cape Darby

E43360
Cape Prince of Wales

5/2955
Point Barrow

---

hunting ducks

qaukkiaq-

"to go duck hunting"

(North Slope Iñupiaq)

E63623
Diomede Islands

E44367
Cape Nome

24/6479
Alaska

E63802
Point Hope

hunting seal in the water

natchiqsiuq-
"to be seal hunting"

(North Slope Iñupiaq)

E33189
Pastolik

E45346
Cape Nome

E44209
Cape Darby

E64152
Hotham Inlet

hunting seal on the ice

niqsamik tiġiktatuq
"He is creeping up on a seal."

(Bering Strait Inupiaq)

E24539
Norton Sound

E63802
Point Hope

E38886
Norton Sound

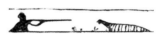

E33187
St. Michael

hunting walrus

aivaniaqtut
"They are hunting walrus."

(Bering Strait Inupiaq)

E24545
Norton Sound

E43360
Cape Prince of Wales

E44367
Cape Nome

E176194
Cape Darby

hunting whale

aġvaniaqtut
"They are hunting bowheads."

(Bering Strait Inupiaq)

E48527
St. Michael

E67904
Alaska

E44398
Cape Nome

E45333
Cape Nome

ice fishing

aulazaaqtut
"They are jigging for fish."

(Bering Strait Inupiaq)

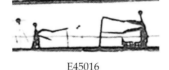

E45016
Sledge Island

E45025
Sledge Island

E45020
Sledge Island

pulling a kayak

qamigaa
"He transported a kayak on a sled."

(Bering Strait Inupiaq)

E44398
Cape Nome

E44367
Cape Nome

sexual activity

kuyaktuk

"They are having intercourse."

(Bering Strait Inupiaq)

E48518
Kotzebue Sound

E44467
Cape Nome

E38886
Norton Sound

E67904
Alaska

shooting a bow

pitiksa.tuq

"He shot a bow and arrow."

(Bering Strait Inupiaq)

E24553
Norton Sound

E48527
St. Michael

E48525
Kotzebue Sound

E48526
Kotzebue Sound

smoking a pipe

qayuqtuq

"He is smoking a pipe."

(Bering Strait Inupiaq)

E24541
Norton Sound

E24539
Norton Sound

E45333
Cape Nome

E24553
Norton Sound

trading

tauqsiġniaqtut

"They are trading."

(Bering Strait Inupiaq)

E176172
Golovin Bay

E45020
Sledge Island

E45333
Cape Nome

E176171
Unalakleet

traveling

umiaqtut

"They are traveling by skin boat."

(Bering Strait Inupiaq)

E44399
Cape Nome

E44367
Cape Nome

E45017
Sledge Island

E44464
Cape Nome

warfare

aŋuyaktut

"They are fighting a war."

(Bering Strait Inupiaq)

E176191
Sledge Island

E24557
Norton Sound

E45016
Sledge Island

E44467
Cape Nome

OUR STORIES ETCHED IN IVORY

wrestling

tiuruk
"They are wrestling."
(Bering Strait Inupiaq)

5/2955
Point Barrow

E45022
Sledge Island

5/4337
Point Barrow

24/6479
Alaska

Abstract

barbed band

E24540
Norton Sound

E48527
St. Michael

E24554
Norton Sound

E33186
Kigiktauik

barbed line

E63623
Diomede Islands

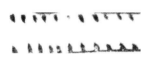

E379814
Point Hope

E24541
Norton Sound

ET16060
Alaska

nucleated circle

aqvaluqtaaq
"a circle, something circular."
(North Slope Iñupiaq)

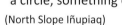

ET1076-1
Alaska

E24550
Norton Sound

4488
Point Hope

E63803
Point Hope

pronged line

E24549
Norton Sound

E24533
Norton Sound

E24554
Norton Sound

E33189
Pastolik

star

uvluġiaq
(Bering Strait Inupiaq)

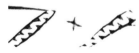

E24533
Norton Sound

ET1076-1
Alaska

E33191
Unalakleet

E45020
Sledge Island

Contributions to Circumpolar Anthropology